Overdue in Paradise

The Library History of
Palm Beach County

Palmango

Overdue in Paradise

The Library History of
Palm Beach County

Janet DeVries, Graham Brunk, Ginger L. Pedersen,
Shellie A. Labell, and Rosa Sophia
Editors

Foreword by Dawn Frood

Published by Palmango Press
West Palm Beach, FL 33401
www.palmango.com

Cover Images: Tropical Sun Photography, Inc.

First Edition 2017

Printed in the United States

ISBN 978-1548627515

Library of Congress CIP data applied for.

10 9 8 7 6 5 4 3 2

This book is dedicated to Mrs. Joy O'Laughlin, a friend and children's librarian who presented me with my first pop-up children's book. That enchanting fairy tale, and Joy's love of books, was the beginning of my lifelong love of books and my career as a librarian, archivist, author, and historian.

—Janet DeVries

Contents

Part III: Special Libraries

Part IV: Library Consortiums & Literary Festivals

Foreword

From our smallest libraries located in farming communities, to our larger multi-story libraries in the heart of Palm Beach County's biggest cities, the libraries of this county are as varied as the people they serve. We are fortunate to live in a county that has libraries with a collective scope that include the arts, science, and special collections that represent the unique cultural and religious identity of our region. The reader will find that many of our libraries began with very humble beginnings in storefronts, post offices, churches, and even closets.

Today libraries are the hub of their communities, places where people can socialize, stay up on current events, and better themselves. Our libraries provide access for users to fully participate in their communities, leveling the playing field for many. For libraries, it is not just the building that adds value, but also the librarians, other library workers and our all-important patrons. These people, with their ideas, innovative solutions, and engaging programming have made libraries a considerable value to their communities from their inception. In this book, the reader will see examples of this and learn about the beginnings and how we got to where we are today with libraries in Palm Beach County.

I started my personal journey in Palm Beach County libraries working in adult literacy. In my own very small way I have been able to make a difference in the lives of the people I have served. I have often reflected on all of the lives that have been made better by the library professionals throughout the county. These persons, for many decades, have one by one been giving a little bit of themselves to enrich the lives of Palm Beach County residents.

Not only have we helped individuals, but for many years our library professionals have added significant value to our communities. We collectively have helped lawyers vindicate clients, religious leaders write sermons, doctors diagnose illnesses, researchers make discoveries, and business executives seal the deal. We have promoted social justice and access by all by ensuring that the blind and other persons facing obstacles do not have barriers keeping them from information. We ensure that the neediest in our community have access to the Internet, computers, and other media devices thus helping to close the digital divide. Libraries in this county have done all of this and much more, while also supporting the education and entertainment of our children all the way into adulthood and beyond. Our libraries have also supported our local, state, and federal governments. Libraries are polling centers, they provide support for persons needing immigration assistance, and they serve as a location for civic meetings to take place. We are a true American institution where civil rights are valued and protected every day.

I was fortunate to study under Dr. Donald Riggs. He was one of the greatest modern library leaders to come to South Florida. Dr. Riggs spearheaded the idea of joint-use libraries in our region. He broke all the traditional library molds by having the vision to create a public-academic library hybrid that also housed a state-of-the-art performing arts center. This pooling of resources furthered the good for all involved. It is with that spirit and vision that I invite you to take in the rich history of our libraries.

Through the historical accounts in this book the reader will most certainly learn of the humble, innovative and at times, scandalous beginnings of what have become the collective libraries of Palm Beach County. Our libraries have even been known as a place for budding love and romance, and I am not talking about fiction. I will leave it to you, the reader, to explore. I could go on and on about the value of libraries, but instead, I now invite you to take a trip back in time through this inspirational and collaborative historical sketch. Enjoy.

Dawn Frood, M.L.I.S., M.I.S.T.
President, Palm Beach County Library Association
West Palm Beach, Florida

Acknowledgments

A remarkable team of valued friends and colleagues collaborated to produce this library history book. The essays were researched and written by librarians, paraprofessionals, and historians throughout Palm Beach County. An assortment of libraries, historical societies, and photo archives shared photographs to illustrate our evolution over time. Graham Brunk, Ginger Pedersen, Shellie Labell, and Rosa Sophia generously afforded editorial and layout assistance and provided valuable critique and advice. Michelle Quigley tediously prepped the photograph submissions and helped write photo captions. The cooperative spirit of the library and community resulted in this work—a gift to future generations. Many other people supplied information or supported a family member or coworker who generously gave their time and talent to make Overdue in Paradise a reality. This book would not be so rich without the assistance and collaboration of the following people:

Lois Albertson, Sammy Alzofon, Ruth Andrews, Susie Rambeau Best, Todd Bol, Brett Brown, Penelope Brown, Joanne Cameron, Angelica Shirley Carpenter, Donna Clarke, Angelica Cortez, Zachary Delia, Michelle McCormick Donahue, Virginia K. Farace, Vicky Fitzsimmons, Dawn Frood, Susan Gillis, Lisa Hogan, Ruby Lynn Holden, Nicole Hughes, Vickie Joslin, Ralph Krugler, Robert Krull, Beverly Jones, Mary Kate Leming, Josh Liller, Mary Lindsay, Karen Mahnk, Suvi Manner, Jenny Noel, Tina Maura, Dr. William Miller, Christopher Murray, Debi Murray, Barbara S. Nowak, Charlotte Olson, L. J. Parker, Sid Patchett, Lisa Petersen, Rich Ploch, James Powell, Arthur G. Quinn, Ellen Randolph, Gail Marie Reece, Anjana Roy, Carlos Ruth, David Scott, Leslie Siegel, Gwen Surface, Christine Thrower, Vicki Thur, Connie Tuisku, Paige Turner, Theresa Van Dyke, Paula Vick, Marsha Warfield, and Helen Zientek.

Introduction

Janet DeVries

The oldest structure in Palm Beach County is the light station at the Jupiter Inlet. Designed by General George Meade, the now iconic Jupiter Lighthouse shone its first beacon in 1860. The light aided ships' navigation and helped guide them safely around southeast Florida's coastal reefs. Palm Beach County was then part of Dade County, and would not become Palm Beach for another fifty years.

The United States Department of Commerce Lighthouse Service contracted station keepers whose job it was to ensure that the light functioned in all types of weather. The keepers and their families lived onsite in these isolated outposts. The sparsely populated region saw few visitors, and there was no outside entertainment. To remedy this loneliness, the lighthouse service generated the first library extension to the region in the form of traveling trunk libraries. The heavy wooden, brass-hinged carrying cases were filled with fifty to sixty books each, the case serving as a bookshelf.

Lighthouse keepers curated the collection, dutifully recording the date, book title, and borrower's name in their government-issued logbooks, the same journal used to record the weather and other observations. Most of the time, the lighthouse keeper's family were the only ones to use the library. Within six months, a new traveling library trunk with fresh reading material arrived by lighthouse tender, with each library eventually traveling the entire circuit of lighthouses in the country.

In 1919, the American Library Association partnered with the lighthouse service to supply lighthouse inhabitants with new reading matter for light stations. Professional librarians curated damaged and obsolete books, helping to develop balanced library collections to circulate among light stations.

Industrialist Henry Morrison Flagler's railroad and hotel systems transformed Palm Beach County from a remote saw palmetto and pine tree covered island into a luxury winter resort in the early 1890s. As man and machine tamed the wilderness, little settlements gradually appeared along the railway route. At the dawn of the twentieth century, farmers, merchants, construction and railroad workers added to the region's population. Pioneering women organized clubs to develop structured educational, cultural, and health endeavors, as well as to push for better roads. This included creating libraries.

West Palm Beach designated the area's first library and reading room in 1896. It initially occupied a corner in a church building and then in a yacht club on the western shore of Lake Worth (today part of the Intracoastal Waterway). By 1906, the Florida Federation of Women's Clubs established a library extension committee, who shipped book trunks by railway to small settlements in need of reading material, including at least three in Palm Beach County. Local woman's clubs developed small libraries within their respective towns. Books were collected and organized in churches, post offices, closets, firehouses, and other available spaces.

The stalwart pioneers and tireless volunteers used old-fashioned hard work as well as forward-thinking ingenuity to advocate for community libraries. From grassroots fundraisers like coconut and pineapple sales, rummage and bake sales, picnics, and the ever-popular fish fry, to effective library campaigns resulting in philanthropic donations, library supporters worked relentlessly to garner the needed support.

As the population grew and literacy levels rose, libraries expanded their services and developed programming to meet the communities' needs. During the Great Depression and other economic down-cycles, libraries stayed open, often with the librarian foregoing a paycheck. The number of government-funded libraries grew along with the baby-boom after World War II. As small farming and fishing villages became metropolises, myriad municipal, county, academic, and special libraries were nurtured by professional librarians, support staff, Friends of the Library, and other volunteer groups who took on the challenge of growing literacy, research, and supporting their community's needs.

Part I
Public Libraries

FREE READING ROOM. West Palm Beach waterfront. *Courtesy of the Mandel Public Library of West Palm Beach.*

Palm Beach County Library System

Graham Brunk

Prior to the 1960s, few countywide library systems existed in Florida. Larger municipalities maintained their own well-established libraries and often created reciprocal agreements with neighboring municipalities without a library, or with the county for unincorporated areas, as was the case here in Palm Beach County. Florida's larger municipalities attempted to create a singular library system. The City of Miami Library System, which began in 1942, ultimately became the Miami-Dade Public Library System. Jacksonville also established an innovative library system in the 1920s. Jacksonville's system to regionally control the area's public libraries continues to flourish today.

Before 1965, the Palm Beach County Board of County Commissioners made at least two attempts to establish a county library system. One of those early endeavors was in the 1940s through the efforts of the Palm Beach County Library Association. A consortium of area librarians governed this organization. In an attempt to align community library services and promote resource sharing in 1943, the association operated exclusively under this name, however, it faded into obscurity within a few years.

In 1959, residents living in unincorporated areas requested that the Palm Beach County government find a way to offer library service. Libraries in operation were located a significant distance from each other and they did not have a cost-efficient way to loan library materials. At this point in time, Palm Beach County was not interested in pursuing the cause, but reconsidered when the League of Women Voters approached them in June 1965 asking them to reevaluate the issue.

Several public meetings and workshops were held in the commission chambers as well as in the meeting rooms of our largest public library at the time, the West Palm Beach Public Library on Clematis Street, located in the heart of downtown. Lake Lytal, chairman of the board, spearheaded an effort to find a cost-efficient way to provide library services to residents all around the county while possibly partnering with many of the existing libraries.

A library committee was formed to examine the viability of the library, to investigate the existing operations of the public libraries in the county, and articulate how it could all work together. The committee consisted of directors from West Palm Beach, Riviera Beach, and Delray Beach libraries.

The committee's report indicated that there were fourteen municipal libraries serving about 217,000 people, leaving about 107,000 individuals without easy access to library services—some not at all since they were not paying into taxes that funded those libraries. The committee recommended that a library system be developed and overseen by the county, but consist of a cooperating effort that streamlined the operations of municipal libraries that agreed to participate. Furthermore, the county allocation would be funded via a special ad valorem tax on unincorporated areas and incorporated areas that were not already contributing to a library. This would be known as the Palm Beach County Library Taxing District. The library system is still funded this way today.

For existing libraries to become part of the system, they were obligated to meet certain requirements and allow anyone residing in the taxing district and participating municipalities to use their services free of charge. The county would provide local interlibrary loan services so that the participating libraries could share materials. Hillsborough and Pinellas counties created similar cooperative systems that still exist today.

On October 1, 1967, the Palm Beach County Library System was established. North Palm Beach, Lake Park, Riviera Beach, West Palm Beach, Delray Beach, Boca Raton, and Belle Glade all agreed to participate in the new system. Libraries in Boynton Beach and Lake Worth to join the library system. Libraries in Briny Breezes, Greenacres City, Lantana, Pahokee, Palm Beach, and Palm Springs were not eligible to join because they did not meet requirements established by the committee. The directors and governing boards of the libraries that joined expressed concern about dual taxation and ensuring operational autonomy.

The county set up a library advisory board to ensure the Library System continues to grow and operate efficiently. The members Ingrid Eckler, Elsie Leviton, Marion Nye, Mami Shannon, Paul Speicher, Bobbe Taffel, Herbert Gildan, and John Opel represented different areas of the county. Municipal library directors served as advisors to the Library Advisory Board and helped create a system of checks and balances. The board was tasked with finding a library system director to lead the library and serve as a liaison to the county administrator. Eighteen applicants applied for the position which paid $10,000 annually. Florence Biller of the State Library in Tallahassee accepted the position and began work in December 1, 1968 as the first female county department director.

A three-room leased suite in the Harvey Building in West Palm Beach became the first physical location for the library system. The suite consisted of an office for Biller and her assistant, Helen White. The offices soon relocated to a former Palm Beach Air Force Base barracks building S-962 at the Palm Beach International Airport. This building became the central nonpublic facility. The library system consisted of a rotating set of books and films that municipal branches could borrow.

TEQUESTA BRANCH. The Tequesta Branch opened in the Gallery Square strip-mall on Tequesta Drive in 1969. *Courtesy of the PBCLS.*

The initial five years of the system's existence were full of firsts. A budget was approved, collection development policies were written, an interlibrary loan program set up, and state aid/grants were received. Biller also began exploring the idea of providing library service to the Jupiter/Tequesta area since there had never been public library service in northern Palm Beach County. The system leased a small 1,361 square-foot space in a strip mall on Tequesta Drive which became the first library fully operated by the county. The branch officially opened September 25, 1969. Five days later, the county implemented bookmobile service for areas of the county that did not have easy access to library materials. The municipal libraries of Pahokee and Boynton Beach joined the system at this time.

PALM BEACH COUNTY LIBRARY SYSTEM. The Library System's main office at the Palm Beach International Airport barracks off Belvedere Road, 1970. *Courtesy of the PBCLS.*

As the library system grew, the library outgrew the airport headquarters. After much deliberation on the part of the advisory board and the system director, five acres of land on Summit Boulevard in unincorporated West Palm Beach was turned over to the library system for development. The land, which had originally been for airport expansion, became the site of a state-of-the-art Central Library facility. The Central Library opened in 1972 with roughly 12,000 square feet. The public facility featured a circulating collection, meeting rooms, administrative offices and technical service.

The Tequesta Branch found much success but could not serve the growing population in the northwestern part of the county. Administrators soon realized that the northwestern parts of the county, particularly the PGA Boulevard and Military Trail area, were still very distant to a physical location. Due to the construction of Interstate 95 and its termination at the time at PGA Boulevard, the region's population was beginning to flourish. A 740-square-foot branch opened in Palm Beach Garden's Tanglewood Plaza in 1975. A few years later, the branch library relocated to the lobby of the nearby newly built Sun Building. The location was much larger at 2,000 square feet. The size of the branch increased again when it moved across the street in 1983.

The Mid-County Branch in Greenacres City opened in a 1,600-square-foot storefront in June 1975. The Southwest County Branch in Boca Raton opened in the Sandalfoot Cove shopping center a few months later. The Okeechobee Boulevard Branch opened in a 1,430-square-foot storefront space in November 1976 in Century Plaza serving the newly completed Century Village retirement community.

The initial 1967 agreement stipulated that the library system was to be

MAIN LIBRARY. The Palm Beach County Library System's Main Branch on Summit Boulevard in West Palm Beach. *Courtesy of the PBCLS.*

reevaluated by an outside independent contractor in 1976. In February, the Orange County Library System in Orlando visited to survey patrons and staff. The advisory board met with the system director and municipal directors to review the study results. Part of the initial 1967 agreement stated that the county was to help fund municipal participants with its Library Taxing District. The Board of County Commissioners began pressuring the advisory board and the system director to end this, or to significantly reduce the amount. The state of Florida Division of Library and Information Services recommended that large metropolitan areas create a single library system administered by the largest branch of government, in this case, the county. The state became more reluctant to award grant money to municipal libraries in large districts. The advisory board also developed a set of new recommended guidelines that essentially took away the capacity of the municipal branches to make suggestions to improve the system's operations and governance.

The municipalities responded unfavorably to the revised terms but continued to cooperate with Biller and the county government find a reasonable solution and to continue without interrupting normal operations. Municipal libraries argued that the extra money was necessary because of the substantial increase in the cost to maintain a collection for residents in incorporated areas. The West Palm Beach Public Library provided materials for residents from unincorporated areas to the west, Riviera Beach to the north, and Lake Worth citizens to the south. Residents in eastern areas of Palm Beach Gardens and Juno Beach were more likely to use the smaller North Palm Beach Public Library rather than the Gardens Branch since it was farther west.

In late 1977, West Palm Beach, Delray Beach and North Palm Beach withdrew from the Palm Beach County library system. Residents in those municipalities were once again restricted to using only their local designated library and residents in surrounding areas were no longer allowed free borrowing privileges. This created a big quandary in the northern part of the county since Riviera Beach was the only participating library and was inundated with new memberships. The local media reported on the disagreements in Palm Beach County, and the story became widespread among librarians in the state.

In an interview with *The Palm Beach Post*, Biller spoke of the issues and stated that the true bottom line of the issue was that municipal libraries just wanted their cut. Area library directors complained that it was not just about the money. They asserted that the municipal libraries were rarely informed of countywide system activities, there was no centralized reference system for efficiently sharing resources—which had been promised in the system's inception—and they felt the library system was looking out for its patrons in the taxing district rather than viewing all participants as one library system.

As a result of the disagreement between the county library and the municipal libraries, Biller's employment was terminated on December 27, 1977. Biller's inability to handle the situation was cited as the cause of her termination. Assistant director Kathleen Perinoff was named acting director until they could find a suitable replacement. In commemoration for Biller's decade of service with the county, the professional library science collection at the Main Library on Summit Boulevard was dedicated to her. Biller went on to manage the Jacksonville Public Library before retiring and became an ordained reverend before her death in 2005.

The county advertised the directorship as a $27,000 salaried position. Eighteen people from seventeen different states applied for the library director position. The advisory board interviewed the applicants with the assistance of Cecil Beach, Broward County library system director and Palm Beach County administrator John Sansbury. Jerry Brownlee of Savannah, Georgia was selected and became the director in September 1979.

Brownlee immediately took action to rectify the falling out between the county library system and the municipal libraries. A revised system was

implemented that gave the municipal locations complete control over their libraries, the county provided courier service and resource sharing benefits if they agreed to provide service to the partnering institutions' residents. This agreement became known as the Library Cooperative of the Palm Beaches which is still in place today. The only library

MICROFILM READER. A researcher using Microfilm in the Main Library on Summit Blvd. in the 1970s. *Courtesy of the PBCLS.*

originally part of the initial system that did not rejoin this effort was Boca Raton. After a lengthy presentation by Brownlee to their city council, the City of Riviera Beach considered turning its library over to Palm Beach County, but ultimately decided to retain their library.

In the 1970s, none of the public libraries in Palm Beach County were automated, and each location maintained its own card catalog. This made sharing materials in the cooperative difficult because of the ambiguity between the libraries and their collections. A vendor called Science Press was contracted to create bound volumes of each library's collection so that librarians and patrons could see what the holdings were at each location. These would later be replaced with microfilm versions of those same books.

In 1979, the Audubon Society of the Everglades donated funds to the library system to establish an ornithological collection at the Main Library. The society's library committee selected the best of the new books published on birds and birding for the collection. Included in the collection are books on birdwatching and field guides to birds from all regions of the globe, with a special focus on North and South American regions.

Following a bid process, the library system selected a library automation system, ALIS by Dataphase, implemented by 1983. ALIS provided the status of any item in the system. Initially, plans were to roll out ALIS to the municipal libraries as a cost-sharing initiative. Dataphase was unsure if their system would be able to handle the records and patron information for libraries with different policies. The cooperative libraries purchased their own Dynix system that went live in 1984-locally known as COALA: Cooperative Authority for Library Automation (see COALA chapter).

In addition to automation, the 1980s brought significant groundwork and library success to the twenty-first century. A new branch was added to the system in 1982 in the south county. The West Atlantic Avenue Branch in Delray Beach was the first standalone county-owned building other than the Central Library. The 11,500-square-foot building purchased by the county previously served as a sales office for area condominiums.

The library system organized sizable storefront branches to meet the community's needs in Century Plaza on Okeechobee Boulevard, Piccadilly Square in Boca Raton, and Woodlake Plaza in Greenacres. A branch opened in the Jupiter Town Hall (closing the original Tequesta Branch) and a Royal Palm Beach Branch for the growing western communities opened in a facility leased from the Village of Royal Palm Beach.

The Belle Glade Public Library joined the library system in 1987 with the county leasing the facility from the City of Belle Glade. Pahokee would follow in 1989, giving the county their library, staff, and facility as part of the agreement (see Glades area chapter).

In 1986, director Brownlee proposed a tax increase to voters in the taxing district. The increase generated an extra $20 million to increase collection size (which was much needed after losing total municipal library integration), build new county-owned branches in the southern part of the county, in Jupiter, and Royal Palm Beach, Wellington, and suburban Boynton Beach. Money would also be available to renovate the Atlantic Avenue Branch (the system's busiest at the time), expand the North County Branch, and bring the Belle Glade Library up to the same standards as other county libraries.

In the November 1986 election, more than fifty percent of the voters in the taxing district voted in favor of the increase. The vote was the catalyst for moving most of the county libraries into permanent county-owned quarters rather than small makeshift storefront branches. By the early 1990s, Greenacres, Jupiter, Glades Road, Okeechobee Boulevard, and Royal Palm Beach branches were in permanent county buildings. A library was added for the emergent West Boynton population and another in Wellington for the growing area south of Royal Palm Beach. A large regional branch was added in Palm Beach Gardens soon after.

In the late 1980s, the Village of Tequesta, whose branch had closed years earlier, began pleading with the county to open a branch in the village. Initially, Tequesta was to get a small branch, but it seemed more economically feasible to name the new Jupiter Branch, which was to be completed in 1992, the

BOOKMOBILE LIBRARY. Patrons outside of the Palm Beach County Library System bookmobile, 1993. *Courtesy of the PBCLS.*

Jupiter/Tequesta Branch. Residents and village council members openly expressed frustration over this. Four opinion letters from concerned citizens were published in *The Palm Beach Post* on the same day in March 1991.

The county ultimately decided to keep the initial promise. One commissioner had warned the others that if they did not make good on using the bond money to replace the Tequesta Library, it might make voters reject future bond issues for the library system. About $700,000 was set aside to build the Tequesta Branch, using the same design as the new South Bay Branch that was near completion at the time. The Tequesta Branch on Old Dixie Highway opened in 1995 on property given to the county by the Village of Tequesta.

In 2002, Palm Beach County voters approved a $55 million bond to further expand library service within the taxing district. The bond would add new library branches and remodel all older buildings. Once the bond passed, the library system immediately outlined the various projects and sought out library architects and designers. The plan called for enlarging the Main Library on Summit Boulevard from 78,000 square feet to 122,480 square feet. Nearly every existing branch was scheduled to undergo complete renovation. Colorful tones adorned the walls of each library and a new logo and branding for the library system was put in place. Some bookshelves gave way for more space for computers. Branches in West Boca, unincorporated Lantana, and in the rural Acreage area were all built from scratch with the Acreage Branch being the county's first Leadership in Energy and Environmental Design (LEED) certified building. The Atlantic Avenue Branch was relocated to a new location around the corner on Hagen Ranch Road. The Library System Annex, which houses the library system's outreach services, bookmobile, and cataloging facilities was also slated to be replaced in a new contemporary building on Cherry Road in West Palm Beach.

In 2005, Hurricane Wilma tore the roof off of the Loula V. York Branch in Pahokee which required an entire building renovation and collection replacement. The building, which opened in 1967, is the library system's oldest operating facility.

Additional work was needed on other branches that were affected by the hurricanes of 2005 and that came at the cost of the large-scale renovations planned for the Main Library on Summit Boulevard. Initially, the library planned an additional 30,000-square-foot expansion and a completely remodeled interior and exterior. With a $44.1 million shortfall, the county decided that the Main Library's own renovation would be delayed indefinitely in favor of using that money to complete renovations at other branch libraries.

The Main Library received renovations so the interior matched the branch remodels. New carpet, wall color tones, and artwork adorn the building including a mosaic floor mural at the entrance entitled "Books on a Library Floor" by Suzi K. Edwards.

At the onset of the library expansion project II, library system director Jerry Brownlee retired after twenty-five years of service. He oversaw the library through its successful growth of the 1980s from storefront locations to permanent stand-alone locations and staffing level from forty-five employees to 450. Delray Beach Public Library director John Callahan replaced Brownlee.

As director, Callahan implemented the completion of the 2002 bond issue with the final project—the opening of a new library annex on Cherry Road— shortly after his retirement in 2015. Some new initiatives were created during Callahan's tenure. The library was rebranded in 2010 to reflect the changing paradigm of library as a community gathering place. Many self-service features including electronic sorters, self-check devices, and self-service hold pickups. The Main Library unveiled the CreationStation. The digital media lab includes equipment for creating videos, audio, podcasts and image editing. The Florida Library Association named the Palm Beach County Library System the Florida Library of the Year in 2014 for the wide variety of activities offered to meet the needs of the diverse community throughout Palm Beach County. Talking Books was also recognized as the Sub-Regional Library of the Year by the Library of Congress.

In October 2014, Callahan retired and was replaced by Douglas Crane, an experienced local librarian who had worked in the Palm Beach County system for sixteen years, beginning as a children's librarian who worked his way up the ranks. Crane has continued to make the system a focal point for the community by establishing a new mission for the library to connect communities, inspire thought, and enrich lives. He also set a vision for the system to open minds to a world of unlimited possibilities through education, technology, and growth.

The library system continues to expand with a deposit collection in the Town of Mangonia Park and addition of a branch in the Canyon area of suburban Boynton Beach in 2019.

The Palm Beach County Library System with its seventeen libraries, the newly donated bookmobile, and outreach services continues to be the largest provider of library services in the county and is the backbone of cooperation among the many other existing libraries.

Library Memories

Ginger L. Pedersen

Books have always held a magical power to me. As a small child, I loved turning the pages, examining the pictures before the words made any sense to me. I loved the Golden Books Nature Guides, a nice size for little hands, and the Golden Books stories sold in grocery stores. We lived in Tequesta, just a few yards north of the Palm Beach County line. Because of that, I had to take the school bus north to the Hobe Sound Elementary School some ten miles away; no local library was near our home.

As the small community grew in the late 1960s, the Palm Beach County Library System began planning a small branch that could serve Tequesta, Jupiter, and Jupiter Inlet Colony. The Tri-Community Library Association oversaw development of the library, and a small store that had served as Howard's Meat Market became available for lease in Gallery Square. Renovations began to convert the butcher shop to a library, and local officials dedicated the library September 25, 1969, just as I had entered first grade.

I quickly learned to read within a few weeks of entering school, and our weekly trip to the tiny library was part of our Saturday routine of grocery shopping and a library stop. I first read my favorites, the complete collection of Beatrix Potter books. I wanted to go back and always find one I had missed, but alas, I had read them all. I read "boy" books like Tom Swift because they were my dad's favorites when he was a boy, so I wanted to know those stories too. I read the Bobbsey Twins books, and also checked out nature books, and any space book I could find, as Apollo 11 had made its historic moon voyage that summer of 1969.

In my mind, I can see, and hear, that library. The hearing part was the wonderful "clunk" of the checkout machine as it printed your library card number on the book card, and the awful sound when a card got jammed in the machine. I think checkout limit was six books, and many times I had picked out more than that, so I had to quickly choose which ones I wanted. Although the building where the library was still stands, the Tequesta library has moved on to a larger location on Old Dixie Highway. This library is more than twice the size the original library, but can never match the magic of that tiny Tequesta library, the first library I called mine.

North Palm Beach Public Library

Rosa Sophia

Behind the village hall, which faces U.S. Highway 1, the North Palm Beach Public Library is surrounded by shrubs, palm trees, and the North Palm Beach Veterans Memorial, which was dedicated on Veterans Day in 2013. Bright pink hibiscus flowers bloom between the library and the village hall.

In 1959 while living in North Palm Beach, Thelma Obert became one of the founders of the local branch of the American Association of University Women. Thelma and her husband were pioneers in the village, the first family to move in. Thelma set out to create a library by forming the Library Study committee. The library committee requested that the village council set aside some of the recreation budget to form a library, asking for space in the old country club building. For two years, the committee worked to garner support from residents and local government, as well as collect books.

On September 19, 1963, the library announced their hours for autumn. It would be open Monday through Friday from ten to four, and Tuesday, Wednesday, and Thursday evenings from seven to nine. A call was made for volunteers for Saturday mornings, and students' ages sixteen to eighteen were also invited to volunteer. The North Palm Beach Library Society announced a masquerade frolic for fundraising. The event, held on October 26 at Captain Alex's Restaurant, offered prizes, including a grand prize of a weekend in Bimini for the best-costumed couple. Tickets were six dollars per couple and all proceeds went to the library for general operations and the purchase of books.

In 1964, the North Palm Beach Public Library opened inside the old country club building—also known as the Palm Beach Winter Club, or the Oakes Mansion. By that point, the building that was built by Harry Kelsey in 1925—the man who founded Kelsey City, which eventually became Lake

SPECIAL DELIVERY. Mr. Gene Armstrong delivers new bookcases to the Library in 1964. *Courtesy of the Village of North Palm Beach.*

Park—and subsequently sold by Kelsey to Sir Harry Oakes, wasn't being used for a country club anymore. The Library Society, with Thelma on the committee, hosted a dance and buffet in June of that year to raise money for the effort. While the Library Society had operated the library, in 1965 it was turned over to the Village of North Palm Beach. The village council library board helped manage the library and aid in its future growth. Members of the board at the time were Mrs. Herbert Gildan, Seymour Bellak, Howard Campbell, James Gill, and Martin Gold. Despite handing over administrative duties, the Library Society actively continued, and one of their gifts included thirty-five books intended for the library's Florida collection. While the library thrived in service to the village's close-knit community, those living outside the village could also get a library card for one dollar per year.

Nancy Fant Moore, who eventually became the library's first director, started out as a volunteer when the library was housed in the Winter Club. She recalled how the circulation desk was in the old barroom with a mirror behind it. Shelves were brought over on the back of a truck while volunteers brought in donated books, and a sign was painted. Nancy was a member of the North Palm Beach Library Society and the Woman's Club. Both groups were active in forming the library. Some folks said the library was in the men's locker room, others said it was the ladies' locker room, and Nancy recalled that Thelma Obert referred to it as "the men's bathroom." It was actually housed in a room by the old dining room. Nancy added, "They started bringing books in and that's when I realized I never wanted to see another *Reader's Digest Condensed Book* in my life."

JAYCEES HELP OUT. The local Jaycees club help to prepare the library sign, 1964. *Courtesy of the Village of North Palm Beach.*

No one wanted to work evenings at the library because the Oakes Mansion was supposedly haunted, but Nancy worked Thursday nights until closing. "It was the [old] country club," she recalled. "I had the pleasure and honor of going there when it was the country club, and we had many good parties in that room. I remember it as the dining room and the library."

Nancy stated she had never loved a job so much as she did when she worked in the old Winter Club. The dining room had a beautiful stone fireplace, but kids had gotten the idea that the spirit of Sir Harry Oakes haunted the building. He had been murdered in the Bahamas, and his body had been found burned in his own bed, the murderer never identified. Children in North Palm Beach believed Oakes had died in the Winter Club, and some said he was killed in the fireplace. Imaginations took flight, leading to the birth of a village legend. "They would sit around the fireplace and tell stories about Sir Harry Oakes burning in that fireplace," Nancy added.

Although she began her work as a volunteer, Nancy eventually became a paid employee. One day, the village manager called and asked if she would be interested in a job. When she said she was not sure, he told her that if she did not like the job, she could just quit. With that assurance, she began working as a paid library employee in 1967. Her job included a variety of duties, not simply library-related. With the library positioned right next to the pool, children would often come in dressed in their bathing suits, dripping water all over the floor. Repeatedly, Nancy had to mop the floor and it became very frustrating for her. "One day, the village manager came in and the kids had just come in before he did," she said. "I was mopping, and I said, 'These kids should really stay out of here, look at this mess,' and he said, 'You know what, if those kids didn't come in here, you wouldn't have a job…I learned to be very careful about what I said."

Over the years, the Friends of the Library kept scrapbooks demonstrating the library's progress, including articles about fundraisers. Photographs showed men cleaning out the room in the old Winter Club and preparing it for books. Another photo showed a truck pulling up, stacked high with shelves, proud citizens standing by the vehicle and posing for the picture. Still more photographs showed ladies gathering books and placing them on the new shelves.

On October 24, 1968, at noon, the groundbreaking for the new library took place, with Mayor Thomas Lewis presiding over the occasion. Guests included the librarians, and those who had served as presidents of the North Palm Beach Library Society, both past and present. The chairwoman of the North Palm Beach library board was there, as well—Mrs. Herbert Gildan. Councilmen including Herb Watt, Tom Bell, and Dave Clark attended the groundbreaking.

Others in attendance included engineers and architects; the president of the First American Bank in North Palm Beach, along with the executive president and senior vice president; and those representing the contractor. The building cost $200,000 at the time, and that price did not include the purchase of books or other library materials. That amount, plus $100,000 supplied by the

DEDICATION CEREMONY. Mayor Thomas Lewis introduces the speaker at the library dedication in 1969. *Courtesy of the Village of North Palm Beach.*

government, went to the creation of the North Palm Beach Public Library as it is today. To help cover the cost of books and other materials, the Library Society sponsored fundraising events, including a horse show at the Saddle and Gun Club on Hood Road. Nancy recalled the library started at its new location with just her and two pages, plus volunteers.

The dedication took place in 1969, and Mayor Thomas Lewis was again present to conduct the event. Building the collection was the most important focus for the librarians and volunteers. Nancy Fant Moore was soon given the official title of reference librarian. She had a hand in ordering books for the collection, and planned all of the library's programs. One day, a couple came into the library and talked with the young woman who worked at the front desk.

The library employee eventually came over to Nancy and said, "This lady says her name is Mrs. James Michener. Do you think it's the real one?"

Nancy, being uncertain, went into the stacks and pulled one of James Michener's books off the shelf. She opened the back of the book and looked at his photograph, then at the man visiting the library with his wife. Sure enough, it was really him. Nancy told him how glad they were to have him visiting, and then went to the acting library director and told her, "You're not going to believe who's here."

James Michener, author of many novels including *Hawaii* and *Tales of the South Pacific*, became a good friend of the library, according to Nancy. Later on, he even complimented the library on its wonderful reference collection. He always found exactly what he needed whenever he visited. He and his wife were living in Juno Beach at the time. When he gave a book talk on the first floor of the library, about two hundred people showed up.

Additionally, Elmore Leonard was a regular visitor. According to Nancy, he lived at Old Port Cove, and he came in often. "He'd come in and no one would know who he was," she said.

Another high point of Nancy's career was when the grandson of the infamous Dr. James Munyon—for whom Munyon Island in the Intracoastal Waterway is named—walked into the library. He was on a journey to explore the area where his grandfather lived, and later sent a photograph of Munyon to the library, which currently resides in the village history archives.

The groundbreaking for North Palm Beach Elementary School had already taken place in February 1958, and soon working there was Henrietta Jeanne Saunders, teacher and friend of Nancy Moore. Jeanne, born in 1926 at Good Samaritan Hospital in West Palm Beach, taught at the elementary school for thirty-six years before retiring from teaching and going to work at the library in 1999. She started in the children's department, and then moved into reference where she later processed inter-library loans.

As the new library quickly became the heart of the community, other activities went on at the old Winter Club, where the library was previously housed. The new country club building had already been built in 1963, and the aging Mediterranean-style building next door was quickly becoming neglected. Art classes were held there, and the building was something of a community center. It was added to the National Register of Historic Places in 1980, but subsequently demolished in 1984.

Nancy Fant Moore was officially appointed library director in 1984. She joked that she had never actually applied for any job, but she had loved every moment of it, nonetheless. The village manager approached her and offered her the job when she was still a reference librarian, but she turned him down. Sometime later, he asked her again, this time telling Nancy that she'd only have to take the job for a little while—just until he found someone else. "I lasted twenty-two years," she said, adding that she had later asked the village manager if he had ever found anyone who might replace her, and he admitted that he had never actually looked.

Nancy was also present when the village's twenty-fifth anniversary time capsule was put into the ground, and when it was pulled up she was there, too. Pratt & Whitney had built both time capsules. When the twenty-fifth anniversary time capsule was extracted, Nancy recalled the capsule being taken into the meeting room, where tables were set up and all kinds of memorabilia—such as photographs of what the area looked like when Northlake Boulevard didn't exist—were placed on tables.

In her time at the library, she saw many changes, and finally retired in February 2005. The card catalogs were still there when she left, despite the fact that computers were now being used. Nancy said that patrons who did not want to use the computer had once warned her, "If you ever move that card catalog out of here, we're going to have your job!" It seemed like wise advice to adhere to.

When Nancy retired, Kathie Olds, who had served as the reference librarian for about a year, became the director. The library has had a short history of dedicated directors. After Kathie Olds, Donna Riegel served as director for about four years, and Betty Sammis for the following six years, and most recently, Zakariya Sherman, July 18, 2016 to present. Before her retirement, Nancy hired Betty Lou Marlow, who is a current part-time staff member. Nancy recognized her as a long-time patron when the two met by chance on a plane trip, and she offered her a job right away. It is believed that Betty Lou is the last person that Nancy hired before her retirement.

Reference librarians included, of course, Nancy Moore; Karen White; Kathie Olds; Ann Burton; Betty Sammis; and finally, Diana Kirby. After working many years in the reference department, Jeanne Saunders resigned just after her 91st birthday in 2016.

Children's librarians included Marsha Warfield, who held the position in the 1970s, and Nancy Palmer in the early 1990s. Doris Pierce worked part-time in the children's department around the same time. In 1999, Susan Holmes started in the children's department and ran two story hours—four to six-year-olds, and seven to eight-year-olds—along with Mary Ann Caruso, who ran a story hour for toddlers. Susan worked with the youth for about eight years, and later moved to the cataloging department, where she is currently technical services manager. Finally, Nancy Hodges—a retired school teacher—worked in the children's department, and retired around December of 2013. As of this writing, Dawn Hahn handles the children's department.

Other notable staff include Elvie Wright, administrative assistant; Mary "Betsy" Taylor, circulation supervisor; and Lynn Ruiz, who is currently the circulation supervisor, but started part-time in October 2005.

According to an article published February 25, 2005 in the Weekday, Nancy's final thoughts at her retirement concerned the future of the library she adored. She wanted the village to keep its municipal status, rather than become a more integrated part of the county. "To see it doing so very well makes me very proud and happy," Nancy said in an interview in 2011, adding, "You always have a place in my heart." Nancy, who was born on November 30, 1928, passed away at home on June 19, 2014. She had been with the library for forty-two years.

The North Palm Beach Public Library continues to be an independent library just as Nancy had hoped, serving patrons with welcomed small-town charm and an enduring sense of community.

Lake Park
Public Library

Karen Mahnk

One cannot understand the history of the Lake Park Public Library without first learning the history of the Town of Lake Park—a unique riches to rags to riches story. The town developed in four distinct phases: the Kelsey Period of the 1920s, the Great Depression era, the World War II era, and the present day.

Kelsey City was the brainchild of Harry Seymour Kelsey of Boston. The young president of national restaurant chain Waldorf Systems, Inc. developed Kelsey City during the Florida land boom of the early 1920s. Harry Kelsey made millions selling his restaurants, bakeries, and farm, and subsequently moved to Florida in 1917.

Kelsey engaged the services of the Olmstead brothers, renowned for their design of New York City's Central Park and other notable projects such as the National Mall in Washington, D.C., the White House grounds, the Jefferson Memorial, and the Bok Tower in Lake Wales, Florida to create Kelsey City. As the founder of Florida's first planned community, Kelsey imagined an ideal community, comprehensively designed from its inception. With the Olmstead brothers, Kelsey developed a community design that was well ahead of its time. A city must, of course, include a library, and the Kelsey City Free Library was erected downtown.

The stock market crash of 1929 and an onslaught of hurricanes in the late 1920s and 1930s led to the dwindling size of Kelsey City, which by that point had been reduced to the 2.35 square miles it covers today. In 1939, the local Garden Club renamed Kelsey City, rechristening it as the Town of Lake Park. The streets of Lake Park were named after trees, bushes, plants or flowers to enhance the town's image. At this time, Lake Park's population sat just under four hundred.

KELSEY CITY FREE LIBRARY. The Kelsey City Free
Library in the 1920s. *Courtesy of the Lake Park Historical Society.*

Much of the land that had served as farms during the Kelsey City era was
purchased by Sir Harry Oakes and incorporated in 1956 into the Village of
North Palm Beach.

Lake Park's Free Library was replaced with a small library on the second
floor of the Town Hall building and tended to by retired Lake Park Elementary
school principal, Marjorie Ross, along with the Woman's Club. Mary Kiernan
of the Purple Sage Book Club recalls working in the library, bringing books
from upstairs and helping with the archives. In
1969, the town built a small dedicated library
building next to town hall. The inaugural staff
consisted of Gertrude McIntyre as the first
librarian and director, followed by her then
assistant Lorna Adams, who would go on to
become the first library director. Local residents
Virginia Tellier and Marian Drake served as the
library's clerks. By this point, Lake Park's

LAKE PARK LIBRARY DEDICATION
PROGRAM. Dedication ceremony held on
Saturday, March 3, 1969. *Courtesy of the Lake Park
Historical Society.*

LAKE PARK LIBRARY SUMMER READING CLUB. Children enjoying a summer reading club event. *Courtesy of the Lake Park Historical Society.*

population had grown to over 6,000 residents. The library's collection consisted of 11,187 books and served 1,500 resident cardholders, as well as almost as many patrons from Riviera Beach, West Palm Beach and other areas of Palm Beach County. In 1969, over 100 children enrolled in the summer reading program.

In 1986, director Lorna Adams with the assistance of Lake Park resident James Faulkner established the Friends of the Lake Park Library, which was incorporated in 1986.

The library continued to flourish over the next few decades, and by 1990 the library's book collection had grown tremendously. As the population of the town increased, it became necessary to add a separate children's room and a meeting room to the library.

After Lorna Adams' sudden passing in 1992, Joy White followed as the library's director. This was a time of rapid change in Lake Park. The town's population continued to grow and the library experienced several building renovations, quickly embracing the digital era, facilitated by funds made available from the Lake Park Bond Issue and a construction grant from the Florida State Library. Soon after, the library joined the local library lending consortium, nicknamed COALA, and also became a member of the Library Cooperative of the Palm Beaches.

In 1996, Friends of the library members Mildred DeMarco and Rose and Stanley Schuyler contributed funds to add new furnishings, a computer lab, and a new multi-purpose meeting room designed to showcase local artists' works as well as renovating the north lobby.

LAKE PARK LIBRARY ADDITION RIBBON CUTTING. 2000.
Courtesy of the Lake Park Historical Society.

Joy White retired in 2000 and Sally Bailey became the interim library director. White's retirement was followed by a major structural renovation, during which the roof was raised. The library's goal was to add a second floor, but new regulations required adding an elevator the library could not afford, so a second floor was never built. The unique design of the library's high ceiling and large transom windows surrounded by trees gave the interior of the library its signature feel of sitting in a cozy arboretum. Embracing library automation and electronic resources increased variety of types of materials available in the library. By the end of the 1990s, the library had once again outgrown its facility, and construction on a second expansion was completed in 2000. The library addition was dedicated on October 21, 2000, shortly after Jane Terwillegar replaced Sally Bailey as library director. The following year saw repair of storm damage as well as a complete renovation of the facility.

By 2004, the Lake Park Library had the second highest number of public access computers per capita. The Friends of the Lake Park Library played an important role in the library.

Rose and Stanley Schuyler, ardent Friends of the Library, provided a dedicated activities and exhibit room, as well as a computer lab and overhaul of the north lobby. Over the course of the decade, library management changed hands several times. 2004 saw an economic downturn; the town's economy suffered, requiring layoffs and shortened hours at the library.

As a result of rising unemployment, the library was filled with residents using the library computers to apply for jobs and file for unemployment benefits. New Lake Park residents also used the library's computers to apply for legal immigration status. The library expanded its collection of language media and materials, and offered computer classes in response to high demand from the community. Changeover in library administration in 2010 brought Karen Mahnk aboard as library director. The addition of a teen room with computers, a game room and two additional study rooms, were made possible by the Friends of the Lake Park Library.

Today, the Town of Lake Park has grown to nearly 9,000 residents and is a diverse family community. The library's collection now houses over 34,000 items, including multimedia and multilingual resources. In 2017, the Lake Park Library celebrated the graduation of twelve local high school students who had spent their childhoods in the library, visiting each day after school and participating in the annual summer reading programs. All twelve graduates are the first in their family to attend college. Long-time residents and active Friends such as Diane Sophinos have raised their families in Lake Park and have witnessed the many changes over the years but note that it is still a family oriented town.

Over the decades, the library has offered a number of unique programs, such as the Book Buggy, annual book sales, fundraising events, and a Homebound Book Delivery Program for town residents, all made possible by the library's community partners including the Friends of the Lake Park Public Library. The Friends always have, and always will, play a vital role for the Lake Park Public Library.

Riviera Beach Public Library

Graham Brunk

Prior to 1954, if a resident lived in what was then known as Riviera, Florida, the library patron would have had no choice but to visit the West Palm Beach library as there was no library in Riviera. The municipality was fortunate enough to be allotted a very small budget which permitted those citizens free use of the West Palm Beach library.

With a bustling post World War II economy, Riviera experienced a large population increase, as did much of Palm Beach County. The town quickly realized it needed a library of its very own. With that in mind, an interim "library" was formed on Avenue E until a brand-new library could be constructed on 22nd Street.

When the library finally relocated to its permanent quarters, Ms. Rachel Van Berkum was hired to develop the library's initial collection and begin library operations. Van Berkum was well-qualified; she held a professional library degree and had worked for sixteen years as a teacher for the School District of Palm Beach County. An additional two library assistants were eventually hired to complete the staffing at the Riviera Beach Public Library.

By 1963, the library had an active programming schedule and the facility held 25,000 volumes. Much of the library's early collection was donated. Van Berkum orchestrated a relationship with libraries up north where their weeded books were donated to the

RACHEL VAN BERKUM.
Riviera Beach's first library director.
Courtesy of the Riviera Beach Public Library.

RIVIERA BEACH PUBLIC LIBRARY. Librarians working in the original
Riviera Beach Public Library. *Courtesy of the Riviera Beach Public Library.*

Riviera library. Due to her familiarity with local schools, she generated
widespread use of the children's area through school story times and other
programming. Van Berkum passed away at age 78 in February 1966, and she
worked in the library up to the day that she died.

The Riviera Beach Public Library's only male director was Charles Huber,
an Air Force veteran, hired six months after Van Berkum passed away. Huber
held a library degree from Florida State University and formerly served as the
adult services director at the Fort Lauderdale Public Library (now a part of the
Broward County Library System). He began his career in Riviera Beach with an
annual salary of $7,500.

In his first year as director, Huber advocated the city for funding to
modestly renovate the nearly ten-year-old library facility and to increase its
operating budget to just over $25,000 annually. He had steel shelving installed,
ordered a new card catalog, new book carts, and newspaper racks. He
vigorously weeded the collection, culling many duplicate volumes. The new
budget allowed him to hire Mrs. Rosemary Beaumont, a dedicated employee
who generously gave over twenty-five years of service to the library and
continued to volunteer well into her retirement. During Huber's leadership, the
library instituted offering Riviera Beach residents' library services for free.
Previously, the library charged a membership fee of one dollar a year.

In 1968, Huber left Riviera Beach to take on the directorship of the Cocoa
Library in Brevard County. Ms. Evelyn Thomas, a Pennsylvania native, took

over the library leadership. She earned her degree from Florida State University and had taken additional courses at Columbia University's now defunct library school. An experienced librarian, Thomas previous worked as the hospital librarian for St. Mary's Hospital in West Palm Beach, and also worked abroad as the director of a public library in Lima, Peru.

During Thomas' tenure, the library featured weekly film nights and grew its patron base by about twenty-five percent in 1969. Library usage grew faster than the City of Riviera Beach. The library hired a second professional librarian to focus solely on children's services.

In 1972, Thomas was replaced by Mary (Lynn) Brink, then wife of renowned *Palm Beach Post* columnist and author, Bob Brink. Brink probably doesn't get enough recognition from the City of Riviera Beach today for the work she did at the library. Upon starting her career at the Riviera Beach Public Library, she found herself in the midst of a changes and challenges in Palm Beach County's library world.

At this time, the county was attempting to set up a single county library system, per state recommendation. The county would operate the library system with municipal libraries as system members, but the libraries would maintain their municipal identities and operations. Just before Brink's arrival, Riviera Beach agreed to take part in this new initiative. Later, Brink and other area municipal directors allied to express their disinterest in participating in this form of operation. They felt they were now servicing surrounding municipalities without the assistance the county had intended to provide. By

CHILDREN'S PROGRAM. The Riviera Beach Public Library crowded with youngsters in the 1970s. *Courtesy of the Riviera Beach Public Library.*

1979 many—including Riviera Beach—opted out of the proposal.

In commemoration of the 1976 United States Bicentennial, Brink and a few library volunteers authored the only known history book written about the City of Riviera Beach called *Riviera Beach, A History*. The book was authorized by the city and remains the official history book today.

Brink also found a way to involve teenagers in the library and its operations. She organized a program called "Library Lynx" where teens aided in library clerical work and helped Brink in new book selection. The teens were paid $2.30 an hour for four weeks. The students worked for one month, then the program rotated so other teenagers could participate.

It became clear around this time, that the library was quickly outgrowing its space. Brink often complained of lack of space for children's and adult programs. The Riviera Beach Public Library had no meeting room, and lacked space to add any new materials. The building didn't even have air-conditioning until Brink had a small window unit added in 1974. The city planned to construct a new city hall, police station, and fire headquarters in a central location on Blue Heron Boulevard, however, the library was not a part of this plan.

The city commission did not support Brink's funding requests for a newer, larger, more up-to-date library. The commission at the time did not feel the library was incompetent at meeting demands of a city's whose population was now pushing 27,000. At this time, the library had 7,500 registered library cardholders.

Brink organized the library's first Friends of the Library group to raise money for more programming and arranged for a visit by an outside consultant who could compare the library to other similar sized municipalities. This consultant concluded that the library was one-fifth the size recommended by the state, and that the city was seriously under budgeting the library considering the amount of service it was providing. The city's argument was that they didn't increase the budget because they knew the library was incapable of holding more materials. They agreed to incorporate a library building in the municipal complex.

By September 1977, the city was ready to begin preparation for opening the complex. It was discovered the city had never planned a budget to purchase supplies and furniture for the modern building. City commissioners had assumed Brink and staff were going to simply relocate the furniture and equipment they already had. Brink argued in a council meeting that this was unacceptable, as much of the furniture was from the 1950s and falling apart;

the new building was to be 17,000 square feet, more than eight times the size of the current facility, and the old furniture would be inadequate.

A stroke of luck occurred one evening when Brink brought her newly formed Friends group to a city council meeting; the volunteers expressed anger regarding the lack of city support in replacing supplies and furniture. City councilman Gary Nikolits agreed. He was quoted that night saying, "It's a tragedy to have a facility that cannot be used to its potential on opening day."

That night the council took $15,000 from its federal revenue sharing funds to apply toward the cost of purchasing state-of-the-art library equipment for the modern facility.

RIVIERA BEACH PUBLIC LIBRARY. The library in the municipal complex on opening day in 1977. *Courtesy of the Riviera Beach Public Library.*

The new facility opened September 18, 1977 to much fanfare. A book fashion show was created to celebrate the opening with adults while a free showing of Walt Disney's *Treasure Island* was offered for kids along with a small party.

The new library featured an open room in the entrance, graced with six skylights bringing natural light into the facility. It was one of the first libraries in Palm Beach County to feature a full programming room roughly the size of the old library. A large wooden circulation desk matching the bookshelves would allow for quick processing of materials. The director's office sat just off the desk connecting with a modernistic library workroom. Two study rooms occupied the first floor and a large children's area occupied the entire second floor with windows looking down into the main room.

On its opening day, the library had 30,000 volumes with what seemed like endless space to expand. New staff members were hired to assist with the increased workload and more programs were created to keep people interested on a daily basis.

Initially Brink's passion for her job and constant efforts to reach higher didn't go unnoticed. When Palm Beach County Library System director Florence Biller was released from the county director job, late Palm Beach County Commissioner Dennis Koehler encouraged Brink to apply for that position. Brink, described as someone who couldn't simply settle down, had other ideas for her future. Seeking to escape her routine life, she divorced her husband and in 1981 left Riviera Beach for the Findhorn Foundation in Scotland, a utopian society of sorts, where its residents made their own clothes and harvested their own food.

In early 1982 the city started a search for a new director. The city's goal was to make sure this new person could align well with the growing African-American community in the area and would continue to grow the library in a positive direction.

After conducting interviews with the few qualified applicants, the city appointed forty-six-year-old Anne Sutton, a long-time local second grade teacher as the new library director. Sutton's husband was a coach at Suncoast High School. The couple was well-known in the community and the city felt confident Sutton would be a great face for the library.

Because Sutton knew so many city employees already, she was able to work with other departments to create unique ideas to bring people into the library. One of her first big programs was a production of Cinderella which she implemented in partnership with the Riviera Beach recreation department.

Throughout the 1980s, Sutton continued to find creative ways for the library to appeal to young people. She coordinated more play production efforts, egg painting workshops, film showings, trivia nights and even created African-American history month programming with materials in the children's department. By 1988 it was decided to switch the children's department by relocating it downstairs and moving adult non-fiction upstairs. Sutton had a new office constructed for herself upstairs in a new administrative area constructed partially from an old children's workroom. The other part of this room became a designated African-American literature room. The room holds a collection of several thousand books, mostly donated. Sutton was also able to orchestrate the donation of unique decorative traditional African-American artwork to be displayed around the room, including a detailed vertical file with local and national African-American events.

Sutton worked well with other city departments and made the library appealing to children and the African-American population. She had little library collection development experience, especially with adult books. Every year she gave a portion of the library's budget back to the city. Only a barebones collection developed over her twenty-six-year tenure, leaving a gaping hole in literature that the library continues to try to mitigate with its modern budget. Sutton rarely participated in cooperative efforts and even at one point withdrew the library from the cooperative until local residents complained that by doing so they were unable to use other area libraries without paying a fee.

Positive changes Sutton undertook included guiding the library through perhaps its largest undertaking by a small staff. In 1985, she ordered a $7,400 security system. In the previous fiscal year, she claimed that the library had lost more than five hundred books. The system used electromagnetic strips that would be placed in all books and videotapes. The library adopted Sagebrush's Athena library automation software and added electromagnetic sensitive security gates. With the assistance of the vender, all the books were barcoded and cataloged into this system.

The 1990s were mostly uneventful as far as library changes. The seven-member staff team remained the same into the 2000s. The thirty-year-old Riviera Beach Public Library Friends group Brink had spearheaded dwindled as its members aged. Without active recruitment of new members, the volunteer group ceased to exist.

In 2008, the City of Riviera Beach began to search for a new director to replace the retiring Anne Sutton. She agreed to remain in place to train the new director. The city hired former Lee County Library System director Cynthia N. Cobb, a professional librarian and graduate of Florida Agricultural and Mechanical University (FAMU).

Cobb is currently the director of the library and has, over time, implemented new library etiquette codes to deal with ongoing homelessness around the library. She also hired new, younger staff to help implement a more technical approach in the library, such as researching ways to offer new e-services like Over Drive, Zinio, and Hoopla. She also worked with designers to freshen up the look of the library which was still sporting its 1970s-era orange and yellow colors when Cobb took over. New carpet was installed and the building's interior was painted with more modern color tones.

At the time of this writing, Cobb is working on two major projects. To replace the Friends group no longer in existence she established a Riviera Beach

Public Library Foundation to explore even more ways to leverage money to improve the library. This began with an upgraded teen space that had been designated in the 1980s via a willed donation, but had been ignored. The new space featured fresh paint and advanced computers. The conference/public meeting space was also given a major overhaul, turning half of it into a computer lab to offer computer classes.

The second project currently in the works is exploration of a new library building the residents so much deserve. The current building, while an amazing achievement in the 1970s, is plagued with issues including a leaky roof and insufficient electrical outlets for laptops and other technologies. Library workflows and shelving need updating. At 17,000 square feet, the building barely meets state recommendations to service a city of now over 30,000 that also participates in a cooperative servicing surrounding municipalities beyond Riviera Beach.

The library's future is optimistic and full of promise especially now that the city has completely remodeled its waterfront to one of the most attractive on the east coast, and is currently redoing its entire marina area. The city hired consultants to explore the possibility of replacing the library. The consultants found the current library was grossly inadequate.

The same study is examining the replacement of other municipal buildings slated to be replaced by the city. Currently, if the plan continues to gain merit, a new three-story library could rise across the street from the current site where the Wells Recreational Center is located.

The Mandel Public Library of West Palm Beach

Jennifer Noel

Church and Free Reading Room – 1895-1924

The City of West Palm Beach was incorporated on November 5, 1894, that much is known for sure. Less certain, however, is the beginning of the city's library, today known as the Mandel Public Library of West Palm Beach. The story begins with the city's first church, the Union Congregational Church, which moved to the corner of Datura Street and Olive Avenue from Palm Beach around the same time the city was formed. In 1895, Reverend Asbury Caldwell started collecting books, "cheap paperback novels" to be exact, for a reading club. Legend has it that the initial intent of the book collection was to draw construction workers away from Banyan Street (also known as First Street or "Thirst Street"), home of the fledgling city's drinking establishments, and toward more productive pursuits of reading and writing.

Reverend Caldwell is credited with impressing the importance of this undertaking upon those of influence. He secured a permanent location for the reading club when Commodore Charles J. Clarke offered the Palm Beach Yacht Club building for its use. The two-story building was partially deconstructed and moved from the island of Palm Beach across the lake to West Palm Beach. Henry Flagler granted permission for the move, as owner of riparian (referring to the land along the water) rights on the west side. The building was rebuilt next to the city dock, partly over the water.

This small reading club existed for a short period, but floundered, as Reverend Caldwell left West Palm Beach soon after its formation. With no official stewards for the books or the building, there was very little reading going on, and a lack of funds prohibited even the purchase of shelves for the

THE FREE READING ROOOM. The Free Reading Room in the former Yacht Club, 1912. *Courtesy of the Mandel Public Library of West Palm Beach.*

small collection of books and periodicals. The building was left open at all hours, and folks simply walked off with any items they wished to have, including lamps and other fixtures!

It wasn't until a few years later, in 1899, that the West Palm Beach Public Library got its official start. For renewing the interest in the reading room and creating the city library, the people of West Palm Beach owe a debt of gratitude to the ladies of the Lake Worth Literary and Social Club, led by Olivia Burnham. Flagler had earlier pledged a monetary donation of one hundred dollars to augment the library's collection, but this gift was delayed until the Literary Club took charge. The ladies coordinated raising funds for the painting and renovating of the building, and added tables and shelving for a reading room.

For the first year, the reading room occupied only the first floor of the building, as the Yacht Club still existed upstairs. The first librarian was Mrs. Rankin, who came to West Palm Beach from Fernandina. At that time, the library relied heavily on donations of books and other materials to fill its shelves. When the Yacht Club temporarily disbanded in 1900, the library received its assets and expanded to the second floor. In 1903, the library reported holdings of five hundred volumes.

The earliest images and maps including the building show its location over the water, next to a city dock. Dora Doster Utz, West Palm Beach pioneer, remembered: "We had an excellent library or 'Reading Room' as we called it. It was facing a dock at the edge of the lake by the little park. Part of it was built on piling out over the water, and we could go there in the afternoons, select a book, and sit out on the breeze-swept porch and read to our heart's content." In later images from the 1920s, the city park has been filled in, and the building is completely on land, with shrubs and palm trees surrounding it. The building remained in use by the West Palm Beach Tourist Club after the library moved in 1924, but was destroyed in the 1928 hurricane.

Annie Metcalfe, an early pioneer of West Palm Beach, was a schoolteacher who later joined the library as a librarian. Her skills in devising recipes utilizing local fruits such as coconuts, avocados, and mangos did not go unnoticed, and she composed a collection of recipes titled *Palm Beach Dainties*, published in 1915. The pamphlet still resides in the library's archives with the following afterword: "This little booklet is prepared in response to one line of inquiries made at the librarian's table in the little reading room and library of West Palm Beach, Florida."

The Free Reading Room was very much a building for the community. Many groups and local organizations (including churches, political groups, the Woman's Club, and a number of others) got their starts and held meetings in the wooden building overlooking the Intracoastal Waterway. During World War I, the library shared space with the Palm Beach County chapter of the American Red Cross on the second floor. Later, artist Charles Bosseron Chambers used the extra space upstairs for his studio. Librarian Maude Clarke recalled Mr. Chambers accidentally turning off all the lights in the library with the single switch that controlled the building, when attempting to darken his workspace.

In 1918, the West Palm Beach Public Library established rules of membership to include residents of West Palm Beach "and community" with annual dues of one dollar per person. Membership included borrowing privileges of one book at a time, for one week at a time, along with an option for renewal for an additional week. In the 1920s, the library conducted "homecoming" days, in which calls for library patrons to bring library books back to their "home"—that is, the library—were issued in *The Palm Beach Post*. These efforts were successful in getting library books back into the collection. The library officially became a municipal institution of the City of West Palm Beach in January 1919, but it was not until 1960 that library workers were recognized as city employees.

Memorial Library – 125 N. Flagler Drive – 1924-1962

By the early 1920s, the library had outgrown its first home and needed a new one. In 1922, contractor H.C. Daniels won the bid to build Memorial Library for $28,413. Designed by architect Henry Stephen Harvey, the building's final cost was closer to $40,000. To bring the building to completion, the City of West Palm Beach floated a bond issue of $13,000.

Memorial Library opened to the public on January 26, 1924. The Spanish Revival design of the building was widely admired and appreciated. Approximately 7,000 volumes were moved from the reading room to the new library, and that collection almost doubled in size soon after. This is largely thanks to a very generous bequest in the amount of $10,000 from Marie Brown, who passed away in 1918. There were originally some questions about using the funds toward the building, but Brown's will stipulated that the bequest was to go toward books alone and that the library shall be known as the "Duke Public Library," in memory of her father. Instead of renaming the library, a separate reference collection contained in the LeDuc Memorial Room on the second floor of the library opened in September of 1924. The original $10,000 ballooned to $13,000 with interest–the equivalent of over $185,000 in 2017, and the funds were used to fill the room with a first-rate collection of reference materials. George Graham Currie, former secretary then director of the library board, selected this collection, which included rare and out-of-print books on Florida history.

MEMORIAL LIBRARY. Children's program on the lawn of the Memorial Library, 1926. *Courtesy of the Mandel Public Library of West Palm Beach.*

WEST PALM BEACH MEMORIAL LIBRARY. Reading room
interior, 1922. *Courtesy of the Mandel Public Library of West Palm Beach.*

As its name suggests, Memorial Library stood as a reminder of the
sacrifices of our military personnel in the Great War. Included in the building
were a bronze tablet bearing the names of the soldiers from Palm Beach County
who fought in the war, and a stained-glass window depicting a fallen soldier
and an angel. The window was created by an unknown artist for a commission
from D.H. Conkling of *The Palm Beach Post* and existed in Memorial Library
until it was torn down in the 1960s. It then hung in the 100 Clematis Street
library until 2009, when that building was razed.

NOTABLE LIBRARIAN – MAUDE CLARKE
Starting as a volunteer assistant in 1909, Maude Clarke
would go on to become head librarian from 1915 to
1947. She continued working at the library as a
cataloger until 1958. During her near-half-century
tenure, she would institute a modern classification
system, introduce the keeping of circulation records,
and supervise the library's move from the Reading
Room to Memorial Library. *Courtesy of the Mandel Public
Library of West Palm Beach.*

Phillis Wheatley Branch – 1949-1966

PHILLIS WHEATLEY. The Phillis Wheatley Branch of the West Palm Beach Library was named for Wheatley, an eighteenth century African-American poet and slave. *Courtesy of the Library of Congress.*

In 1949, West Palm Beach opened the Phillis Wheatley Branch library for African-Americans. At the time, Memorial Library was not open to these citizens. An increase in the library's annual budget allowed for the creation of this new branch, including two staff members: a librarian (Fannie Payne was the first) and a page. There was no room in the budget for collecting materials, but Zella Adams from Memorial Library ensured that duplicate copies of books would go toward the new branch and solicited for book donations. When the new library opened in December 1949, the collection was comprised of 1,500 books. The Phillis Wheatley Branch was originally located at St. Patrick's Church at 416 N. Sapodilla Street but moved in 1954 to 2001 ½ N. Tamarind Avenue. Named for Phillis Wheatley, an eighteenth century African-American poet and slave, the branch library existed until 1966, when the city's budget no longer allowed for its continuation. Harriet Washington and Ida Mae Burns were the librarians at that time, and they, along with the branch's full collection, moved to the library on Clematis Street.

West Palm Beach Public Library – 100 Clematis Street – 1962-2009

Ground broke for West Palm Beach's next library building on September 5, 1961 and the library opened on April 30, 1962. Designed by Norman Robson, the modernist $484,000 library would stand at the foot of Clematis Street on the Intracoastal Waterway for the remainder of the twentieth century. With an abstract mural on metal frieze panels and thin columns surrounding the rectangular perimeter, the building drew much attention and strong opinions (not all of them positive) from members of the public.

WEST PALM BEACH LIBRARY. City Library, 100 E. Clematis. Note the artistic facade adorning the building, 1960s. *Courtesy of the Mandel Public Library of West Palm Beach.*

This iteration of the West Palm Beach Public Library would see the introduction of automation, computers, and the Internet. While both librarians and patrons evolved with this new technology, the library itself remained, as ever, a place for the community to come together. A 250-seat auditorium in the basement, completed in 1964, allowed for meetings, performances, seminars, and many other gatherings. With 28,000 books on the shelves on opening day, and room for up to 80,000, the library's collection drew throngs of citizens to its doors. The library received its first microfilm reader, along with The *New York Times* on microfilm, when the new building opened. That same year, a photocopier was also installed for the first time. Later, vinyl records, VHS tapes, and CDs were available for patrons to borrow, and the West Palm Beach Public Library was the first library in Palm Beach, Martin, and St. Lucie counties to begin loaning DVDs in 2001. Free Wi-Fi arrived in 2005.

West Palm Beach Public Library faced tough times, however, in 1993. That year, the City of West Palm Beach considered closing the library altogether in order to balance the budget. Facing a deficit of $7 million, city commissioners and Mayor Nancy Graham weighed the options of closing the library, reducing pay for all city employees, and numerous other cuts. A contingent of library supporters made an impassioned plea at a city commission meeting regarding the importance of the library to the West Palm Beach community. Graham, a proponent of the library herself, did not support the library's closing, and after much debate, the budget was passed with a reduction of city employees through voluntary layoffs. It became necessary for the library to cut opening hours, including closing on Fridays.

NOTABLE LIBRARIAN – ZELLA ADAMS
Zella Adams joined Memorial Library as head librarian in 1947. Following a brief job in Tallahassee as Library Extension Director for the State Library Board from 1952 to 1956, Adams returned to her post in West Palm Beach until her retirement in 1971. She oversaw the transition from Memorial Library to 100 Clematis Street. *Courtesy of the Mandel Public Library of West Palm Beach.*

In October 2006, First Lady and former librarian Laura Bush visited the library and led a story time. Mrs. Bush treated the children of West Palm Beach to a reading of *The Spider and the Fly*, just in time for Halloween, and the First Lady emphasized the importance of reading as much as possible. Other notable speakers at the library included authors Jackie Collins, Daniel Silva, Barbara Taylor Bradford, James Patterson, and Nicholas Sparks. John Kerry spoke in front of the library during his Presidential campaign in 2004.

Murmurings of moving, rebuilding, or renovating the library started as early as the 1980s and the decorative frieze was removed in 1985 due to rust. Architect Robson himself expressed apathy toward the decision, later saying that the building barely resembled his original design. *The Palm Beach Post* archives include hundreds of op-eds, letters to the editor, and articles that discussed keeping the library where it was or moving it to a new location. Both sides had valid points: "The library has always been on the waterfront; we have an amazing view!" vs. "We should be using the waterfront park space for festivals, concerts, etc.; the library is old and in the way." The debate continued amongst mayors, city commission members, newspaper editors, and citizens into the twenty-first century.

Under Mayor Joel Daves, the city held a design competition among four renowned architects to plan the next library in 2001. The winning design from Demetri Porphyrios of Porphyrios and Associates featured a Mediterranean design and one-hundred-foot tower. The proposal, intended to be paid for with private funds, never got off the ground, and with new mayor Lois Frankel, a new idea was born: City Center. The plan included a new city hall complex comprising the library, a three hundred space parking garage, and the inclusion of the Palm Beach Photographic Centre, which would move to West Palm from Delray Beach. After many years of controversy, the new library in City Center officially opened in April 2009.

City Center – 2009

Mayor Frankel is credited with the manifestation of the City Center complex on the 400 block of Clematis Street, which the city purchased in 2003. Even with a lawsuit calling for a referendum on the project midstream, she ensured that the project stayed on track. Designed by Song and Associates and built by Catalfumo Construction and Development, the new library's final price tag came in at $31 million. Frankel made use of the city's Community Redevelopment Agency to appropriate the majority of the funds for the project.

The current library is two and one-half times the size of the previous building, with four floors. The first floor of the library is entirely dedicated to new and popular materials with a café. The second floor is the Technology Floor with spaces allotted to teens and media. KidSpace, a separate children's library, and meeting room spaces, including an auditorium, are on the third floor. Finally, the 270-foot long reading room on the fourth floor has a thirty-five-foot-high barrel-shaped ceiling. While many patrons pine for the location and view of the old library, scores more sing the praises of the attractive, contemporary building. Aside from the structure itself, patrons admire the excellent customer service, the wide array of offerings, and the sense of community the library brings to downtown.

Comparing the first full year in the new library to the last full year in the 100 Clematis Street library, the number of items loaned increased fifty-four percent. Reference questions answered increased seventy-seven percent, visits to the library increased thirty-five percent, computer use increased fifty-one percent, adult and computer class attendance increased nearly 200 percent, and even the always-popular children and teen classes and programs increased twenty-three percent. With only three additional staff added for the technology floor, one of the reasons the library was able to keep up with the tremendous increase in use—especially in the labor-intensive area of items loaned and returned—was the addition of RFID technology for both self-checkout and self-returns. Self-check in the new library increased by 426 percent. Using the "Value of Library Services Calculator," provided by the Florida State Library, to see what services were worth to citizens based on what can actually be measured, the final year in the old library delivered $7.8 million in services. The first full year in the new library—that figure was just under $15.5 million in services to the public—saw an increase of 198 percent.

Mandel Public Library of West Palm Beach – 2012

2012 was a very exciting year for the West Palm Beach Public Library. The West Palm Beach Library Foundation received a five-million-dollar grant from the Mandel Foundation. Four million was used to create an endowment to support the library for years to come. The rest went to support three years of Library Foundation infrastructure and four years of funding for classes offered by the library. This funding allowed the library to significantly improve classes offered to the public, and "increMental-U" was one aspect of that improvement. A lifelong learning experience for adults, it developed over several years and in 2016 won two national awards: The Association for Continuing Higher Education South (ACHE South) 2016 Distinguished Program Award for an outstanding non-credit initiative, and the Harvard Kennedy School Ash Center Bright Ideas Award. In addition, it was a second-round finalist in the 2016 U.S. Conference of Mayors City Livability Awards Program, and the Public Programs Office at the American Library Association invited the library to write a program model based on the lifelong learning program.

The library's name was formally changed to Mandel Public Library of West Palm Beach. The grant also provided funds for the change in signage, and a photograph of the Mandel brothers, Joseph, Morton, and Jack, was installed near the entrance to the library with the following quote: "The hallmark of our philanthropy is our commitment to invest in people with the values, ability, and passion to change the world."

The West Palm Beach Library Foundation, which secured the five-million-dollar grant from the Mandel Foundation, also secured funding to support many of the library's new and traditional services: Elementary Homework Center, Teen Homework Center, the aforementioned "increMental-U," Summer Academy, Healthy You, Get That Job, Let's Read, summer reading programs, and Dog Tales. The Friends of the Mandel Public Library of West Palm Beach (reestablished in 2009), and the Library Advisory Board support the library both financially and via advocacy efforts to raise awareness about the library.

So much of the library's one hundred year plus legacy lives on. Many volumes in the Florida Room and Special Reference collection bear a "Memorial Library" imprint from the early twentieth century. The library's own scrapbooks, with painstakingly collected newspaper clippings proclaiming a children's story hour or list of new books, were most likely maintained by

Maude Clarke herself. Our most veteran employee, Marsha Warfield, joined the library staff in 1980 and even recalls working with the librarians from the Phillis Wheatley Branch. As the oldest continuously operating library in Palm Beach County, the Mandel Public Library of West Palm Beach staff and administrators take great pride in the library's history. The staff is delighted to represent the wonderful City of West Palm Beach and welcome visitors from all over the world, every day.

Library Memories

Barbara Storch
Technical Services Manager, library employee since 1987

For SunFest, I remember supervisors having to spend a good amount of time figuring out alternate schedules for staff so that they could get their forty hours in when we were closed on the Friday of SunFest. This usually meant four ten-hour days. Eventually we were able to stay open during SunFest, and we got to hear much of the music, as there was not much insulation in the walls of the old building and we did not have high impact windows. This was also a challenge, as we got frequent visitors looking for restrooms.

I also remember how different Clematis Street was. When I came here for my first interview in June 1987, I had lunch at a little country style restaurant in the 200 block in the space that was subsequently occupied by a pizza place and then became a trendier café. I also used to get my lunch just about every day at Robinson's bakery, which was a little farther north on the same block.

When I started my job, I had six years of cataloging experience and had to schedule time at the one cataloging computer. Quite a change has taken place since then. A good amount of the physical processing was done in house, with the help of volunteers. At that time, we were using 3M security strips and we had to put them into each item manually.

I remember the "great third floor flood of January 1987" when our leaky roof finally gave way during a heavy rainstorm. I had foolishly come to work that day even though I was getting sick. I came into my department and everyone was standing around amid soggy roof tiles and wet books. It was quite a challenge to take stock of the damages and get back to normal, but the staff pulled together and we did it.

We also started bookmobile service in 1997. I remember riding around the city with Jose Aponte, former library director, while we were in the planning stage, evaluating neighborhoods for potential bookmobile stops.

Tara Moreno
Hispanic Outreach Librarian, library employee since 2004

When I came for my interview, in early fall of 2004, there were tarps over some of the adult stacks and the entire children's area was out of service, due to Hurricanes Jeanne and Frances. People in New Jersey thought I was crazy to be moving to Florida at that time. I just thought it would be cool to experience a hurricane. All I heard from my new coworkers for a few months were hurricane stories, about roof repairs, lines for gas, showering at friends' houses, and camping out on patios in the heat. Everything around town was recovering, too, for a while, like the Palm Beach Zoo and Mounts Botanical Garden. As it turns out, I've only really experienced one hurricane in the twelve years that I've been here: Wilma in 2005. But she brought a cool front in, and electricity was restored quickly. So that wasn't too bad at all. Ironically, New Jersey has had worse storms than Florida over these years (most notably, super storm Sandy). Meanwhile, I have enjoyed every year of living and working in West Palm Beach.

Janet Norton
E-Government Librarian, library employee since 2003

This is a library story from several years back during the recession – Note: The Life Support Workshop is now on Monday mornings.

Each Monday afternoon on the second floor, something special happens. Airplane pilots and art teachers, cooks and carpenters meet in one spot and try to accomplish the same thing—improve their lives. Mondays from 1:30 - 3:30 p.m. we have the Life Support Workshop in our computer lab. Folks can come by and work on résumés, job search, fill out online applications and government forms or just see if they can find someone to network with using additional computer time. I'm there to offer assistance, so I have had the pleasure of getting to know the faces and stories of many of our area's unemployed. I can tell you there are some hardworking, dedicated people out there doing everything they can to make a change in their lives.

I recall one gentleman, with a more than slightly apprehensive expression on his face, enter the computer lab and sign in. He said he had been told from other library staff that he could receive help with his résumé in the lab. We sat down and began to talk about what type of work he did and if he had his job history information. As with so many of the people that come to Life Support workshops, you can't start talking about their jobs without it intertwining with their lives. The stories of concerned parents, last resort efforts, etc. often spill into the conversation. This gentleman was no exception. Job history? He had worked at the same restaurant most of his career. Computer skills to type out a résumé? Not really. In need of a job immediately? You bet.

Together we were able to decipher the skills and tasks he had been doing all along, but had never put into words. His résumé turned out to showcase his strengths and he left with his five free copies, a newfound realization of his job talents and the idea of how much he had to offer a perspective employer. The very next day he came back into the library and walked right up to me to proudly announce he had gotten a job the very same day. After leaving the library, he had visited restaurants and dropped off his shiny new résumé. He was hired the same day—much to his surprise and relief! He then proceeded to offer me money, food and everything short of his first-born child in gratitude for my help. I informed him the best thing he could he do for the library was to write a comment card and tell a friend. Next staff meeting I was pleased to hear the card read that "...I would love to say thank you ... I attended her workshop on November 3, 2009. I know she went above and beyond her duties to help me. Also, I got a job on November 4, 2009. Thanks..." The next week at the workshop I saw another gentleman with that same look of hesitation walk into the computer lab. He said, "A friend told to me come to the library. They help you here."

This story came from Polar Express MANY years ago:

One of my favorite stories involving the library is one that occurred during our Youth Services Polar Express event. Every child wants to climb on Santa's lap, but unfortunately not all are able. Not because of the unanticipated hundreds of people that showed up, or time constraints, but for the fact that they may not have the physical ability to make the climb.

As the line for Santa began to grow and twist its way into our hallway, parents soon began to feel the tug of small restless hands accompanied with their little ones asking, "When will I get to see Santa?" In Santa's room, elves and Mrs. Claus tried their best to move the line along. At one point, two boys came in with their Mom, one jumped into Santa's lap, the other could not—he had multiple sclerosis and was secured in his chair. Mom snapped her photo while the restlessness of the crowd was tangible. While the body of the younger brother may have been different than that of the older sibling seated on Santa's lap, his eyes showed the same wonder and excitement. Disregarding the "need for speed" our Santa came down from his dais, knelt down to the child and began to engage him. Mom was grateful and teary-eyed as she snapped the photos of her wiggling and smiling young son. Those who saw came quickly to the realization that this was not some mall picture line. Here at the library, there are no sales to pitch or dollars to be made by the minute. Instead we offer community—free to those that choose to embrace it.

I am proud to say: that event was created by my Youth Services Department and that Santa was my husband—and this is My City Library.

Another Polar Express favorite story:

Because of the unanticipated number of attendees one year, we ran out of bells to hand out to the kids. We started cutting off jingle bells from every decoration and costume we had, tying on a red ribbon and making sure each child left a believer with a bell to hear the "sweet sound" of Christmas.

Lena Safi
Technical Services Librarian, library employee since 1997

Before moving into the new building in 2009, we ordered thousands of new books on a great variety of subjects for which we would have dozens of separate sections on the first floor—a luxury we could not afford with the limited space in the old library. The sections would range from pets and plants to art, to true crime, to just for laughs, to world literature to… you name it. The books were not to circulate until after the move. When we opened the doors to the public in the new location, there was so much to choose from for everybody, including staff (naturally). At some point, I had more than fifty brand new books on a wide number of subjects checked out to myself. I was bringing books home almost every day and of course could not read them as quickly so they were piling up like a tower, on my side table next to the armchair by my living room window. At that time, I lived in the apartment on the first floor with a wide French door facing the backyard lawn that was not my private patio. Anybody who walked behind the building and came close to the window could see what's inside my living room unless I had closed blinds protecting my privacy. Actually, it was not that bad as hardly anybody ever walked there except for an occasional drop by from neighboring kids. One Sunday afternoon, I was at home letting bright sunshine in through the open blinds. Kids were running outside and I was finishing my kitchen chores in anticipation of sitting down in the armchair with one of the books from my "Eiffel tower." At some point a girl of about five or six years old stopped by my window, saw a tower of books on my side table, and shouted to her playmates, "Look, look! It's a LIBRARY in there!" The effort she put into articulating the difficult word and the admiration in her voice clearly indicated her awe and surprise at seeing so many books in my apartment. Her two friends came closer to check out the "library." After a little discussion of their discovery, they were gone like a small flock of birds chirping about their business. I finished my chores and spent the rest of the afternoon with books. The entire collection on loan from then City of West Palm Beach Public Library (now Mandel Public Library of West Palm Beach).

Mitzie Vincentz, library patron

I am remembering my youth and how I would stay cool on a hot, humid day in the Palm Beaches—those memorable years of the 1940s and early 1950s when there was no escape to the beach, lake, or canals with my friends. A cooling apparatus was a rare luxury, and there were no malls to meander about. So off to the downtown library, an old two-story building that housed a large inventory of reading materials, and a welcoming librarian. No air-conditioning, but some adventure book covers promised to vicariously carry a person to the freezing summits of mountains. I climbed those squeaky wooden stairs, and perched by an open window, I viewed the lake's activity filled with sailboats and prams; I could almost feel the cool spray from winds across their bows. The palm fronds brushed against the window screen, a fan provided by nature. A heard a purring noise from below at the park. I saw Sally the Seminole Indian, stitching with her hand machine, bright pieces of fabric into native skirts and dolls—for the tourists' delight. Jovial old men played board games and reminisced under an open shelter. Across the street stood the Palms Theatre, where one could view a movie in air-cooled comfort. This was a landmark, after Elvis Presley gave a live performance. But what girl could stay "cool" being in his presence? Next stop, down the street to Woolworth's or McCrory's Five & Dime store's lunch counter for ice cream. Oh, and maybe a bottle of a new nail polish. After all, we had to have pretty toes for the beach. Now my Great Pyrenees are begging me to hit the cool switch!

OVERDUE IN PARADISE

Susie Rambeau Best, library patron

I remember on rainy days going to the downtown West Palm Beach Library. It was so cozy and was always cool and comfortable. The staff was very dedicated to their job. The main floor had a small Florida Room. The Florida Room was kept locked at all times. You could only enter the room with permission. It had old local yearbooks, photos, phone directories, and more. I remember how important that room was to all. The items can't be replaced. The genealogy room was downstairs on the north side of the library. We always parked on the north side of the library under the huge banyan trees. The parking lot was also where we parked when going to the Greyhound bus station. I remember story time, too. It was such a happy time in that building. I will always cherish the memories.

Jeanette J. Guerty
Palm Springs Public Library

Virginia K. Farace and Suvi Manner

In the early 1960s, Bobbe Taffel proposed a resolution to the Palm Springs Village Council to start a library. Taffel is quoted in the 1988 Library Souvenir Booklet as declaring, "I pushed it at each meeting ... and then when I was Vice-Mayor...they said yes and it knocked me off my feet." The library's first location was a closet in the village hall.

The village published a flier, asking residents to donate books, and books started pouring in. Taffel recruited her friend Janet Walker to assist with the library project. Both women were classroom teachers, and both were taking graduate library science classes at the time.

Walker volunteered to organize and catalog the collection. She is quoted in that same souvenir booklet as saying "...here are all of these books totally unclassified...it was a big mess! I worked six weeks, taking a lot of that work home, and put them in some semblance of order."

A bevy of volunteers, including Ban Robinson, Shirley Kohl, Mary Lou Seaman, Mary Schwenk, Norma Lasko, and Charlotte Lynch worked at the new library, making sure to keep regular hours so residents would know when it was open. The village council established a library board, with Barbara Jette as chairman. Other early board members included Thelma Lowenkron, George Silverman, Moses Lennon, Victor Muller, Bobbe Taffel, Frances Mooney, and Janet Walker.

When the library outgrew village hall, a doublewide trailer was placed on land just north of the current library where the rear parking lot is now. The library shared this space with the recreation department. Charlotte Lynch became the first paid staff member. Lynch had bookmarks printed at her own expense. She closed the library two hours in the afternoon so that she could eat dinner. Once a month she made out a list requesting best-selling books and handed it in to the village manager's office. "I don't know where the list went," she said, "but they gave me the money or the books."

Jeanette J. Guerty was elected to the village council in the early 1970s. Her favorite cause was the library. She lobbied for monies to fund the first designated library building. Soft-spoken but determined, Guerty urged that revenue from the 1976 Capital Improvements Bond issue be used to construct the library. To honor her efforts, the village council named the library after her: The Jeanette J. Guerty Palm Springs Library. Guerty died in September, 1978, just before the opening of the first library building.

The Village of Palm Springs appointed Janeen Campanero as library director in 1978, the first professional librarian to hold that position. Dedication ceremonies for the new building were held on November 11 of that year. That new facility offered 6,000 square feet for books and activities. Additional staff members were employed, including Eve Johnson as children's librarian.

JEANETTE J. GUERTY LIBRARY GARDEN. The library has garden space for outdoor reading and library programming.
Courtesy of the Palm Springs Public Library.

A group of library supporters organized the Friends of the Library in 1979. The inaugural officers were Berenice Bluestone, President; Lil Newell, Vice-President; Anne Dee, Secretary; Lee Locatelli, Treasurer; and Harry Scholes, Historian. Sarah Gay was elected president in 1980 and she and her husband Harry, as Treasurer, served the Friends and Library for many years. The Friends began to sponsor many programs throughout the years including an annual book and author luncheon featuring best-selling authors, art exhibits, talent shows, a library gift shop, a library cookbook, and the annual children's bookmark contest.

When Angelica Carpenter came as the library director in 1982, there were over 20,000 items in the collection and additional space was needed. In 1985, voters approved a bond issue to enlarge the library by fifty percent.

During the mid-1990s, the library automated by joining COALA (Cooperative Authority for Library Automation) using Sirsi Unicorn software. Circulation on the system began in December 1997 with about twenty-five percent of the retrospective conversion to complete. Around this same time, the library offered Free-Net access to the public and in January 1998 began to offer full, unfiltered Internet access.

On October 1, 1997, the library joined The Library Cooperative of the Palm Beaches. Through the Cooperative, the library received State Aid for the first time. Public library directors worked hard for many years to win State Aid for municipal libraries. As part of that effort, the Palm Springs Library took a leadership role in the Florida Public Library Association. The organization's articles of incorporation were signed in this library. At one point, Carpenter served as president and longtime Palm Springs Library Friends' President Sarah Gay served on the founding FPLA board.

The Palm Springs Library also played a major role in organizing BookFest, an annual, regional literary festival. It started in 1991 under the leadership of Angelica Carpenter and was presented annually by the Palm Beach County Library Association. Again, Sarah and Harry Gay from the Friends' Board also served on the founding BookFest board. The village provided strong support for BookFest, donating money and other resources. This included encouraging residents to attend the event or to volunteer. BookFest grew and prospered, outgrowing the volunteers of the library association. The Palm Beach County Cultural Council took over BookFest starting in 1998 before canceling the event a few years later.

The Palm Springs Library was state headquarters for the Florida Chapter of the Society of Children's Book Writers and Illustrators. Carpenter's mother, Jean Shirley, began a local critique group for this organization when she moved to Palm Springs in 1984 and later became the Florida Regional Advisor. After Shirley's death in 1995, Barbara Casey took her place. The Palm Springs Library hosted a statewide workshop each September, co-sponsored by the SCBWI and the Florida Public Library Association.

YOUTH PROGRAM. Children participate in a Pokémon event at the Palm Springs Public Library. Have to catch them all!
Courtesy of the Palm Springs Public Library.

Starting in 1990, Shirley and Carpenter published three biographies for young people, all from Lerner Publications: Frances Hodgson Burnett, L. Frank Baum, and Robert Louis Stevenson. In 1999, Carpenter moved to Fresno, California, to become director of The Arne Nixon Center for the Study of Children's Literature at the Henry Madden Library of the California State University at Fresno.

Another library expansion followed in the early 2000s almost doubling the original 6,000 square feet size to its current 11,800 square feet. This was accomplished under library directors Don "Pete" Daniels followed by Elena Romeo. As of today, under the directorship of Suvi Manner, the library boasts multiple free use public access computers, wireless computer access, classes, programs and activities for all age groups and for bi-lingual users, more than 50,000 materials that include books, movies, documentaries, newspapers, magazines, music and audio book CDs, and e-books.

Assistant director and children's librarian Mary Helen Sakellarios, who retired in 2016 after thirty-one years, was honored and recognized at both the local and state level for her contributions to youth programming and community outreach. According to current children's librarian Rebekah Stewart, "whenever I attended a workshop with Mary Helen, she was treated like a rock star!"

Currently, Vicki Webber is the longest serving library employee at thirty-six years as the Technical Services Supervisor. Since 1978, the library directors were Janeen Campanero, Angelica Carpenter, Don "Pete" Daniels, Elena Romeo, and currently, Suvi Manner. Webber has served with them all.

Webber said, "Just as each director brought a unique leadership style and skill set to the library, so have they encouraged our staff to develop and share our own strengths and talents both personally and professionally. As a result, we continue to enthusiastically find new ways to engage and encourage our community to discover and enjoy what libraries have to offer."

The Jeanette J. Guerty Palm Springs Library continues its tradition of providing Palm Springs residents the best possible public library service, offering cultural, educational, and recreational benefits through its collection, staff, and services.

Greenacres City Library

David Scott

In 1926, Greenacres City was officially incorporated with a population of 1,250. Twenty-five years later in July 1951, local resident Mrs. Elmer Leonard volunteered as the first town librarian and housed the library in a closet in her home. Town residents and the Lake Worth City Library donated the books.

In 1952, a local chapter of the Home Demonstration Club (HDC), a women's organization, took over the library duties and transferred the collection to a small room built behind the town fire station with Ms. Hester Allen as librarian. By June 1953, the collection was comprised of five hundred books. The HDC relinquished its library duties by 1956, leading to a series of volunteer librarians over several years.

The town council appointed Ms. Joyce Simmons as part-time librarian with a modest twenty-five dollars per month salary in February 1963. A city hall complex was built on Perry Avenue and Fourth Street that same year. A 920-square-foot facility as part of the Greenacres City Hall complex at 500 Perry Avenue was to house the city library. It was initially anticipated that the entire building would be designated for library use, but over the years it became a shared space with the Public Works Department and Police Department at various times.

The library had irregular and limited hours until the early 1970s at which time it established a regular weekday-only schedule of forty-four hours per week. Throughout the 1970s, the library collection continued to grow to the point of outgrowing the available space. The town was also growing, as was the need for more administrative office space to accommodate the demands of an expanding population.

One of the first moves to address the overcrowding issue was a resolution and subsequent agreement between the town council and the county to turn library service in Greenacres over to the county. The town joined the Library Taxing District in the spring of 1982 and formally closed the city library. The

MID-COUNTY BRANCH. The Mid-County Branch in Greenacres shortly before its merger with the Greenacres City Library in the 1970s. *Courtesy of the PBCLS.*

collection, along with city library staff, would move to a new storefront library location for the county. In February 1983, the new 5,500-square-foot Greenacres Branch of the Palm Beach County Library System (PBCLS), with combined collections from PBCLS's Mid-County Branch and the City of Greenacres Library, opened on 6135 Lake Worth Road in the former Lake Worth Center Plaza.

Lake Worth Public Library

Ginger L. Pedersen

In 1909, Palm Beach County had just emerged after being carved out of Dade County. Many could see the potential of this tropical paradise, and land sales were picking up. A corporation began quietly acquiring large tracts of land along the body of water known as Lake Worth, about seven miles south of West Palm Beach. This high land, mostly covered with its primeval oak and sand pine forest, was farmed by hardy pioneers such as Samuel and Fannie James, the first homesteaders in what would become Lake Worth. The settlers grew pineapple, citrus, and tomatoes on the sandy soil. The land parcels were stitched together by Harold J. Bryant, Frederick Edward Bryant and William Greenwood, who formed the Bryant and Greenwood Corporation. Their grand scheme was to offer prospective Floridians farmland west of the proposed town site. The three men also owned the Palm Beach Farms Company, which had thousands of acres of land west of the coastal area. If one bought five acres of farmland, they received a free twenty-five-foot lot in the proposed Town of Lucerne. Many investors bought acreage, but many more people simply bought a town lot or two and set to build their cottage in paradise.

The proposed Lucerne town name went to the United States Post Office for approval, but Bryant and Greenwood had to quickly think of a new name for their settlement because Lucerne was already taken. Given its prime location on Lake Worth, the name became self-evident–the town of Lake Worth.

Although the town officially incorporated in 1913, settlement had already begun. In 1912, still bearing the Lucerne name, a newspaper began publication to chronicle the new settlement's story. There was no printer in Lake Worth, so the fledging *Lucerne Herald* was printed in West Palm Beach with R.D. Strong as publisher. Bryant and Greenwood mailed the paper's first issues in 1912 by the thousands across the nation as an advertising vehicle for selling their town lots and farm acreage. However, within that paper was an interesting plea—to send books to start a library. Those first pioneer residents of Lake Worth knew that to grow a community, a library was needed to help adults and children in their avocational and personal interests.

That plea for book donations was heard across the nation, and books began to pile up in the stock room at the printery in West Palm Beach. A narrow, gleaming white shell rock road connected West Palm Beach and Lake Worth, not yet given the name Dixie Highway. It was simply called the "Rock Road" and its dusty, sandy stretch was walked by many, or ridden on by bicycle. Automobiles were making their first appearance, and were a luxury most could not afford. As if by magic, a couple volunteered to transport all those books to Lake Worth, and even set up a makeshift library in their new home. John L. McKissock, a plumber by trade from Pennsylvania, and his wife Retta, pedaled all the books back to their home on O Street from West Palm Beach. They helped catalog the books, keeping records as patrons checked them out. On November 30, 1912, R.D. Strong, the publisher of the *Lucerne Herald*, and the McKissocks founded the Library Association.

As the collection grew, a larger home was needed for the fledgling library, and the newly built Lake Worth Club House was selected. Fundraising began for the dream of having a dedicated library building for the town. The collection soon outgrew the club house, and the library board made arrangements with the town to move the collection to a room in the city hall building. Finally, in 1926, the Lake Worth Public Library was formally established as part of the Town of Lake Worth by the town voters. A budget of $6,000 was allocated for the library by a vote of 188 to 24. Lots were purchased on M Street and Lucerne Avenue, and the sums of money began to grow, but not enough to erect a facility.

Local residents hatched an idea to have the proposed library be a memorial to General William Jenkins Worth, for whom soldiers had named the body of water as they were scouting the area in 1842. Fort Worth in Texas was named for the general, as well as Worth Square in New York City, yet no memorial existed for him in Florida. In 1939, Senators Claude Pepper and C.O. Andrews proposed a bill in Congress that $60,000 be appropriated to build the Major General William Jenkins Worth Memorial Library to commemorate the one hundredth anniversary of the naming of the body of water. Congress approved the bill, but President Franklin D. Roosevelt vetoed the measure, dashing the hopes of residents and the library board.

Local fundraising efforts were pushed, and enough funds were in the bank to begin construction in 1940. Architect Edgar S. Wortman received the commission for the library building. His design was a Mediterranean-style

UNDER CONSTRUCTION. The new Lake Worth Public Library, designed by architect Edgar Wortman under construction, November, 1940. *Courtesy of the Lake Worth Public Library.*

building that would complement other buildings in the downtown Lake Worth area. Just as construction began, two longtime winter residents, twin brothers James D. Strait and William S. Strait, made a $10,000 donation to the library board for the erection of a museum. A museum wing was added to the library plans, and the Strait Museum added to the cultural offerings of the town.

Ground was broken October 7, 1940; by February, 1941, the building was substantially complete. Although funds were not available for air-conditioning, the building was constructed to allow for its eventual installation with ducts and a small room for the plant. The dedication took place on August 12, 1941.

LAKE WORTH PUBLIC LIBRARY. The nearly complete library in January, 1941. *Courtesy of the Lake Worth Public Library.*

REFERENCE ROO.M. The new reference room at the Lake Worth Public Library, 1940s. *Courtesy of the Lake Worth Public Library.*

The Lake Worth Art League took up residence in the Strait Museum, and patrons enjoyed many years of art instruction and exhibitions. The design of the building, with its high ceilings and open spaces, also made it a wonderful venue for paintings and other forms of art, including the R. Sherman Winton collection of paintings, and many other paintings depicting historic and colorful subjects.

During the 1950s, the Lake Worth Library had the highest number of patrons and circulation among all Palm Beach County libraries by a wide margin, and seasonal patrons especially enjoyed its spacious rooms and customer service.

By the early 1960s, sufficient funds were collected to install a heating and air-conditioning plant. This would keep patrons more comfortable, especially in the hot Florida summers, but more importantly allow the book collection to be kept under better conditions for preservation.

As the decades passed, the library kept up with the needs of patrons. LP vinyl records were replaced by cassettes and CDs; books on tape became books on CD. Lake Worth installed one of the first library security systems to reduce theft of library materials, and in 1982 the library became handicapped accessible. In the 1990s, computers for patron use were introduced, and soon the Internet became a service the library offered its patrons.

As the City of Lake Worth celebrated its centennial in 2013, the library played a central role in the festivities. A groundbreaking look into the city's hidden history revealed the town's original inhabitants, Samuel and Fannie James, and resulted in the publication of *Pioneers of Jewell*. All proceeds from the book benefited the library.

The evolution continues into the twenty-first century. Most recently the library opened its "CreatE-Lab" where children and teens can study and explore technology to support their studies and interests.

Over its more than one hundred years, the Lake Worth Public Library has served thousands of patrons, from locals to winter residents. The library building is the focal point of downtown Lake Worth, as it has been for more than seven decades, and it will continue to serve its patrons with information and services for education, entertainment, and enjoyment that only a good book, or new knowledge, can bring.

Lantana Public Library

Sid Patchett

Lantana's library started like many other public libraries: through community involvement. In 1947, the Lantana Woman's Club established a circulating library collection in the Community Church on Oak Street. The library was stocked with nine hundred books donated by the Society of the Four Arts in Palm Beach. For the next four years, Lantana's library, like many fledgling libraries across the country, relied on donations for collection development. The library was open to patrons a few hours per week and was staffed by enthusiastic volunteers. Book donations from the community, purchases by the Woman's Club, and growth of the church's membership compelled the Woman's Club to seek new quarters. This posed a challenge; the town, with less than eight hundred residents, could not afford to build a library and the club had insufficient funds to rent a new facility.

A 1947 hurricane changed the library's history. The storm destroyed the wooden drawbridge that connected Lantana and nearby Hypoluxo Island. However, the bridge tender's house remained intact, and when a concrete bridge replaced its wooden predecessor, the town moved the house to a site near the new bridge. There it languished until 1952, first as a fisherman's shanty and later as an empty eyesore, when it caught the eyes of Mrs. Donna Hickam, chairwoman of the Woman's Club building committee, and club president Mrs. Abbie Wadell. These women persuaded Lantana's town council to lease the building to the club for just one dollar per year. Following monetary donations from Madam Jacques Balsan, a Hypoluxo resident and the former Duchess of Marlborough, and Mrs. Harold Vanderbilt, as well as smaller donations from local businesses, the club enlisted the help of members' husbands and generous contractors. These members of Lantana's community worked to improve the building, refinish its interior, paint the exterior, and install shelves and furniture. Lantana's new library opened to the public in late 1952. This imaginative

LANTANA COMMUNITY LIBRARY.
The Woman's Club and the Town of
Lantana operated the free library.
Private Collection.

repurposing of a piece of Lantana's history gave the town the only library in Florida once housed in a drawbridge.

For four decades, the Lantana Woman's Club, assisted by the Town of Lantana and generous private donors, supported Lantana with a free public library. In the 1950s, experienced librarian Mrs. Nancy Bauskett cataloged the collection. Her colleague, children's radio host Mrs. Lena Carson, held popular story hours at the library. The Town of Lantana gave the club an annual stipend, maintained the building, and paid for electricity and insurance. Afternoon tea fundraisers were held at the library, supplementing community book donations and raising money for the library's first sign, which listed the library's hours of operation. It is unknown when these hours were, but they probably did not exceed six hours a week, as recorded in the early 1960s. In 1963, Mrs. Norman Ball became the chairwoman of the Woman's Club's library committee, which worked hard that year to process incoming book donations. Club members' families built new shelves to house the books. By the end of the decade, the library held 7,000 volumes and spent $1,200 a year on book purchases. The town allocated additional funding for the library, and the library teas and open houses continued to support the library's finances.

By 1971, the library had outgrown its facility, and a twelve-foot extension was added to the building. The Town of Lantana provided $1,100 for materials as well as a volunteer crew led by councilman Paul Seppalla, who built the walls and roof. After the library's expansion was complete, it reopened to serve one thousand patrons, prompting an expansion of the library's hours of operation from six to eight hours per week. Chairwoman Ball cataloged the collection using the Dewey Decimal Classification system, after which she retired, having served on the library's committee for fifteen years. By the end of the 1970s, the

LANTANA COMMUNITY LIBRARY. The Lantana Library housed in the repurposed bridge-tender's house in a park next to the Intracoastal Waterway. *Courtesy of the Lantana Public Library.*

library was open to patrons twenty hours per week and offered over 8,000 books.

In the 1980s, Mrs. Ginny Spence was serving as the committee's chairwoman. Eighteen volunteers worked nearly 4,000 hours in less than two years, lending over 15,000 books to community patrons. The library now offered the rental of best-selling novels for ten cents per week. By 1986, the town's grant was $1,500. Overdue fines theoretically supplemented the library's funds, but Mrs. Spence was known for forgiving the fines and collecting overdue books at borrowers' front doors, which was quite an unusual practice.

From 1947 through 1986, the Woman's Club Library flourished. Library volunteers enjoyed offering community service, and by providing a small grant of taxpayer money, the Town of Lantana avoided being absorbed into the new Palm Beach County Public Library Special Taxing District. In 1986, Mayor Robert McDonald and councilman Dave Adams suggested that the library occupied valuable land which could be used for commercial purposes. This proposal provoked a spirited defense of the library over the next months by members of the Woman's Club, library

GINNY SPENCE LIBRARY CHAIRWOMAN. Ginny Spence. Library chairwoman and volunteer extraordinaire. *Courtesy of the Lantana Public Library.*

patrons, and even some town council members. The privatization proponents then perused the forty-five-year-old State of Florida document granting the Town of Lantana the land comprising Independence Park, including the land where the library stood. It contained a deed restriction limiting the property's use to a public purpose. The library issue faded away, but it left a general feeling that Lantana's library service needed to move to an expanded level.

In 1994, McDonald saw a sign inviting bids for a half-acre property in downtown Lantana. The town council enthusiastically agreed that the building on the land would be an ideal space for a new level of library service. Lantana's town manager won the bid for the property, and the property was sold to Lantana for $226,000. What followed was the building's renovation and modification for library use, the purchase and installation of furniture and equipment, and employment of a professionally qualified library director. The town also established the Lantana Library Foundation, a charitable organization chaired by Mrs. Nancy Canter. Mrs. Canter and her fellow board members raised over $16,000 within a year.

The Lantana Woman's Club was instrumental in planning and stocking the new library. Interviewed by the *Coastal Observer* in 1996, Mrs. Ginny Spence proudly reported that the opening of the new library was "the greatest event for the Town of Lantana" and that she hoped the town's residents would volunteer their time, effort, and money to help support the library. That same year, Brandon Moving and Storage donated their equipment and staff to pack and move the library's 9,000 volumes to their new home. After nearly five decades, the bridge tender's house was retired and relocated to the South Florida Fair's Yesteryear Village.

The library's transition from a private organization to a public institution was unique and cost effective, as the library was staffed solely by volunteers, led by a single professional director. The Town of Lantana dedicated its new public library in a grand ceremony on the afternoon of Sunday, April 21, 1996, and the library served its first patrons the next day. Lantana's public library has maintained its original tradition of providing a free public library in which services are available to all, regardless of ability to pay. In recent decades, the library has offered faxing and photocopying services, charging only nominal fees, a quite unusual practice in modern libraries. Automated circulation and publicly available computers and printers became available to patrons in 1997, and grant money from the Gates Foundation's Library Initiative over the next decade allowed the library to expand and maintain its electronic offerings. The availability of library computers, printing services, and computer basics courses has provided countless patrons with free electronic resources, even for non-members. Since the late 1990s, the library has maintained a digital catalog. Volunteers have enthusiastically mastered the computer skills required to loan books, enter new borrower records, run overdue notices, and assist users of the online catalog.

As of 2017, the Lantana Public Library is open fifty-one hours per week and has a carefully curated collection that now contains over 9,000 volumes. The library's extended hours made it eligible for a variety of grants, and since 2001 has met the requirements for membership in the Library Cooperative of the Palm Beaches. This co-op includes the Palm Beach County Public Library, as well as city libraries in Delray Beach, Boynton Beach, Palm Springs, Lake Worth, Lake Park, West Palm Beach, North Palm Beach and Riviera Beach. Membership in the co-op provides reciprocal borrowing privileges to the residents of each member town.

Local support groups have raised community awareness of the library's services, as well as funds to supplement the library's budget. The Lantana Library Foundation has continuously solicited donations, raising thousands of dollars for book purchases. The Friends of the Lantana Public Library provide publicity for the library in local newspapers, raise funds through book sales and auctions, organize monthly meetings that feature local lecturers and authors on topics of interest to Lantana's residents, and run the library's book discussion group. The Friends' semi-annual newsletter, *The Bugle* (bearing the subtitle "We Blow the Library's Horn"), was first published in 1999 and alerts readers to local events and new library services.

The Lantana Public Library also holds an invaluable collection of slides depicting Lantana's historic buildings. Collected over many years by the town's official historian, Mary Linehan, these slides were donated to the library by Mrs. Linehan's daughter and digitized by volunteers. In addition to the slide collection, a team of Chancellor Charter School students created a collection of videotaped oral histories of some of Lantana's older residents. Both the oral history collection and the Linehan Photograph Collection are available online through the library's website.

In 2009, the Palm Beach County Public Library system opened its largest branch, a 29,000-square-foot building less than three miles west of Lantana's library. This handsome facility has much to offer, including extended hours of operation, public computers, DVDs and audiobooks, multiple copies of bestsellers, a vast children's room staffed by experts in youth programming, and many highly qualified staff members to serve patrons. Despite initial fears that the Lantana Public Library would succumb to the "Walmart Effect," a frequent retail phenomenon in which big-box stores open in a town and drive small "mom and pop" stores out of business, the libraries have in fact complemented each other. Palm Beach County's Lantana Road Branch has provided Lantana's residents with the county library's resources at no additional cost.

As a result of this partnership, Lantana's town library now attracts a smaller group of users seeking a quiet and comfortable space in which to read and work. Many visitors have remarked upon the friendliness and unhurried attention of the library's volunteers. In recent years, the library has expanded its services to include wireless Internet and computers reserved by appointment. Patrons reserving a computer, whether by telephone or in person, have continued to enjoy the library's generous time limits and free color printing. Far from a competitor, Lantana's town library perceives its neighboring library as a tremendous complement to its own services. Marching to the beat of different drums, both libraries have exponentially increased resources available to Lantana's residents.

Serving a coastal town which began as a fishing village, and located for almost fifty years directly adjacent to the water, Lantana's library has had a unique atmosphere from its inception. Like the protagonist of Robert Frost's famous poem "The Road Not Taken," Lantana's library has taken the road less traveled for seven decades. Its reliance on volunteer librarians, adherence to the concept of a truly free public library, and its vision of complementing rather than competing with the behemoth next door all demonstrate the library's uniqueness. Honoring the generations of volunteers who painstakingly developed it, the Lantana Public Library will continue its march to the beat of a different drum as the twenty-first century unfolds.

J. Turner Moore Memorial Library, Manalapan

Michelle McCormick Donahue

The unique history and story of the Manalapan Library goes beyond its books and building; it is a story of the land and people who occupied the area. From the early days of settlement along the shores of Lake Worth to the modern-day design and innovation, the Manalapan Library is a one-of-a-kind monument. Nestled within the residential community of Point Manalapan, the J. Turner Moore Memorial Library may be considered the oldest site of Palm Beach County's first library. To better understand Manalapan Library's treasured place in Florida history, it is necessary to understand and acknowledge the deep, rich history of this island location and how this library came to be a "Fountain of Knowledge."

In 1873, Hannibal Dillingham Pierce and his family moved from Chicago and settled on Hypoluxo Island, in the area known today as Point Manalapan, and filed the second homestead claim in what is now Palm Beach County. A cousin to brothers Franklin Pierce, 14th United States President and Benjamin Pierce, a lieutenant colonel in the Seminole Indian War for whom Fort Pierce is named, Hannibal and his pioneering wife, Margretta Moore Pierce, were well educated and well connected.

They built their home on the south end of Hypoluxo Island with timber and lumber-board salvaged along the Atlantic Ocean beach from ships that were no match for Florida's notoriously deadly storms. Hannibal was a romantic adventurer who traveled the world before marrying his beloved Margretta, an intelligent and refined woman from Illinois. She was a lover of books with an affection for writing, keeping detailed journals of her pioneer life in Florida.

Throughout the Pierce's early years in Manalapan, Hannibal's extended family, well-known members of Maine's literary circle, sent magazines, books, and countless educational supplies to their family in the wild tropical jungle. The Maine branch of the Pierce family was instrumental in establishing the town's first library, located in the Pierce home on Hypoluxo Island. Margretta's son Charles William, one of Florida's legendary barefoot mailmen, wrote a 690-page manuscript using the family's written recollections of their lives in Florida. Florida Atlantic University professor Donald Curl edited the memories into a book entitled *Pioneer Life in Southeast Florida*. The significance of Hypoluxo Island to Florida's history cannot be overstated; the next few decades brought great prosperity to the region, which continued to develop as a fount of knowledge and cultural importance.

After Hannibal's death in 1898, the property was acquired by Florida State Senator E.N. "Cap" Dimick, fellow pioneer and family friend. By the spring of 1914, the Hopkins family, heirs to the Listerine mouthwash fortune, purchased it as a family leisure resort. In 1925, businessman and Palm Beach socialite John Demarest and his wife purchased the approximately forty-acre plot of land. The Demarest family built a large estate surrounding the original Pierce home. Demarest and other local oceanfront landowners Harold Vanderbilt, E.E. Allyne, Jerome Gedney, and Romyn Pierson successfully petitioned the State of Florida to incorporate the Town of Manalapan. While the remainder of Hypoluxo Island remained relatively untouched until the 1940s, this land continued to thrive.

In 1934, the Demarest estate was sold to Colonel Louis Jacques Balsan, celebrated French aviator and flying pioneer. Accompanying Balsan was his wife, Consuelo Vanderbilt Balsan, the former Duchess of Marlborough and sister of Harold Vanderbilt. This purchase brought far-reaching attention. British Prime Minister Winston Churchill visited the Balsans and wrote a portion of his Iron Curtain speech at their Florida estate. The Balsans remodeled the Demarest house, transforming it into servants' quarters, a laundry room and a garage, also building an extraordinary mansion on the original home site.

In early 1957, Bill Benjamin, real estate developer and great-grandson of Standard Oil partner Henry Huttleston Rogers, purchased the Balsan estate and created the exclusive "Manalapan Club," dedicating the exquisite Balsan home as its clubhouse. For the next several decades, Benjamin continued to develop the southern end of the island, building a premier luxury residential neighborhood and community known as Point Manalapan.

In 1967, during this time of explosive growth, town commissioner J. Turner Moore learned about a newly created Palm Beach County library system

J. TURNER MOORE MEMORIAL LIBRARY. A large porch graced the front of J. Turner Moore Library from its inception, 2008. *Courtesy of Mary Ann Kunkle.*

and taxing district. The implementation of this new district directly impacted the residents of Manalapan, as the town did not have a library of their own. Moore wanted to secede from the taxing district, but the only way to do so was to create a town library. Three years later, Moore's library referendum was put to the voters, and all but one voted in favor of creating the town's library.

During this same election, Moore was elected mayor. He made the library his top priority, pouring his heart, soul, and mind into the project. His friend Bill Benjamin rallied support for the initiative. Six weeks after the mayoral election, the original Manalapan Library, funded by private citizens, was established in an old ten-foot by twenty-foot building on the grounds of the Manalapan Club. The library was located in the Balsan's former laundry quarters on the original property that was first settled by the Pierce family nearly a century earlier. This laundry-room-turned-library offered more than just books; it was a community center for social and cultural events, as well as a venue for annual cocktail parties. In 1977, almost a year after Moore's death, the library was formally dedicated as the J. Turner Moore Memorial Library Reading Room.

When the library first opened in 1970, Manalapan was home to 205 residents and 144 homes. By 1981, the population had grown to 350 full-time or seasonal residents and 230 homes. In order to keep up with the growth and demand for services from the increasing population, town officials introduced a unique partnership between the library and water utilities department. The area's direct-filtration water plant was established in the Town of Lantana across the Lake Worth Lagoon. It was the first of its kind, as it did not use the lime-softening process that was standard in the area. This partnership created a challenge for residents and town officials, as the water had to be pumped

LECTURE HALL. Interior library and lecture hall. *Courtesy of the J. Turner Moore Library.*

from the plant along a pipe under the Intracoastal Waterway to a 400,000-gallon holding tank.

To disguise the distracting and unsightly massive holding tank located in the middle of a wealthy residential island neighborhood, the town proposed an innovative idea; a library that literally surrounded the water tank. It was a novel concept, one that town residents embraced and supported. By the end of 1981, a 2,000-square-foot Spanish-style building with pink stucco walls and a barrel tile roof was complete. Other than the curved walls on the inside, the water tank was undetectable from the outside.

Poised at the southwest entrance to the former Balsan mansion along Land's End Road, and only a few hundred feet away from its original site, the J. Turner Moore Memorial Library, a virtual "Fountain of Knowledge," has continued to inspire residents and institutions since its inception. The library has received rave reviews in Architectural Digest, was awarded the 1981 Florida League of Cities Innovative Showcase Award, and its technology advanced structure is much admired, marveled and respected.

In 2010, the library underwent an interior refurbishment paid for by generous patrons. These improvements increased library membership and led to the distinguished lecture series. Lecture attendance soon exceeded space, and within five years, the library once again grew in size. A portion of the front porch was enclosed; the lecture hall extended, and new wooden flooring and a sound system were provided by a private donation from the Strauss Family Foundation.

What started as a pioneer family's collection of books and educational materials in 1873, to a tax savings initiative that included a handful of donated books, Manalapan's J. Turner Moore Memorial Library is a thriving organization supported and funded by the community through membership dues, donations, and subsidies from the General Revenue Budget of the Town of Manalapan. Since its genesis, the library has provided "access to knowledge, information, and works of the imagination through a range of resources and services." Growing with the needs of the community, the J. Turner Moore Memorial Library's mission is to "meet the informational and recreational reading needs of people of all ages." The library's collection consists of a large selection of books, DVDs, CDs, audio books, and children's literature. The library also provides Internet access to its patrons. Library membership also includes an invitation to the Annual Open House and Lecture Series.

Boynton Beach City Library

Janet DeVries and Virginia K. Farace

At the heart of any thriving city or town is a public library, and the Boynton Beach area has had a library of circulating books for over a century. Just as the town has grown, so has the library. From its humble beginnings as a modest library located at the local post office to today's state-of-the-art 63,000-square-foot library, residents and visitors to the Boynton Beach area have enjoyed a free public library.

In 1910, the unincorporated Town of Boynton, as it was known then, had under five hundred full-time residents, most of whom were farmers growing pineapples, tomatoes, and other vegetables. The town had a railroad depot, two schools, several churches, two hotels, one restaurant, as well as a few general stores. The first public library in Boynton was informally established in 1910, when Byrd Spilman Dewey and husband Fred S. Dewey donated a large collection of books to the pioneers living in Boynton for a lending library. Mr. and Mrs. Dewey founded the Town of Boynton in 1898, laying out the streets

BYRD SPILMAN DEWEY AND FRED S. DEWEY. The Deweys founded the Town of Boynton in 1898. *Courtesy of the Dewey Family Archives.*

and naming the settlement after their friend, Major Nathan S. Boynton. The Deweys were avid readers; Byrd Spilman Dewey was a well-known author, writing several books including the national bestseller *Bruno*. Her other works included *From Pine Woods to Palm Groves, The Blessed Isle and its Happy Families*, and *Peter the Tramp*. She also wrote for the area's first newspaper, *The Tropical Sun*. Fred Dewey was a cousin to Melvil

BOYNTON POST OFFICE. The Boynton Post Office on
Ocean Avenue where postmistress Ethel Pierce circulated a
lending library of donated books. *Private collection.*

Dewey, who established the Dewey Decimal Classification system in 1876,
creating a new standard for library organization. Melvil Dewey also helped
found the American Library Association.

The donated books were kept at the post office, located on the north side
of Ocean Avenue. Ethel Pierce, wife of Charles W. Pierce (one of South
Florida's barefoot mailmen and longtime Boynton postmaster), was
postmistress. She curated the library's collection and loaned the books to local
residents. The collection consisted mostly of standard literature. According to
the *Miami Metropolis*, the Deweys were instrumental in providing a free reading
library to the area's residents, demonstrating their love for both reading and
their community.

BOYNTON WOMAN'S CLUB. The original two-story
Boynton Woman's Club on the south side of Ocean Avenue.
The library was located on the second floor, 1911. *Private collection.*

MIZNER DESIGNED WOMAN'S CLUB. Addison Mizner designed the 1925 Boynton Woman's Club. The library was located on the first floor and Clara White served as the first paid librarian. *Private collection.*

The Boynton Woman's Club raised money to fund the construction of a two-story building using lumber salvaged from the cargo of the shipwreck "Coquimbo." The club met on the second floor, also home to the nascent volunteer library. When guests staying at Major Nathan Boynton's oceanfront hotel learned about the Woman's Club library, many hotel guests, including renowned author Edgar Guest, donated their books to the library before returning north for the summer.

In 1925, famous South Florida architect Addison Mizner designed the beautiful Mediterranean Revival style building that would house the new Woman's Club. Part-time Boynton resident Mrs. Edward C. Cameron donated a bookcase and books to start a formal lending library in the new clubhouse building, encouraging others to donate books. Former Woman's Club president Clara White was selected to be custodian of the new library, and shortly thereafter, the club formed an official library committee. Individuals such as local farmer Oscar Winchester, as well as by the Boy Scouts and other civic groups generously donated to the library, adding more books and bookcases to the collection.

By the 1940s, the Woman's Club was able to pay Mrs. White a yearly salary of fifty dollars, paid monthly and often supplemented by donations from local civic groups. The library boasted a catalog of 2,000 books and magazines. The population of Boynton continued to grow, and in 1941, the town changed its name to the City of Boynton Beach. In the 1950s, the city allocated funds for the librarian's salary, as well as books and part-time employees. The library was open just six hours per week.

Before 1954, there was no formal library for use by Boynton Beach's African-American citizens. The idea of a branch library in the north side of town was explored; after a church-based library branch was unsuccessful, the City of Boynton Beach agreed to set up a branch library in the Wilson Recreation Center. Local community member Mrs. Ezell Hester took over the management of the branch.

The library room in the Boynton Woman's Club had outgrown its facility by the end of the 1950s. Residents complained that the building was on a busy street, too far for children walk to safely without parental supervision. The city council began exploring options for a structure suitable for a new city library. Resident Emery LeMieux offered to donate to the city a wood frame house on a lot where he had originally planned to build a new home. The Woman's Club library committee and librarian agreed, but town council refused, citing safety concerns.

The Boynton Jaycees (members of the Junior Chamber of Commerce), proposed building a new dedicated library building. The town council also vetoed this, citing financial obstacles. Desperate for a new facility, the Woman's Club library committee pledged to give their books and bookcases to the City of Boynton Beach on the condition that city council provide a facility for the library, employ a professionally educated librarian, and keep two of the Woman's Club members on the library advisory board for five years. In 1960, the City of Boynton Beach purchased a residential home from Mrs. William Rolff. The cement block house on the corner of Ocean Avenue and Seacrest Boulevard was connected to other city-owned property. Architect Dirk Grootenboaer designed an addition to the house, preparing it to become Boynton Beach's new library. After a renovation, the library's 3,000 books and bookshelves were moved into the new building in 1961. Mayor John L. Archie and Louis Smitzes, Boynton Beach's first city manager, dedicated the new Boynton Beach Public Library. Smitzes commended the library committee of the Boynton Woman's Club for their foresight and persistence in creating a library for all the citizens of Boynton Beach.

The new library offered tables and chairs for patron use and had a capacity of thirty-four. The city hired Mildred Zwart and Sue Miller to assist library director Florence Sullivan. Within months, the library was open to the public thirty-four hours per week and had over eight hundred patrons. In less than a year, book donations overwhelmed library staff. By the middle of 1962, the library had collected over eight thousand volumes and needed to weed out duplicate and worn books. These books were donated to nursing homes and other organizations that helped disadvantaged families.

In 1963, the Boynton Beach Rotary Club began a local branch of the Friends of the Library Association. The first slate of officers included John Alden as president, Mrs. Norris Saltzman of the Junior Woman's Club as treasurer, and librarian Mrs. Edward Sullivan as secretary. The library quickly became the city's activity hub, much as it is today. Patrons of all ages enjoyed using the library. Over 11,000 books were cataloged, with one thousand items circulating each week. In response to the library's ever-growing needs, the city council funded additions to the library facility in 1963, and again in 1966.

In 1968, members of the newly formed Boynton Beach Historical Society dedicated a new "Florida History Room." The Florida Room housed donated and collected items chronicling local history and was manned by volunteers from the Boynton Beach Historical Society. The tiny library established over five decades earlier had grown to nearly 5,000 square feet, filled to capacity with books, newspapers, magazines, and reference materials.

Rutgers University graduate Virginia Kapes Farace moved to Florida in 1970, becoming the new director of the Boynton Beach City Library. Her first task was to research state law and to find any available financial support from the state. Farace learned of aid that the state library gave out and immediately applied, but was told that only county library systems could obtain these funds. Thus began a long struggle to allow the Boynton Beach City Library and other municipal libraries to obtain a share of state library funding. Prior to Farace's arrival, a committee of citizens was appointed in 1965 by the Palm Beach County commission to study the situation of library service. Their study showed that as of January 1967, there were fourteen municipal libraries serving 217,100 people, leaving 107,000 with no library service. The following month, the committee made a presentation to the board of county commissioners detailing its recommendations:

A county library system should be established with a federation of the existing municipal libraries as the foundation; supplemented by county funds with contractual arrangements between the respective official bodies and

VIRGINIA KAPES FARACE.
Private collection.

99

the Board of County Commissioners. The county funds would come from an ad valorem tax on the unincorporated area plus those incorporated municipalities not now supporting libraries with tax monies.

For a library to become a part of the federation, it must spend a minimum of $1.00 per capita or .25 mills per annum for library operation and be open a minimum of thirty (30) hours per week. As a member of the federation, the library will provide free library service and free use of its library facilities to all county residents living in the unincorporated area, the incorporated municipalities not now having libraries and those municipalities whose libraries joined the system. The local library will be completely autonomous insofar as its rules and regulations, selection of books, personnel, etc.

In return for service to those outside its community, the county will pay to the municipal library a sum equal to fifteen percent of the monies spent the previous year on library operation. The library will also benefit from the additional services such as professional help, central purchasing and processing, central catalog, and the avoidance of much duplication. Such a system would also make possible the acquisition of materials which cannot now be purchased by an individual library due to cost and/or limited demand.

In the 1967 session, the state passed a legislative act to approve a Palm Beach County special taxing district to tax unincorporated county residents for library service. In December 1968, the county hired Florence Biller as its first female library director to organize the taxing district library. Eligible city libraries that opened their doors to county residents began receiving county funds. In 1971, Farace won city council approval to join the taxing district and

JUVENILE SECTION. Students peruse the paperback book selections, 1970s. *Private collection.*

the library started to serve all of the surrounding areas and receive county funds starting in 1971. The board of county commissioners accepted the library advisory board's proposal that the criteria be increased to require at least forty business hours per week with an expenditure of $1.50 per capita, based on federal standards for receiving financial aid.

In 1976, the county library advisory board again made recommendations to change the ways and means of reimbursing city libraries. This conflict led to the dismissal of the county library director in 1977. Discussion of the issue continued until 1979, when the board of county commissioners passed a resolution providing for financial aid to cooperating municipalities; the funds were to be taken from the county's library budget.

In 1979, new county library director Jerry W. Brownlee joined Farace, working together with other municipal librarians to implement a reciprocal cooperative agreement. By 1980, Boynton Beach, Riviera Beach, Belle Glade, Pahokee, and Lake Park had agreed to participate. West Palm Beach joined the following year. The agreement provided for the taxing district library to provide annual leased book services for the benefit of the participating municipalities as well as permanent library materials to be placed in the participating municipal libraries.

A committee of library directors was charged with the equitable distribution of leased books and library materials. Library staff would oversee the selection of materials for purchase or lease. The cities agreed to serve all library taxing district residents, as well as residents of all other participating cities, on the same terms as residents of their own cities. Palm Beach County agreed to register and service residents of the participating cities on the same basis and conditions as residents of the Library Taxing District. The cities also agreed to maintain records of Library Taxing District residents who were registered with each city for use of its library, and the county agreed to maintain records of city residents who were registered with the county library system for use of its services.

This compromise led to the founding of the Library Cooperative of the Palm Beaches, with additional city libraries joining the cooperative. The battle for state financial aid continued through the 1970s and 1980s, with municipal libraries throughout the state forming the Florida Public Library Association (FPLA). Farace was one of the founding members and served as one of the association's presidents. Eventually a compromise was reached and city libraries became eligible for state funding.

Another of the first projects Farace took on when she was hired was finding a larger facility for the growing library. Farace and the library's board of directors successfully convinced city council that a new library was needed. Citizens expressed their desire for a new facility by approving a bond referendum in 1972. Seeing widespread community support, the council decided to fund the building from general funds rather than sell bonds.

A new 12,000-square-foot library built next to the existing library was dedicated on August 24, 1974. This library served all residents of Boynton Beach and surrounding areas. The new library offered areas for children and young adults, a large meeting room, a typing room, a multimedia room, and a quiet study area. Special departments included business and investment, Florida-specific materials, circulating prints and posters, large print books, songbooks, and a reference section.

The Boynton Beach Library Quilters began meeting in 1979, led by retired library staff member Connie Baish, who volunteered to conduct weekly quilting sessions. Farace saw the quilting sessions as a way to provide an extension of the library's information services, a way for patrons to learn about the tradition of quilting, and the opportunity to contribute to the perpetuation of quilting as a cultural folk art. The Quilters currently meet on Thursday mornings at the library and the members share instruction and planning concepts. Proceeds from quilt sales are donated to the library. A Florida history quilt, on display in the library's lobby, was designed and sewn by the Quilters and officially registered with the state.

BOYNTON BEACH CITY LIBRARY QUILTERS. The Quilters donate the profits from selling their quilted creations back to the library for youth and adult programming, 2010. *Private collection.*

In November 1980, library director Farace sought the support of the library board to reactivate the Friends of the Library group, which had become inactive after the successful 1974 building project. The Friends' stated mission was to improve library service and use their talents, funds, and influence to promote, nurture and expand the library and have long been an asset to the library. By 1982, the library was open over sixty hours per week and the collection contained 65,000 items. In addition to books, the library housed periodicals, newspapers, out-of-town telephone directories, maps, records, jigsaw puzzles, and framed art.

The library catalog and circulation system was automated during the 1980s. Boynton Beach, along with the Delray Beach and West Palm Beach municipal libraries, formed the Cooperative Authority for Library Automation (COALA). Library staff undertook the monumental task of manually entering collection data and patron information into the new digital system. COALA has since expanded to include other municipal libraries, but the Boynton Beach City Library hosts the primary for the online catalog system.

By the mid-1980s, Boynton Beach's population had reached nearly 45,000. Citizens again expressed their wish for an expanded facility by passing a bond issue in March 1985. Renovation and an addition brought the size of the library to nearly 28,000 square feet. In 2000, yet another expansion was needed. One of Farace's last projects at the start of the new millennium was building yet a larger library for the city. The building program allotted space for a used bookstore, a café, a large program room, as well as a local history archive. The updated facility offered more shelf space for books, more seating, computer and audio-visual equipment, independent study rooms, and a computer-training lab. Over the next several years, the existing 28,000-square-foot building was completely renovated and a new two-story addition of 35,000 square feet was constructed. The Friends of the Library, now a registered non-profit organization, donated funds to purchase new furniture for the library.

Farace was involved in many of the civic groups in the city and understood the needs of the Boynton Beach community. She twice served as president of the Palm Beach County Library Association, sat on the Boynton Beach Historical Society's board of directors, and helped establish BookFest! Farace's "community librarianship" style of service helped move the Boynton Beach City Library from a small facility into a large, modern, technically advanced, community-centered entity. When Farace retired in 2006 after thirty-five years of service, Craig B. Clark of Detroit, Michigan replaced her as library director. Clark oversaw the completion of the construction project and continued the

REFERENCE AND QUIET STUDY AREA. The modern second
floor reference room and study area, 2010. *Private collection.*

mission of providing quality library service to the local community. The library
remained open to the public during construction, and in 2009, the new $7
million state-of-the-art facility was unveiled to the public.

In September 2009, the library collaborated with Literacy AmeriCorps
Palm Beach County, a national service program that recruits recent college
graduates to bring literacy to adults, children, and youth. A Literacy
AmeriCorps program volunteer provides homework help to students each
week at the library.

By the library's centennial in 2010, the library's collection size was about
140,000 items. The library had a computer lab and almost one hundred
computers available for public use. The library not only had circulating books,
but also DVDs, CDs, audiobooks, and eReaders. Today, patrons of all ages–
preschoolers, grade school children, and young adults–have their respective
spaces with unique seating arrangements and age appropriate décor. The
building is equipped with wireless Internet service, and the second-floor
reference department offers tables and ample seating for patrons. The Local
History & Archives department includes a climate controlled storage room,
housing photographs, maps, postcards, newspapers, and other items
chronicling the history of Boynton Beach and surrounding areas.

Libraries have always been a central hub in any community, and the
Boynton Beach City Library is no exception. The library is busy with activity
from the moment the doors open until they close. Since its humble beginnings
when community members donated library books, Boynton Beach's library has
grown with the population and continually transforms to accommodate the
needs of the community.

Library Memories

Graham Brunk

In my elementary school years in the early 1990s, I would spend the summer days with my grandparents who lived near me and my parents in Boynton Beach. One of our weekly traditions was visiting the Boynton Beach City Library. It was always a treat to run up and down the aisles with my grandfather trying to find something interesting to read. It was also the first place I ever used the Internet. I vividly remember the white archways lining the library and the giant card catalog always with a crowd surrounding it. What was not crowded were the Sirsi terminals just next to the card catalog, which had the entire collection cataloged electronically. I always found it easier to locate things that way...such as a Generation Y'er might say. I found the card catalog however, equally as fascinating.

Perhaps the most fascinating thing of all is my vivid memory of a strange daytime program that my grandparents once took me to. It was a kid's film program, held in the programming room in the front of the library. I remember going into the room and there were about twenty or so kids in attendance. The lights were turned off and a library technician rolled a 16-mm film projector out and a film began to play. The film was about a young boy and his mother who move away from the bustling city and into a mysterious Victorian era house. In settling into the old house, the boy discovers that a witch is living in the attic. She mentions that she has lived in the house for years and is not budging for the boy and his mother.

The next thing I remember about the film was that the witch started making pancakes every morning for the boy and his mother and when they ate the pancakes they would start to see all these trippy colors and become happy and giggly. Soon all the neighborhood kids wanted these witches' pancakes.

Years later, as an adult, I recalled this memory and could not even decide if this was for real or my imagination, but with Google search now at my disposal I tackled the issue one day by Googling "witch with magical pancakes." I was surprised to find literally hundreds of online posts about people who had similar memories. All described the same witch that looks like a homeless woman making psychedelic pancakes. It was clear to me my memory was definitely not false.

From my research, I finally learned the film's name: The Winter of the Witch was a 1969 film starring Hermione Gingold. The film was a 23-minute short produced by Parent's Magazine and was screened at schools and libraries for generations. There is even a fan-site about the film at http://www.happypancakewitch.com/with the tagline "It wasn't your imagination, and you aren't crazy! Your search is now over."

I saw this film at the library in about 1993 or 1994. I doubt that anyone in my generation knows who Hermione Gingold even is and I am not sure why this was selected as a suitable program for kids in the 1990s.

As a librarian myself now, I have learned that the State Department of Library and Information Services did have a 16-mm film program that they distributed to public libraries and the program was in operation until the late 1990s. On an interesting note, I have never met a long time Boynton Beach City Library employee who remembers this event. Thanks to YouTube, however, the film is now out of obscurity and anyone can watch it.

G. Yvonne Graham

She was a tiny little lady, not quite five feet tall, sparkling blue eyes, big smile, Bostonian accent. She was a library volunteer. Her name was Marion and she had just turned ninety years old.

I was a free-lance writer working on an article about the library and was introduced to her by the president of the Friends of the Boynton Beach City Library.

She was happy to be interviewed. She told me about her years of living in her native Boston where she first got into various kinds of volunteering. At one time, she helped out in a children's polio research project. This required her to be fitted into an iron lung for size. Being short she was ideal for this project.

When she and her now late husband first moved to Florida, she had no idea just what kind of volunteering she'd get into. A friend told her about the library volunteer program. Well, she'd always liked being around people and books, so it seemed like a good fit!

She helped start the accommodation desk near the entrance, which volunteer staffed. It gave her such a feeling of satisfaction to engage with patrons and help them find the right book. She even had her own shelf to take care of!

Her co-volunteers were a wonderful group, she said, and she was happy to be on the team. They in turn agreed that she had a warm, friendly personality and a great sense of humor and was a worker who could always be relied upon.

I kept in touch with Marion, always stopping to say "hi" whenever I visited the library. After she retired I remembered to call her on her birthdays. She seemed glad to hear from me and we enjoyed our phone talks.

She lived to be almost one hundred years old. I shall never forget Marion and how she made each library visit such a fun occasion always to be looked forward to!

Briny Breezes Library

Donna Clarke

Located east of Boynton Beach between Gulf Stream and Ocean Ridge, Briny Breezes' little mobile home park is one of Palm Beach County's smallest municipalities. Briny Breezes is believed to be the only oceanfront mobile home park in Florida and one of two towns that are mobile home parks. Mostly retirees live in the 487 mobile homes in Briny Breezes either seasonally or year-round.

Briny Breezes started as a five hundred head dairy farm named Shore Acres in 1919 when Ward Beecher Miller came from Michigan and purchased the current forty-three acres of land. In 1925, he turned Shore Acres into Briny Breezes. The Millers raised turkeys and dairy cattle on the west side of A1A and turned Ruthmary Avenue into a strawberry patch. During the Great Depression of the 1930s, Miller allowed tourists to park their travel trailers on his land for three dollars per week.

By 1937, there were forty trailers in the park and Briny Breezes separated from Boynton Beach (now Ocean Ridge). During the 1940s, more than fifty children wintering in Briny rode the public-school bus every day to attend school in Boynton Beach. Sixty-nine children attended the first Sunday school class.

During the World War II years, German submarines torpedoed ships off the coast and campers were asked to keep blinds closed at night. The ladies of the park gathered in the Community Hall each week to knit for the American Red Cross making scarves, socks, sweaters and mittens for the servicemen.

In 1955, the residents started their own town newspaper, *The Briny Bugle*. When a fire burned the old community hall in 1956, construction began on a new auditorium with a capacity for five hundred people. The residents pooled their resources in 1958, purchasing the Miller's land at $2,000 to $2,500 per lot, a total of $1.5 million; they paid off the mortgage in three years. The trailer park

BRINY BREEZES LIBRARY. Exterior view of the Town of Briny Breezes Library, with the entrance located behind the community shuffleboard courts, 2017. *Courtesy of the Briny Breezes Library.*

incorporated as the Town of Briny Breezes in 1963, with a town hall, mayor and library.

The library was, and still is in the building located on the north side of the shuffleboard courts to the east of A1A. This is the site of the original community hall, burned in 1956 then rebuilt. The small building holds two rooms: The West Clubroom, used for shuffleboard meetings and card games, and the East Clubroom, which became the library.

In spring 1958, the recently formed Mobile Home Square Club decided to start a library for the bookworms who had no source of supply. A few shelves were put up in the East Clubroom and folks were asked to bring the books from home that they no longer wanted.

Jean Wood, long-time resident of Briny, until her death in 1961, offered to take the responsibility and that fall the collection of reading material was begun. Following Jean were Bessie Poole, Grace Speery, Peg Tolford and Carol Aspray. Marcella Tennel was also one of the first librarians and a good collector of books. Bob McLean, Rick Rasure and others, built the first shelves.

Gladys Rasbach came along next. It is unclear exactly how many years Gladys devoted to the library, some say maybe twenty years. All of her time was volunteered, as all the library aides. During those years a new book would cost five dollars and be kept under lock and key behind glass cupboards. When Gladys died, she was so well thought of that the Briny Breezes Board of

LIBRARY VOLUNTEERS. Library aides working inside the Briny Breezes Library, 1972. *Courtesy of the Briny Breezes Library.*

Directors purchased a plaque in her memory. That plaque is currently displayed in the library.

Many Briny residents volunteered to work in the library; shelving books and helping people find a book to read. One of those library volunteers was Lu McInnes. Before she died, Gladys told Lu that she had "specially chosen" her to take over and lead the library. Lu and her husband Bob have owned in Briny Breezes since shortly after Briny became a town in 1963. Together, they made many improvements to the library that are still being enjoyed in 2017.

When she took over library duties in 1993, Lu McInnes purchased books from the local Barnes & Noble Bookstore. She focused on the Top 10 Bestsellers for the Briny readers. Lu established sections in the library including fiction, mystery, nonfiction, biographies, westerns and romance (affectionately called "bodice-rippers"). An abbreviated version of the Dewey Decimal System was used to catalog books. A card catalog was maintained with author and title cards all neatly typed. Lu also started a magazine section, including *Vanity Fair*, *Time*, *Better Homes & Gardens* and *Southern Living*. The *Wall Street Journal* was delivered daily throughout the winter season. Bob built additional shelves in the library, most of which are still being used. He turned an old broom closet into a useful and attractive area for the once popular VHS tapes. Bob also built shelves for returning books and tapes, and he recovered and painted two well-loved chairs. Lu McInnes stayed as the Briny lead librarian until January 2014 when she followed in Gladys's footsteps and "specially chose" Donna Clarke to assume the duties of lead librarian.

The Briny Breezes Library started with sole funding from the Town of Briny Breezes. Sometime after she took over in 1993, Lu McInnes found that with all the improvements she and Bob had made and the higher costs of books and supplies, their funds were lacking. At that time, she was receiving a $1,500 yearly budget–the same amount as when the library was started in 1963–and needed double that amount. When the town council continued to delay approving additional funds, in the usual Briny take-charge fashion, a solution was hatched. Briny resident Janet Zerull suggested the library ask for donations and the Briny Angels was started. "Angels" after "Theater Angels" a term used during that time.

Volunteer, Estelle Van Tassell sent out letters to residents about the Library Angels. Letters had a picture of an angel on them and were embossed in gold. She kept meticulous records of each two-dollar donation, sending each "Angel" a membership card into the Briny Library Club. There was no need to ask for additional money from the council after the Library Angels project launched. In fact, today the library receives just $1,250 annually from the town– the rest of the funds are provided by the generous "Angels."

Donna Clarke now has the job of maintaining a much loved and much used Briny library previously headed by very capable and special women. There are currently twenty-three library aides. Since 2014, Donna and the library aides have tried to continue to keep the briny Library a place where residents can find a good book to read or movies to take home, and enjoy a cool and quiet, comfortable spot to read.

In 2015, a group of library aides undertook a big job when they decided to preserve some old photo albums that, over the years, had been donated to the library. With funds from the Briny Bazaar, all the photos were preserved in archive-quality photo albums and are displayed prominently in the library for future generations. Grandchildren and great-grandchildren can see Briny life from the 1920s to 2016.

While there have been some changes since the earlier days, many of the old Briny library ways remain the same today in 2017. They still have the magazines, *Wall Street Journal* newspaper, paperback & hardcover fiction and mysteries, biographies and nonfiction. The westerns and romances are still being read. There is an ever-growing large print section. The Briny residents continue to enjoy reading the Top 10 Best Sellers. They no longer have the locked cupboards for the new books but are not computerized and use circulation checkout cards (they make themselves) for hardcover books. Supplementary materials include a children's section of books, audio books, and a large collection of DVDs. All materials are checked out on the honor system. They now have Wi-Fi in the library.

Photos of Briny life are now on Facebook and there's a tablet in the library for residents to view those photos. Briny historian Joan Nicholls keeps the Facebook page filled with photos of the latest events. Joan started the Briny Breezes Albums Facebook page with both historical and current photos posted. Many Briny residents and their friends and families enjoy these Facebook photos and stories. Joan also started the Briny Breezes Historical Committee of which she is the president.

The Briny Breezes Library is unique in many ways. It is open (to residents only) 365 days a year. The library is open on an honor system basis daily 9:30 a.m. to 6:00 p.m. The staff is entirely volunteer help with someone (usually) on duty 10:00 a.m. to 11:00 a.m. Monday, Wednesday and Friday. The Briny library remains a popular place; on any one day in the season, there are over two hundred books checked out (and that is just hardcover books)!

Library Memories

Lu McInnes spent from 1993 to 2014 as lead librarian for the Briny Breezes Library. She and her husband Bob, have lived in Briny Breezes since the 1960s. Lu recalls her years in the Briny Library fondly, always saying how much she "loved it." It meant a lot to her to be specially chosen to take over the library from Gladys Rasbach. In those days, being in charge of the Briny Library was a "prestigious job" among Brinyites and at the time there were several people "in the running" for the top job.

Once a month she and another library volunteer, would make a trip to the local Barnes & Noble to buy the latest Best Sellers. They would make a day of it, going out to lunch after their purchases. New books were listed on a sheet of paper beside the New Books shelves and residents were asked to keep a new book just 14 days, although fines were never levied. Lu's philosophy of the library was that it be a "Modern Lending Library."

Lu and her husband Bob made many positive changes to the library that are being enjoyed today. She currently attends all the library aide meetings and, to the relief of her successor, is available 24/7 as a library consultant. Lu still

BRINY BREEZES LIBRARIANS. Lead librarians, Donna Clarke, left, and Lu McInnes inside the Briny Breezes Library, 2015. *Courtesy of the Briny Breezes Library.*

enjoys reading the best sellers and keeps up with new books via the *New York Times* Book Review.

Lu recalled Pat Esterman an especially good library aide with great organization skills. At one time, when they needed the money, Pat organized a sale of books that had been donated to the library. She also organized a book discussion group. In a recent interview with Pat, she recalled the Briny Library with great fondness. Pat recalled her love of reading that started with her father, who always encouraged her to read and never minded when she wanted to spend days reading.

Pat's favorite book is *1776* by David McCullough. "The best book EVER!" She thinks it should be made into a movie. When discussing the pitfalls of having an honor system library, Pat put things in perspective stating her belief that as books come up missing–which they do– "Who cares ... as long as they're reading!" Pat complimented the Briny Library as always having "a good selection all the time." On being a library aide, she says your job is to help people. "That's what life is all about ... helping people."

Dorothy Mann McNeice is a long time Briny resident. Dorothy was just 11 years old when her parents started going to Florida for the winters in 1938. Dorothy attended school in Boynton Beach until the war started when she moved back to Michigan year-round. Dorothy lived in Michigan most of her adult life, retiring to Briny Breezes. Her mother kept historical records of Briny Breezes throughout her lifetime. Dorothy remembers the Briny library as a

BRINY BREEZES LIBRARY.
Entrance to the Town of Briny Breezes Library, 2017.
Courtesy of the Briny Breezes Library.

great place, very popular with the residents. Dorothy now spends her summers in Michigan and her winters in Briny Breezes.

Brenda Dooley and her husband Jim retired to Briny Breezes in 2012. Brenda had been a middle school librarian in New Jersey. Brenda and Jim loved the Briny life and since moving to Briny full-time, Brenda has become involved in many activities. So many in fact that Brenda has recently curtailed a few of her activities—except for the Briny Library. Brenda has often said she knows how much work it is to run a library, so she always makes herself available to help. Brenda manages the Library Angels' money, the *Wall Street Journal* newspaper subscription and the magazine subscriptions. She helps process new books and donated books.

Donna Clarke had no idea how much was involved when she said yes to Lu McInnes and took over as lead librarian. Being a retired teacher, she already loved books so the fit seemed natural. The library is a busy place and this is a big volunteer job.

Thanks go out to the twenty-three library aides who help in so many ways. Shelving books, filing circulation cards, straightening shelves along with helping people find a good read are just a few of the library aide jobs. They are organizing our DVDs and keeping our collection up to date with Oscar winning movies. In the summer, volunteers undertake bigger jobs such as sorting the shelves, weeding out books no longer popular to make room for newer books. Books are given to the Friends of the Boynton Beach City Library bookstore or traded to a used bookstore. Thanks to the generous Briny Angels and the Briny Bazaar for all the financial support.

The Village of Golf Library

Janet DeVries

The four-hundred-acre Village of Golf, named after Golf, Illinois, was incorporated by a special act of the Florida legislature on May 30, 1957. The village sprouted from an exclusive resort country club concept. In the 1930s-1950s, dairy cows grazed in pastures northwest of Delray Beach. Chicagoans Carlton Blunt and Robert E. Maxwell purchased the 765 acres of gently rolling farmland in 1955 from seven dairy farmers for $906,000. They considered the sandy ridge, set upon the highest point in Palm Beach County, an ideal location for a golf course and club as well as raising and training horses, and hosting equestrian events.

The golf course, designed by famed architect Robert Bruce Harris, opened in 1956. Initially, many club members considered the location too remote, and called it "a Godforsaken place," lamenting that the area was too far away from the beach and stores. Others called it a refuge, an oasis amid wilderness and nature. The only entrance to the property was a dirt road off Military Trail. Cows roamed across the golf course and skunks, foxes and bobcats lived in the nearby woods.

Residents who lived in the Village of Golf paid for membership to the Par Club and the Par Club paid for services not provided by Palm Beach County. In 1962, the Par Club purchased land on A1A for its Ocean Club, and the golf, equestrian and oceanfront amenities attracted new residents and new construction. In 1982, under village manager John Mosher, Golf became a true village with a taxing body that provided services for its residents.

Village administration moved into their own building with a post office and a library. The Village of Golf maintains a library for the exclusive use of its residents and their guests. Located at village hall, the library stocks current and recent bestsellers, a variety of fiction and non-fiction, paperbacks, audio books, and a small selection of children's books. The *New York Times* bestsellers are a big hit with the residents. A library card for each resident is kept in a file box in the library to record which best-selling (fourteen-day) books they have borrowed. The library collection has more than six hundred books. Once the residents finish reading the books, they donate the gently used books to other libraries or to the Friends of the Boynton Beach City Library bookstore.

VILLAGE OF GOLF LIBRARY. Interior view of the village library, 2015. *Courtesy of the Village of Golf.*

Highland Beach Library

Lois Albertson

The Highland Beach Library is a hidden gem on the Intracoastal Waterway in the tiny town of Highland Beach, Florida. Nestled between the cities of Boca Raton and Delray Beach, Highland Beach encompasses a three-mile long stretch along state road A1A. The residents are primarily part-time retirees who spend the winter months here, along with a number of families and year-round inhabitants. The population is 4,150 permanent residents, doubling during the winter season when the snowbirds arrive. Highland Beach is almost entirely residential; aside from the municipal Town Hall complex and a church, the only commercial entities are a resort hotel and a real estate company.

The Town of Highland Beach was incorporated in 1949 and, until the late 1960s, it did not have a library. When the Palm Beach County Library District was created in 1967, Highland Beach chose to create its own library rather than paying into the county system. According to a March 14, 1982 *Sun Sentinel* article, the Town Commission "bought $100 worth of books, borrowed a few bookshelves and loaded these with donated *Reader's Digest* novels, paperbacks and *National Geographic*'s to make a library." Back then, the system was very informal; residents could stop by Town Hall and take out books on the honor system. From those humble beginnings, the Highland Beach Library has grown and flourished along with the town and its residents.

In the early 1980s, the town hall building was expanded and included dedicated space for the library. A library director, Elizabeth Paulson, and two part-time staff members were hired, and formal circulation procedures were implemented. Town residents eagerly jumped in to help. Former bookstore owner Joanne Freeman provided expertise in developing the collection materials. Theresa Colarullo took a part-time position processing and mending books, as well as assisting patrons. Other enthusiastic local residents formed a Friends of the Highland Beach Library organization to provide support. The library grew steadily over the next few decades, eventually encompassing 1,200

HIGHLAND BEACH LIBRARY. The Highland Beach Library under construction, 2005. *Courtesy of the Highland Beach Library.*

square feet that included a small children's room and space for public computers.

By the early 2000s, the Highland Beach Library outgrew its small space in Town Hall. Not only was more space needed for books, movies and other materials, more public computers were needed as well. In addition, there was little space for programs or activities. Highland Beach staff and residents came together to transform the Library into its next incarnation. In 2012 interview

HIGHLAND BEACH LIBRARY ENTRANCE. *Courtesy of the Highland Beach Library.*

in the *Coastal Star* newspaper, Mari Suarez, library director from 1998 to 2015, stated, "I knew what was important to the residents (other than reading) and from the start requested that we have areas where concerts, movies, discussions, lectures, and a whole new amalgam of activities could be available to the residents." In 2003, staff began working with town officials and residents to design and finance construction of a new freestanding library. On March 16, 2006, the current 11,000-square-foot building opened to the public.

HIGHLAND BEACH LIBRARY. Library terrace, 2006.
Courtesy of Tina K. Valant.

A large, sunny, atrium invites visitors to read and relax in comfortable leather armchairs. Two screened terraces overlook the Intracoastal Waterway, providing views of local wildlife and passing boats. One of the most significant features of the new building was the addition of several meeting spaces. The Sanford H. Goldstein Community Room is a large open space with seating for ninety-nine people; the room is equipped with a baby grand piano, a sound system and theatrical lighting. A smaller meeting room houses historical photographs and the town archives.

The Highland Beach Library is truly a reflection of its residents' interests. Most patrons are seeking materials for personal enjoyment and enrichment. Best-selling novels, newsworthy nonfiction books and popular movies on DVD are the most in-demand items. As patrons become more tech-savvy, demand for eBooks and other digital resources increases every year. One of the features that makes the Highland Beach Library unique is the personal interaction between staff and patrons. Library staff members take pride in getting to know and serving the residents and often work one on one with them to recommend books, assist with using an eReader or share a movie review. If a resident requests a book that is not in the collection, the library purchases it whenever possible.

Residents also increasingly rely on the library for entertainment, classes and social activities. Because Highland Beach has almost no commercial space, the library's community room functions as a de facto meeting place for the town. On any given day, the room is busy from morning to evening with yoga classes, discussion groups, card games, movies and other activities. The Friends of the Library sponsor many cultural events, including concerts and art exhibits.

Current library director Lois Albertson has witnessed firsthand how the Highland Beach Library has evolved over the years. "My grandparents came to Highland Beach as snowbirds in 1970. As a child, I came to the library in town hall with my grandmother. I never dreamed that one day I would work here," she says. "I moved to Florida in 2004 and became a Highland Beach Library patron. In 2008, I began volunteering at the library one evening a week. I enjoyed the experience so much that I went back to school to get my Master's in Library and Information Science." After working at the Southeast Florida Library Information Network (SEFLIN) for five years while continuing to volunteer, she came to the Highland Beach Library in 2015. For all the changes that have occurred over the years, one thing has remained consistent: support from the town and the residents. "Every day residents tell us how much they love this library. The town officials fully support us with anything we need. The Friends of the Library donate time and money to enhance our cultural programs. The library staff comes in every day with smiles on their faces. The Highland Beach Library is a very special place."

Delray Beach Public Library

Michelle Quigley

Like so many public libraries—three out of four by some accounts—the Delray Beach Public Library was established by an organization of the town's women in the early days of its settlement. The Ladies Improvement Association was formed in 1902, a few years after the first northern settlers arrived. Among the association's first projects: Installing a sidewalk along the dirt road that is now Atlantic Avenue, establishing a cemetery, and building a town hall.

On April 11, 1913, the Ladies Improvement Association established a library. *The Delray Progress*, the town's first newspaper, reported on the endeavor: "A number of ladies met at the Booster Hall, each bringing one or more books as a beginning for the Delray Library. Forty books were brought, besides a few that will be used for reference. They were soon neatly covered, as many hands make light work. This is only a beginning and we hope and expect much from it."

Nearly 1,000 people lived in Delray when the library was established, and there were seventy-five books in the library when it officially opened to the public from 2:00 p.m. to 5:00 p.m. on January. 31, 1914. Some of those books were purchased with a gift of ten dollars from Henry Flagler. The first library was housed in a small room between the meeting room and the kitchen in the two-story town hall in the 400 block of East Atlantic Avenue, just east of the historic Arcade Building. The library remained in that building until 1949.

Volunteers staffed the library for the first thirty or so years of its existence. Newspaper accounts say Mrs. Smith and Mrs. Cromer (no first names listed) were the first librarians. Mrs. W.A. (Marcia) Jacobs, who came to Delray in 1918, was librarian from 1921 to 1934. Jacobs described the early days of the library when she was recognized for her service at a library association meeting in 1960: "After the 1928 hurricane, I opened the door to find the floors covered with inches of water. The library was moved temporarily to the Booster Club, later known as the USO building. The Booster Club served as the big meeting place for Delray from elections to Eastern Star meetings."

Jacobs said "the library was entirely self-supporting. The books, cases, supplies, etc., were purchased with fifty cents a year membership dues and fines from overdue books."

One exception was a gift from the popular novelist and screenwriter Nina Wilcox Putnam, who had a winter home on North Swinton Avenue. Jacobs reported that Putnam "visited the library several times and presented me personally with a fine portrait of George Washington and gave the library a check for one hundred dollars. How we did rejoice!"

Jacobs recalled that she shellacked every book in the library to keep the bugs out, and once attended a meeting of South Florida librarians from Miami to West Palm Beach where the discussion turned to censorship. Jacobs said most other librarians dealt with the issue as she did — the few "so-called bad books that had crept in" were hidden under her desk so "teenagers wouldn't find them."

A library volunteer, Edna Copeland, recalled in 1960 that in those early days the library was not only for books, but also a hub of social life. Ladies (and it was mostly ladies who frequented the library in those days) brought their knitting and embroidery, and spent the afternoon visiting.

The Ladies' Improvement Association, renamed the Woman's Club of Delray in 1924, ran the library until 1939, when the Delray Beach Public Library Association was formed. The association's charter was signed by Circuit Judge C.E. Chillingworth of Manalapan, who, along with his wife Marjorie, was murdered in 1955 in what is known as the local murder of the century. The Oct. 12, 1939, contract between the Woman's Club and the Delray Beach Public Library Association said Woman's Club would house the books of the library association until the association had its own building.

During the 1930s and 1940s Delray Beach was known as a place where the rich and famous could vacation more quietly than in Palm Beach. Viscount and Lady Astor — Nancy Langhorne Astor, a Virginia native who became the first woman to sit in the House of Commons in 1919 — were among those visitors. Library association board member Mrs. Lauren C. (Elizabeth S.) Hand met Viscount and Lady Astor after a church service when the Astors were visiting Delray in 1939. The Astors commented on what a pleasant place Delray Beach was. Hand of course agreed, but added that the one thing Delray Beach did not have was a library of its own.

Lady Astor declared that every town should have a library, and advised Hand to convene a meeting of interested residents. More the one hundred people attended the meeting a few days later at St. Paul's parish house, "some of whom were drawn, it must be admitted, by the star attractions of the evening, Lord and Lady Astor," according to an account in the library association annual report. "Charming and enthusiastic Lady Astor gave a rousing talk for the library cause," and at church the following Sunday, gave Hand a check for five hundred dollars.

After the association took over, the library continued to be run by volunteers, under the supervision of Marion Lundquest, a teacher at Delray Beach High School and "a graduate librarian." In 1939, the library held 605 books which were circulated 3,972 times among 328 registered borrowers. Best sellers could be rented for twenty-five cents. The library was open three evenings a week and hosted a weekly story hour.

In 1940, library board member R.E. Turpin, who had been a *New York Times* editor before he moved to Delray Beach, made a "declaration of independence" that the library should not be a tax burden on the community, but would be supported by memberships and contributions. The board adopted a mission statement, vowing to build a collection meeting national standards, to develop the library as cultural center of the community, and "to build a building which would worthily represent the place cultural activities shall hold in the life of a modern community."

The next year, the directors decided to bring the local library up to the minimum requirements as recommended by the American Library Association for a library in a city of this size (population: 3,737). To that end, the association purchased fifty new books in classifications the library was lacking, $150 of new equipment, and constructed shelf space for 1,000 additional volumes. The board also decided to increase the library's hours of service during the summer, "when people had more time to read." Rates on rental books were reduced, and patrons were allowed to take out a many as four books at one time.

During the early 1940s, the library hired its first paid librarians. Works Progress Administration (WPA) funds paid for a thirty-hour-a-week librarian. Mrs. C.H. (Emily A.) Lammrich was hired in December 1941 as a cataloging assistant at a salary of thirty-five cents per hour, and Mrs. Ben (Dorothy) Adams was employed as librarian in October 1942. The 1941 treasurer's report shows the city contributed twenty-five dollars per month for the operation of the library. The city's contribution increased to fifty dollars per month in 1941, $125 in 1943, $250 in 1946, and more than $700 in 1951.

At the December 1940 annual meeting, the board appointed a building committee with the objective of planning for a new library building. The war put building plans on a back burner. The board appointed a committee to contact the commander at the Boca Raton Army Air Field to see what services the library could render. An additional reading room was added to accommodate servicemen, and a sign hung prominently in front of the library welcoming servicemen. In 1943, one-third of the library's book circulation was to servicemen and their families.

The association held three library teas in 1940, to make the townspeople and winter visitors aware of the library association's work to date. The speaker at the first tea was Pulitzer Prize winning author Maud Howe Elliott of Palm Beach, whose mother was women's rights activist, abolitionist and poet (she wrote "The Battle Hymn of the Republic") Julia Ward Howe. According to newspaper accounts, "tea was served from a beautifully appointed tea table and music during the afternoon was furnished by Mrs. LeRoy (Ruth) Diggans, pianist." The library was decorated with pink gladioli and ferns, and "Mrs. Elliott reminisced, mostly in a humorous vein, of her intimate contacts with the literary and artistic great not only of the United States but of England and Italy."

In 1948, the board decided on a location adjoining the USO building (formerly the Booster Club, where the library had been temporarily relocated after the 1928 hurricane) on SE 4th Avenue, just south of Atlantic Avenue.

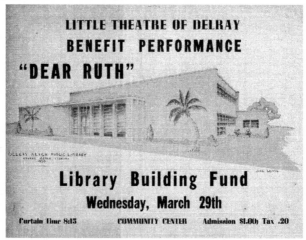

DELRAY BEACH PUBLIC LIBRARY. 1950 building benefit flyer. *Courtesy of the Delray Beach Public Library.*

Two thousand fundraising letters were mailed to residents and businesses. The population of Delray Beach at the time was about 6,000.

Rosalie Norris was hired as librarian in September 1946. She remained until 1952. Flood and fire and the construction of a new building made her tenure perhaps the most challenging of any in the history of the Delray Beach Public Library. The 1947 hurricane blew part of the roof off the Woman's Club building, and flooded the reading room and the children's room. Then in October 1948, a fire at the Woman's Club building left the reading room unusable. In January 1949, the building was sold, and the library was left without a home. John Reid offered the use of a vacant store in his Reid's Village shops on East Atlantic Avenue, east of Gleason Street, as a temporary solution.

BILLY THE BOOKWORM MEMBERSHIP CAMPAIGN. *Palm Beach Post-Times* cartoonist W.J. (Pat) Enright (right) and Mrs. G. Moore Lapham, center, present Billy the Bookworm, as Delray Beach Public Library Association president Edward Schellenberg, left, looks on. Mr. Enright created the Billy the Bookworm cartoon for the library's membership campaign. Photo by Charles J. Wick, II. *Courtesy of the Delray Beach Public Library.*

The library board revised the building schedule with an aim to complete the building shell, rough plumbing (including a restroom for the librarian), and temporary lighting, to permit moving into the new library as soon as possible. Editorials in the *Delray Beach Journal* (on February 3 and April 7, 1949) urged residents to support the library: "Whether we all use a library or not, it is one of those institutions which every town needs. In this modern day, a library is not only a building full of books, but it is the center of all kinds of cultural

DELRAY BEACH PUBLIC LIBRARY. The Delray Beach Public Library in the late 1950s or early 1960s. Photo by Chris Butler. *Courtesy of the Delray Beach Public Library.*

activities and everyone may find some subject of interest to him there. Let everyone support this campaign."

On July 24, 1950, the library moved into the unfinished new building on Southeast 4th Avenue. The children's department was the only completed section. Community volunteers moved and stacked books, and the Little Theater of Delray Beach performed the one-act melodrama, "Curse you, Jack Dalton" at the opening festivities.

It was more than a decade before the new library was truly completed. During a 1988 interview, board member Grace Kreitzberg recalled that the librarian had but "a tiny little school desk to operate out of" in the middle of the bare concrete floor. Cork floors were installed in 1951. The south side of the building was completed the following year. Restrooms were finished in 1953, and ceiling lighting, walls, and shelves were installed in the main reading room in 1954 and 1955. The office

DELRAY BEACH PUBLIC LIBRARY EXTERIOR. 1954. Photo by Hank Cohen. *Courtesy of the Delray Beach Public Library.*

and workroom were completed in 1956. The music room, equipped with record players, opened in 1960. A "solar wall" of openwork Venezuelan tile was installed at the entrance, to provide shade for the west side of the main reading room, and air-conditioning was installed in 1961. The wood entrance doors were replaced with glass doors, and the entryway was dedicated to the memory of H. Anderson Hubbard and Paul S. Knowles in 1964. Soon after, a new sign was installed, and the building was finally considered completed. And then began plans for an addition. The library had been built for a capacity of 20,000 volumes, and by this time, it was accommodating more than 28,000.

In the midst of getting settled into the new library building, the board began discussions of opening a branch in the west part of town to serve the "colored" population. In 1952, the board met with several "prominent and interested colored people to discuss the project." The Carter B. Woodson Branch opened Nov. 10, 1953, in the educational building at Mt. Olive Baptist Church on NW 4th Avenue. The branch was named for historian, author and journalist Carter G. Woodson, known as the father of African-American history. Alberta Palmer was the librarian, and S.D. Spady was chair of the branch committee. The Woodson Branch was open from 5:00 to 8:00 p.m. on Tuesdays and Thursdays, and on Saturday mornings. It housed seven hundred books, and had room for twelve people to comfortably use the library. American Library Association

CARTER B. WOODSON BRANCH. The Delray Beach Public Library opened the Carter B. Woodson Branch on Nov. 10, 1953, in the educational building at Mt. Olive Baptist Church. The branch was named for historian, author and journalist Carter G. Woodson, known as the father of black history. Photo by T.P. Wyatt. *Courtesy of the Delray Beach Public Library.*

documents say the Woodson Branch was at the time the only such municipal library for the African-American community in Palm Beach County.

In April of 1961 the library board discussed moving the Woodson Branch to the city's Teen Town facility, but it was decided that would be unsatisfactory. The Carter B. Woodson Branch closed in 1961, the year Palm Beach County schools were integrated and one year before the municipal beach in Delray Beach was integrated. Library documents do not specify a reason for the closing, but one can presume the Delray Beach Public Library became integrated around that time. At the November 9, 1960, library board meeting, a motion was presented to instruct the library staff to issue a card and books to anyone who comes to the library, regardless of color. The motion passed unanimously.

There was much staff turnover during the 1950s, the library's first decade in the new building. Thelma Rieless replaced Rosalie Norris as librarian in 1953, and she was replaced by Dorothy Hansen three years later. Hansen resigned in 1958, over a disagreement with the board on increasing library hours. Two other staff members left with her. Carolyn Wolf was hired in late 1958, and remained as head librarian, and later as library director, until 1979.

Other events of note during the 1950s and 1960s include a new mechanical charging system to expedite traffic at the front desk in 1954, and a gift of $2,700 for building improvement projects from developer and aviation entrepreneur Warren Grimes in 1956. Grimes donated $2,400 the following year for improvements to the children's department.

A 1962 report to the city manager lists among community services currently rendered: Reference help and information service for all, either at the library or over the phone (in 1961 such service was given in response to 5,450 requests); children's activities during the summer: story hour, stamp club, reading club, Spanish conversation class, origami (Japanese paper folding); six-hour term of classes in music appreciation in 1961; an attractive, quiet and air-conditioned reading room for all who wish to use it for leisure or for purposeful reading; specific collections of books for the convenience of readers; Garden Nook developed from a nucleus gift made several years ago by the garden clubs of the city; Florida collection consisting of both fiction and nonfiction pertaining to Florida, her history, wildlife, marine life, flowers, trees, laws, literature and people; business collection expanded in the last two years to meet the needs of those interested in business and finance and to help on the economic development of Florida; and young adult section with both fiction and nonfiction for the teenager on subjects in which they are interested.

The library staff in 1962 included head librarian Carolyn Wolf, reference librarian Ruth Carson, circulation clerk Eleanor Foust, Mrs. James (Mildred L.) Lane in charge of circulation, children's librarian Ruth Nelson, circulation and display assistant Mrs. Roger (Eve) Schuenaman, and secretary Florence Cowley.

In 1964, the library introduced a circulating art collection featuring twenty reproductions of well-known artists' works, from old masters to modern abstract painters. The paintings were loaned on a five-dollar deposit for a sixty-day period, with overdue fines of twenty-five cents per day. Plastic cards replaced the old paper library cards in 1966.

A hand-typed history of the library (from which much of this chapter is gleaned) says 1965 "saw a new look in the library. All the interior plaster wears a fresh coat of paint. Sheer draperies in willow green hang from the east and west windows in the main reading room, and colorful new rattan chairs replace much of the worn-out furniture."

The end of the 1960s ushered in a new era for the Delray Beach Public Library. A two-story addition completed in 1968 nearly doubled the library's capacity, adding 7,500 square feet. Also in 1968, the Delray Beach Public Library became one of seven municipal libraries to join the Palm Beach County Library System. The Delray library withdrew from the system in 1977, citing dissatisfaction with the level of service provided to municipal libraries in the system. West Palm Beach, North Palm Beach, and Lake Park libraries also withdrew from the county system that year.

LIBRARY BUILDING DRIVE. The library raised money for an extensive addition in 1968.
Courtesy of the Delray Beach Public Library.

A garden room was added in 1975, providing space for gardening books and other special collections. A 1976 news story reported on a new trend in children's room at the Delray library: Parents requesting stories with girls as the active participants instead of boys. Children's librarian Holly Russo remarked, "Women's lib is seen as a contributing factor."

The library installed a $17,000 security system in 1977. A sign beside the now ubiquitous theft-detection checkpoints instructed "If a bell rings, please return your library materials to the circulation desk to be properly checked out." Assistant librarian Mrs. James (Mildred L.) Lane, who had started at the library in 1942, retired in 1977. In 1979, Leslie Strickland was named library director, after longtime director Carolyn Wolf left the library.

The library published a cookbook in 1983, *A Literary Feast: A Cookbook out of Character*. The staff had fun with literary punning in the recipe names: Mutiny on the Brownie, Moby Dish, (shrimp gumbo), Quiche Me Kate, Loaf Story (ham loaf), and Lettuce Eat Right to Keep Fit (nine-layer salad). The library released a second cookbook in 2008, *A Literary Feast: A Second Helping*.

In 1984, the Delray library went online with an automated catalog system shared by the West Palm Beach and Boynton Beach libraries. A 3,100-square-foot auditorium addition was completed in 1985. In 1988 renovations to the children's room, boardroom and quiet study areas were completed.

The youth department took outreach to a new level with a summer Book Caravan in 1997. The first caravan was a used station wagon that brought books to kids at parks, camps, daycare centers, and schools, five days a week for six weeks. The caravan program upgraded to a colorful van, and grew from twenty-one to thirty-four sites in the seven years it ran under the guidance of longtime children's department head Lynda Hunter. In 1998, the library received a state grant to bring Internet access to the library on fifteen workstations with full Internet access, and to make the online catalog available on the library website.

In 1999, with a new library director—John J. Callahan III was hired a few months after Peter Daniels resigned—and with the nearly 100,000 volume collection bursting the library building at the seams, the board began planning for a new library. Not all in community supported a move. Some thought the library should expand by acquiring lots adjoining the existing site on SW 4th Avenue, but others looked forward to a new building where moms with tots wouldn't have to go through the adult mystery section and then a hallway, around the side of the auditorium, and through a set of double doors to get to the elevator to the children's department.

The board decided on a Community Redevelopment Agency owned site in the 100 block of West Atlantic Avenue, east of the county courthouse. The proposed two-story, 47,000-square-foot building would double the size of the library and the book collection, and add one hundred computers. Mayor Jeff

DELRAY BEACH PUBLIC LIBRARY. Second floor, 2016.
Courtesy of the Delray Beach Public Library.

Perlman was among the residents who were not fans of the proposed library design. Some said it looked like a prison. Architect Jose Gelabert-Navia said he modeled the building after the historic Florida East Coast Railway depot and in the spirit of other Delray landmarks. He redesigned parts of the exterior and resolved most concerns.

Construction on the new building began in 2004, and on a January Sunday in 2006, Delray residents celebrated the grand opening of the new library with a ribbon-cutting ceremony and a symbolic book-passing brigade. This event echoed the 1950 move to the 4th Avenue location, when community volunteers moved books from a storeroom in Reid's Village to the new library on Fourth Avenue.

The library has continued to evolve in the new building. The youth department was expanded in 2007, added a computer center in 2011, and was renamed the Lynda Hunter and Virginia Kimmel Children's Library in 2016, featuring an audio recording studio and a technology lab with 3D printers.

The adult education Lifelong Learning Community Institute was established in 2009, and the following year, the Empowerment Zone opened in the computer technology lab, to assist adults resume building, job searching, online research, and computer skills. The Teen Advisory Board was created in 2010, and e-books were added to the collection in 2012.

In 2013, the Delray Beach Public Library celebrated its centennial, and is poised to mark its next 100 years by continuing to offer library service through a partnership between the city of Delray Beach and the Delray Beach Public Library Association. The Delray Beach Public Library is one of just two public libraries in Florida that remains under the governance of a not-for-profit organization.

Boca Raton Public Library

Ellen Randolph and Vicky Fitzsimmons

Editor's Note: Of the original municipalities of today's Palm Beach County, Boca Raton had a late start. When West Palm Beach and Delray were thriving communities, Boca Raton was a sleepy farming village, growing pineapple, tomatoes, and green beans.

That all changed with the 1920s Florida Boom. Developers such as Addison Mizner and George Harvey swooped in and bought land. They planned developments that would have been the grandest in the county, with homes, golf courses and even a gondola canal to Mizner's hotel The Cloisters.

The 1926 and 1928 hurricanes and the stock market crash of 1929 snuffed out the plans. In spite of these hardships, the Boca Raton community came together to create a library legacy.

* * *

In January 1923, the Woman's Club of Boca Raton created the community's first library in the town's municipal building. The vision for a

BOCA RATON WOMAN'S CLUB. The Woman's Club started the first library in Boca Raton, 1923. *Courtesy of the Boca Raton Public Library.*

public library became a reality through hard work, dedication, and volunteerism. Woman's Club member Mrs. Morris Stokes obtained a large donation of fiction books from Chicago friends to form the heart of the new library's collection.

The Woman's Club organized library fundraisers including musicales where the admission price was a book. Architect Addison Mizner convinced his Boca Raton Club members to contribute books at the close of their vacations. The original Boca Raton library flourished in its initial years during the booming economy. However, it closed in the late 1920s, a victim of the "big bust."

In 1946-1947, the Women's Christian and Civic Club, made up of wives of Boca Raton Army Air Field (BRAAF) personnel, along with other civic-minded women of the community felt the lack of a library had a detrimental impact on the city's cultural existence. Led by their president, Mrs. Arnold MacSpadden, the women established a library in the administration building on the Army Air Base and conducted library fundraisers. They raised money through personal donations, books collected from friends and families, card parties, and membership drives. With the determined efforts of a loyal few, the women kept the library open three afternoons and one evening a week.

Two hurricanes struck Boca Raton in September 1947. The Air Force base reported $4.5 million in damages. The roof of the library blew off, and the library closed. A short time later, the Woman's Club itself dissolved, but Eleanor Bebout, the organization's secretary, continued to conduct library meetings at regular intervals, arranging for substitute librarians when necessary and doing everything possible to keep the project alive. On April 26, 1948, the first library board of five directors was elected with Mrs. Bebout as president, Helen Mann as secretary, and Carrie Sperry as treasurer. After receiving permission from the town council to use a room in the municipal building, the committee framed a constitution and by-laws. They selected the name "The Library of Boca Raton," and the books were moved to their new location.

In 1950, Mrs. Hildegarde Schine, wife of J. Meyer Schine of the Boca Raton Club, became interested in the library and redecorated the room, adding bookcases, fluorescent lights, and draperies. The library held an open house and an art exhibit highlighting the work of local artists with paintings from galleries in Miami and Palm Beach. More than eight hundred people attended the event, marking the beginning of the Boca Raton Art Guild. The guild worked effectively with the library to raise funds for a new library building where they planned to house a permanent art museum.

BOCA RATON LIBRARY TEMPORARY QUARTERS. This one-story concrete structure on West Palmetto Park Road served as a temporary library in the late 1950s. Photo by Gene Hyde. *Courtesy of the Boca Raton Historical Society & Museum.*

By late 1955, plans were proceeding for the Boca Raton Library and Cultural Arts Center erected on land donated by Mr. and Mrs. J. M. Schine, overlooking the golf course. The center's first priorities were books and art, but they also planned to host flower shows, art classes, drama groups, musical organizations, craft classes, book reviews, and other civic activities. Facility plans included a two hundred-seat auditorium with complete kitchen facilities for catered events such as buffets, garden parties, and teas.

While the plans were in the approval stage, the library moved to a temporary 680-square-foot space in the administration building of the Garden Apartments on West Palmetto Road. The Boca Raton Town Council subsidized a large percentage of the library's operations; library services continued uninterrupted during the new library facility construction. The library's board of directors approved final plans in 1961 for the new $41,000 library building on NW 2nd Avenue. The Boca Raton Woman's Club arranged to furnish the children's area and organize a story hour in the new 4,000 square foot building.

The Boca Raton Library opened to the public on Monday, November 13, 1961. The air-conditioned facility featured juvenile and adult areas, a conference room, a small room for vinyl music recordings, and a book drop for night deposit. In late 1966, the library was dedicated to the City of Boca Raton and renamed the Boca Raton Public Library. Although the city council previously helped financially support the library, the entity was initially a nonprofit organization, operated by a volunteer library board of directors.

Soon after, city administrators used the same architect to plan a 5,000-square-foot wing costing $120,000. The new wing opened in 1972 providing much-needed space for reading, research, new shelving for additional magazines, books, records, a new card catalog, display case, and a space for the Boca Raton Historical Society. The addition's second floor children's room featured story hours, puppet shows, and other programs.

During the mid-1970s recession, library use increased. Janet Murray, Boca Raton Public Library director, noted, "The library always seems to have an increase in business when things get bad." The increase in use came during a three percent budget decrease in operational funds. Subsequently, the library reduced hours, cut expenditures for supplies, instituted a hiring freeze, and turned down the air-conditioning.

Library patronage nearly doubled from 1972 to 1975. As the library grew, the clientele changed. Patrons ranged from retired senior citizens to IBM employees' kids. A summer reading program for children augmented the winter programs of lectures, travelogues, and book reviews.

Janet Murray, library director since 1961, announced her retirement in early 1978. That July, Michigan librarian Bruce R. Kauffman became the new director. The hiring committee was impressed with Kauffman's broad experience at both public and university libraries and his familiarity with the use of computer applications in library science.

Palm Beach County Commissioners voted to end subsidy payments to seven city libraries, including Boca Raton in mid-1979. The purpose of the subsidy was to reimburse municipalities for library services to residents from unincorporated areas of the county. According to Kauffman, Boca Raton's payments from the tax district in 1979 were about $26,000. In place of the subsidy, the commissioners voted to accept a recommendation from the county library advisory board to encourage cities to enter a reciprocal borrowing agreement for books and other library materials. Under the agreement, unincorporated area residents and city residents could use any library that was a party to the agreement without paying a non-resident fee.

The Boca city library board members and Kauffman decided that the county commission's action was not in the best interests of the taxpayers of this municipality. When the city council reviewed the proposed 1979-1980 budget, it asked to review its agreement with the county library system. The library board requested the council provide money for at least part of the deficit that the local library would experience because of the county's severance of the subsidy payments.

LIBRARIAN FLORENCE MANGUS. 1970s. *Boca Raton News*
Photo Collection. *Courtesy of the Boca Raton Historical Society & Museum.*

When Palm Beach County started its own taxing district library system in 1968, the system invited all libraries in the county's municipalities to participate. The Boca Raton Public Library elected to take part, along with most other city and privately-owned libraries in the county. As Boca Raton's population increased, the administrative and operating costs of servicing thousands of new patrons exceeded the library's resources and the system's level of reimbursement. The City of Boca Raton decided to withdraw following another reimbursement reduction. The city then offered full-time residents and property owners' free library services as a benefit of their municipal taxes. All services previously offered under the prior arrangements were continued. Non-residents, who paid the county library system tax, paid a non-resident fee of twenty dollars annually to use the Boca Raton Public Library.

Thirty volunteers enlisted in the Friends of the Boca Raton Public Library first organizational meeting in November 1979. Kauffman said that typical Friends organizations work to bring public attention to the library. They cooperate with the library staff in developing services, give support to legislation related to libraries, help the library acquire materials, and help raise money for the library. The Friends toured the library and found the facility cramped and outdated. The library Friends group committed to a substantial expansion of the existing library facility, held their first book sale fundraiser—dubbed the Boca Book Bash—and hosted a series of presentations.

The library expanded again in 1982. The city now numbered close to 50,000 residents and the library fell below national library standards in many areas such as the number of books and employee workspaces. Voters passed a $1,920,000 bond issue to expand the library with $100,000 spent on books. The 5,490-square-foot addition would almost double the library's existing floor space. In August, the city council tentatively approved $94,000 to buy new books for the library and $33,000 to buy a new computer [OCLC] to hasten the cataloging of the additional books. The library now had about 64,000 volumes, many in poor condition which needed to be replaced.

The Boca Library Friends hosted a program in 1981 entitled "The Present and Future of Home Computers" with guest speaker Larry Crismond, sales manager for Personal Computers at I.B.M. (International Business Machines) in Boca Raton. A group of twelve engineers led by William C. Lowe had assembled in Boca Raton several years prior to work on a secret project codenamed "Acorn." The result of these efforts was a machine called the "IBM PC." Crismond explained that I.B.M. engaged in an extensive marketing effort to make these new computers available for use at home and in small businesses. He claimed that personal computers would help people accomplish what they wanted to, faster and easier, and that even if you had never used a computer, the interactive system made the I.B.M. PC easy for anyone to use.

Florence Mangus retired on August first, 1986, after seventeen years as children's librarian at the Boca Raton Public Library. During her career, she saw changes resulting from advances in technology and the need for more parents to work. "No two days here are the same," Mangus said. "The point of our job is not to pop up and help children every time they want it, but to teach them to help themselves." Mangus devised story programs for kids aged three to twelve. In a retirement interview, she told a *Boca Chronicle* reporter: "We feel that guidance is important in getting youngsters interested in books early.... We read, tell stories, and even include the care of books. We always throw in a little entertainment to keep it interesting, as their interest span is very short. For this we use hand puppets, film strips, songs, and finger plays."

In addition to updating the juvenile collection with music, film, and computer games, Mangus devised innovative children's programs that included summer reading and holiday programs, writing contests, and costume parades. She insisted that over the years the children themselves changed only slightly. "Maybe they are more visually oriented, but overall their love of a story hasn't changed. There are just more stories to choose from. The popularity of television and computers hasn't seemed to lessen the appeal of books."

STORY TIME. Children's librarian Florence Mangus reads *Harry's Bee* to
Rachel Grooters, age 6, at the Boca Raton Public Library July 28, 1986.
Photo by Zich, Boca Raton News Photo Collection.
Courtesy of the Boca Raton Historical Society & Museum.

In May 1989, the city council approved a ten-year blueprint for Boca
Raton's future, including a second library in the northwest area of the city to
serve those living north of Glades Road and west of Interstate 95. Acting City
Manager Rick Witker advised the city council to hire a facilities planner and to
use data to develop an expansion plan, including information gleaned from the
residents' survey conducted the year before.

The 1990 library phone survey responses included suggestions for a drive-
through book return drop box, adult special interest programs, copy machines
that work, more parking, more quiet space, more books (especially biographies
and true stories) for children, better pay for staff, and more. In the interim, the
library refurbished and expanded its Youth Services area with updated carpet
and color scheme and renovated and expanded the reference area. In 1992, the
library added a high-tech alternative to the White Pages to its reference
resources with a computer database called Phone Disc containing eighty-five
million names, addresses, and telephone numbers of persons and businesses
located throughout the United States. This addition supplemented the
extensive collection of newspapers and business research materials already
owned by the library, plus research materials available through interlibrary loan
services.

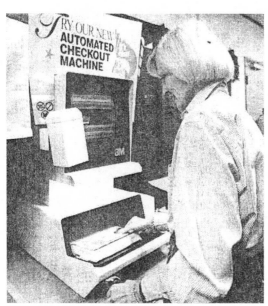

SELF-CHECKOUT MACHINE.
Courtesy of the Boca Raton Public Library.

The Boca Raton Public Library joined other local libraries in 1992 to eliminate functional illiteracy in Palm Beach County after determining that 70,000 adults in the county were reading at less than an eighth-grade level. Joan-Marie Mueller coordinated the library's literacy program with students paired with tutors, supported by donations from the Boca Raton Friends of the Library and an advisory council.

Managing fines in order to protect the collection while allowing as much access as possible has always challenged librarians. In 1982, the city council agreed to implement controls over lending practices and take action against irresponsible borrowers. The new tough penalties were preferable to a poorly stocked library. Borrowers could keep books for up to three weeks and record albums for a week. Under the new policy, overdue book fines were set at ten cents per day up to a maximum of five dollars per item and fines for overdue records raised to twenty-five cents per day per item up to a maximum of ten dollars.

By 1992, overdue fines for any item per day were twenty cents with a five-dollar cap. Pat Michalski, adult services librarian, reasoned that people did not return books due to guilt and lack of money. In order to retrieve long overdue materials, the library implemented an amnesty week waiving overdue charges and charges for lost or damaged materials. If the book in question was returned, no questions were asked. Although only two dozen of the nearly five hundred overdue items were returned, the library staff called the week a success. Some of the long overdue books were no longer in print and could not be replaced.

Another referendum went on the ballot in 1993 for $13.3 million to expand its downtown library facility to 52,300 square feet. If voters approved the proposal, the book collection would increase from 111,000 to 250,000 volumes and the expanded facility would feature four times as many videos, records and compact discs, more computers, rooms for educational films and children's programs, outdoor reading courts surrounded by gardens, as well as additional patron parking.

Supporters emphasized the cost per taxpayer to show the reasonableness of the project's cost and argued that you can't have a first-class city without a first-class library. With 20,000 cardholders and nine hundred regular nonresident users, most people agreed that a good library would not only improve life for current residents, but help attract future residents as well.

Despite popular consensus about the need for expansion, in March, 1994, Boca Raton residents voted down the $12 million bond issue by eighty-eight votes. The cost of the new facility was the main reason for a "no" vote, prompting the city to adjust the plans for expanding the facility to 35,000 square feet, still doubling the existing building. Revisions called for doing away with the gift shop and altering other areas. The revised referendum was delayed to allow for the acquisition of two tracts of land for parking lots and the exploration of resource-sharing agreements with other libraries.

During the late 1990s, the library saw many new technological advances in patron services. Beginning in January 1996, a library patron with a computer and a modem could access the library's catalog along with other information without physically visiting the library. Updates to the library's system were supplemented by the purchase of additional computers and the acquisition of a Newsbank CD system, a collection of newspapers on compact discs.

In May 1996, the library welcomed Catherine O'Connell as the new library director. In addition to building support for a library expansion, her priority was to add new technology such as automatic machines for book checkout to improve patron services. In 1997, the library added the provider Free-Net to the library's automated system, allowing patrons to access a wide range of material via the Southeast Florida Library Information Network both in the library and from home. Free-Net was accessible from any computer in the library and contained local and government news, media resources, arts and entertainment.

By 1998, library expansion was reconsidered, including alternatives such as several full-service branch libraries or smaller branch libraries electronically connected to the Main Library. A library patron survey revealed their top two desires were more reading and study space and more copies of popular books. The library also wanted to offer new technology, such as Internet access, video-conferencing, and graphic imaging systems, which patrons expect to find at their public libraries.

Following several years of inactivity, the Friends of the Boca Raton Public Library reorganized in 1999 with O'Connell as its driving force behind the reorganization. The Friends' goals included advertising the library's facilities, collections, and services to the public; creating exciting programs for the public, and attracting guest speakers and authors to the library; and sponsoring the kickoff of the summer youth reading program.

In November 1999, the library went high-tech with self-checkout to reduce long lines at the circulation desk. The system, the first of its kind in South Florida, looked a bit like an ATM machine. Patrons loved it and said it made checking out of the library much more efficient and convenient. Self-checkout represented the final step of a twenty-year process transitioning from card catalogs and pocket due date cards to a fully automated checkout system using barcodes. Prior to computerization in the 1980s, the library used the Gaylord checkout machine which stamped each book card with the patron's library card number. These book cards were filed by staff alphabetically or by call number in long trays and returned to the book pocket when the item was returned. A stamped due date card was put in the back pocket of the book to remind the patron. Hand-typed cards which described each item in the collection were organized in three card catalogs by author, title, or subject heading.

Computerized cataloging began in 1981 with the $33,000 purchase of an OCLC cataloging computer with dial-up connection which produced printed catalog cards. By 1989, the library had purchased the compatible LS/2000 computer software, had the entire printed catalog entered into the computer catalog, and introduced the online catalog to patrons. In 1995, the library converted to Sirsi Dynix and began to add barcodes to materials. Library staff could scan items for checkout at the circulation desk and provide a printed checkout slip to the patron. By the end of 1999, patrons could check out their books and print a checkout slip online themselves.

Increased patron access through improved technology continued in the early 2000s. In the fall of 2000, the library website debuted, which included information about hours, programs and available services, plus the new library logo and motto, "Expand Your Horizons." In 2001, patrons could browse the online catalog from home and by early 2002 they could also access databases remotely. In June 2006, the library switched from Sirsi Dynix to Millennium which allowed patrons to access their accounts online, place holds, pay fines, and keep reading histories and wish lists.

In early 2003, library employees wanted to ensure that voters turned out to support the bond issue for library expansion. Voters were surveyed to see what they wanted in their library. The library sent a promotional mailing to all registered voters and had volunteers stationed at the library's entrance in the weeks leading up to the election. A promotional video aired in the library as well as on public access station cable channel 20. Friends of the Library paid for spot campaign signs around town. Library workers wore buttons and encouraged patrons to vote "yes" come Election Day. A conceptual artist's rendering of the future downtown library was on display. City officials joined O'Connell in speaking at club and civic group meetings. Mayor Steven Abrams went door to door in many neighborhoods to distribute promotional brochures. The public was also invited to two community meetings on the bond issue. Representatives from the city, the library, the library board, and the Friends of the Library were on hand to answer questions.

The $19.8 million bond issue to build two new library facilities to provide more space for children's programs, computers, and quiet study areas passed by an overwhelming majority on March 11, 2003 despite low voter turnout. Over seventy percent of voters were in favor of the bond. The city planned to repay the $19.8 million loan plus $9.9 million in interest over a twenty-year period. The average cost increase for residents was estimated to be twenty-four dollars, which according to O'Connell was less than the cost of one hardcover book. The two new facilities were scheduled for a 2008 completion date.

On December 14, 2004, the city council approved plans to expand the design of the new western Boca Raton Public Library facility on Spanish River Boulevard. The plans included an additional 12,000 square feet of indoor space, and an additional 14,500 square feet of outdoor space for a total of 55,000 square feet. The plans included outside rooftop terraces to allow patrons to sit outside on sunny days and a footbridge to connect the library grounds with the nearby Pondhawk Natural Area.

The extra space would provide a fundraising opportunity with party and event rentals. The facility planned to add dressing rooms, catering facilities, and a space for a valet parking stand to accommodate the events. The expansion was estimated to add $223,000 to the project's initial cost, but Mayor Steven Abrams stated that the voter-approved $19.8 million bond issue would cover the added expense. Groundbreaking was set for April 2, 2005 with a projected opening date in 2006.

Active hurricane seasons in 2004 and 2005 delayed construction of the new western site of the library. In September 2004, Hurricanes Frances and Jeanne both hit southeast Florida within weeks of each other. In October 2005, Hurricane Wilma struck the southwest Florida coast and quickly crossed the state, exiting near Jupiter as a Category Two storm. The storms damaged the construction site and led to shortages of both materials and laborers. Labor and contract issues forced the city to hire a new contractor in February 2007.

The Friends of the Boca Raton Public Library opened their first bookstore in September, 2007. The next month, the Friends presented the city council with a check for $14,000, a donation earmarked for the purchase of audiobooks for both the Downtown Library and the new Spanish River Library; set to open in January 2008.

The new Spanish River Library opened on January 26, 2008 to huge crowds. O'Connell expected at least 2,000 visitors for opening day, but by noon she said they had probably already reached that number. The library opened with about 45,000 new books in the collection. O'Connell told the *Sun Sentinel*, "A library is always a work in progress. Across the country a lot of library directors are calling their libraries the 'community's living room,' and this is sort of what it is."

Just weeks after the Spanish River Library opened, Boca Raton moved on to the next phase of planning for another library downtown. As the city struggled with its annual budget that included layoffs and program cuts due to economic downturn, city leaders said the plans would cost too much. The resolution was to reduce the size of the building from 50,000 square feet and a cost of $22 million, to 42,000 square feet at a cost of $8.3 million. The downtown library was projected to have a more urban flair than the Spanish River Library, according to Mike Woika, assistant city manager at the time. Both designs would keep the classic Boca Raton style.

A top priority for the Friends of the Boca Raton Public Library was the 250-seat auditorium, as the Spanish River Library's largest meeting room could not accommodate their monthly musical events. Space for a used bookstore, which the Friends would operate, was also on the wish list. The Friends contributed $250,000 to the construction budget to help make those wishes a part of the final design.

The library board and the Friends launched a campaign to build a new downtown library in August 2008. A huge lobbying effort to get the city to move forward began with presentations at community organizations, city boards, city workshops, and a 2010 goal setting session. In September 2010, after two years of public and passionate debate over the location of the new library, a 4.5-acre parcel just one block north of the old library was chosen.

The groundbreaking ceremony was held on April 24, 2012 for what would become a 41,932-square-foot building. In early June 2013, the public was invited to participate in a book brigade—a human chain to move the last one hundred books, hand-to-hand, from the old library building to the new. Over three hundred people turned out, including children from nearby summer camps and preschools, to take part in the historic event.

BOOK BRIGAGE. School children participate in the book brigade moving books from the old library to the new. *Courtesy of the Boca Raton Public Library.*

Following the 50th anniversary of the old downtown library on May 18, 2013, the new downtown library opened June 22, 2013 with a ribbon-cutting ceremony, family carnival and a film screening. The new green-designed building included a large community room, business meeting room, private study rooms, a teen space, seating for 155 people, seventy public access computers, and free Wi-Fi. In May 2015, the Downtown Library was awarded Silver LEED (Leadership in Energy and Environmental Design Certification for its sustainable and green design initiatives. It soon added an electronic car charging station.

From 2013 to 2017, Boca Raton Public Library continued to grow. In 2013, the library added Zinio for digital magazines, and Freegal, which provides access to more than seven million songs available. From 2014, the library added Universal Class, Atomic Training, which provided patrons with online learning courses in software, business, the arts and music instruction, gardening, cooking, health, job preparation, and much more. In 2015, Tumblebooks was added which provided digital books and audiobooks for children. In 2016, the library added Value Line, Lynda.com, Transparent Language, and Hoopla, which significantly increased online classes and access to digital materials. New programming and literacy events included Story Central storytelling series, civic engagement lectures, foreign film series, bilingual story times for preschoolers, and author signings, plus participation in national programming such as Summer Reading, Read for the Record, Teen Read Week, Teen Tech Week, and Money Smart Week. In 2016, the Boca Raton Public Library had more than 560,000 visitors, circulated more than 828,136 items, and hosted more than 1,582 events with over 49,287 attendees. As of July 2017, the library had ninety-five experienced staff of which eleven are librarians, twenty-six are full-time, and fifty-eight are part-time.

In September 2015, Discover Studio was launched at Downtown Library. Funded by the Friends of the Boca Raton Public Library, Discover Studio uses a pop-up space model to teach emerging technologies, including 3D printing, music production, audio podcasting, and photo and film editing as part of the library's role as a partner in education for the community. This unique opportunity connects people with the latest technology to foster creative learning, and develop new talents and skills. Future classes at Discover Studio will teach audio recording and podcasting; music production; digital photo editing; and digital film editing complete with green screen and camera equipment for budding filmmakers and performers.

In December 2015, the Friends of the Boca Raton Public Library presented a gift of $64,000 to fund youth services programs, e-resources, the Discover Studio staff development and the library's signature initiative, Civic Engagement. "The Friends are grateful to our members, donors, and bookstore customers for their continued financial support of our organization," said Cyndi Bloom, then president of the Friends Board of Directors. "Because of this, we are able to give generously to the library for its 2016 programs. It is a true testament to the community's ongoing dedication and support for one of the most important educational and cultural resources for the people of Boca Raton. As their twenty-sixth anniversary year approaches (1990-2016), the Friends celebrate their continued mission to help make Boca Raton libraries vital resources for the well-being of the community."

In May 2017, Boca Raton Public Library introduced Youth Makers and Little Makers coding and robotics classes. Through a generous donation by the Friends of the Library, a series of new classes will launch this summer to teach computer science and coding principles to children and teens. Little Makers introduces kids ages five to eleven to nationally known educational robotics and coding programs such as Squishy Circuits, Cubetto, Little Bits, Ozobot, and Finch Robot. Teens and tweens will learn new skills in Youth Makers classes using Hummingbird Robotics and Sphero.

Reflecting on the past while anticipating the future, Ann Nappa said, "As the BRPL moves further into twenty-first century technology, methods and materials will change. The buildings that we cherish now will be updated and reimagined to meet the emerging needs of a new community of users. The BRPL will add new services and materials that will allow the citizens of Boca Raton to learn and to grow through self-directed education, and instructive and enlightening experiences. The BRPL will always be inspired by our community, our civic leaders, the Friends of Library, and our staff to bring exciting improvements for the benefit of everyone within the City of Boca Raton.

Throughout its history the women and men of the Boca Raton community have understood the educational, cultural, and civic benefits of providing a public library for the citizens of the city. Each generation of BRPL stewards has been faced with similar challenges, from funding to hurricanes, and each generation has continued to build upon the democratic ideal of a free public library.

"Never doubt that a small group of thoughtful, committed citizens can change the world; indeed, it's the only thing that ever has."

~ Margaret Mead

Glades Area Libraries

Graham Brunk

Belle Glade

Library service in Belle Glade dates back to 1926, when it began as a simple bookcase in the Belle Glade Hotel which was destroyed in the infamous 1929 hurricane. The bookcase relocated to the American Red Cross Tent, after which the Belle Glade Woman's Club was tasked with opening a library to serve all the Glades area including South Bay and Pahokee. A small room was set aside in Belle Glade's town hall.

The Woman's Club set up a library committee and through committee chairs Mr. and Mrs. A. Daane, they were able to secure a sizable lending library from the Palm Beach Athletic Club for a town hall space, and opened for four hours a month in the afternoons. The Woman's Club hired a professional librarian, Mrs. J.F. Browne to oversee the collection. They paid her four dollars a month.

In 1940, the Woman's Club was able to convince the City of Belle Glade to begin contributing to its operational costs. They city agreed to contribute ten dollars a month toward the library's operation. By 1946, the collection had grown to a size of over 3,000 volumes and had nearly 350 members throughout the Glades region. The library's budget had grown exponentially from ten dollars per month to an annual $1,500.

Mrs. Browne made some interesting observations while watching patrons select books to take home. She noticed that many patrons would select books with colorful covers rather than those that were plain covered library-bound books. She made a decision to catalog books in their original appearance, a concept not often practiced at other libraries at the time. Since Mylar book jackets were not yet available, she began to cut out the covers of the books and paste them onto the library-bound hard cover books.

Post-World War II days were very positive for the growing Belle Glade Library. It moved to its own building next to the city police department on W. Canal Street. President Roosevelt's administration created a program called the Works Progress Administration (WPA). Its goal was to employ people in all kinds of public service jobs throughout the country. Belle Glade hired Mrs. M. F. George, a professional librarian staffed by WPA for thirty hours a week.

The library grew to a steady 16,000 books and by the mid-1950s and in the 1960s was outgrowing its space. In 1965, librarian Betty Harris started encouraging the Belle Glade City Council to begin exploring the possibility of building a new library from the ground up. Local Glades area architect Chester A. Cone was selected to design the new municipal library and Belle Glade City Hall, which would be built together in the center of town at South Main Street and Avenue E (now Martin Luther King, Jr. Boulevard) in the former McDonald Park. The Woman's Club raised approximately $11,000 to furnish the new building upon its completion.

Despite an unfortunate incident of vandals breaking into the building when it was nearing its completion and causing $800 worth of damage, the new library opened in the spring of 1967. A dedication was held later that year, featured lectures given by several librarians from around the state, local government officials, and Glades historian Lawrence E. Will.

From Halloween parties in the parking lot, to packed children's story times, to adult literacy classes, the permanent facility brought a breath of fresh air to the Glades area. With a very well-established collection, two full-time staff members, meeting rooms, and air-conditioning, the library was a popular spot. The Belle Glade Library joined the new Palm Beach County library system set up in the coastal areas of the county, giving patrons in the Glades access to

BELLE GLADE PUBLIC LIBRARY. Interior view of the Belle Glade Public Library in the 1950s. *Courtesy of the PBCLS.*

many of the benefits of the coastal area libraries. The library opted out of the system in 1979 when it, along with many other municipalities, disagreed with how library taxing district money was being distributed to municipal participants.

In 1976, the library received some noteworthy attention when with the United States bicentennial celebration and the opening of the Lawrence E. Will Museum, named for the popular Glades area historian who attended the opening. The city donated an outside memorial statue that remembered the two thousand people who lost their lives in the1928 hurricane. The museum housed house much of Wills' personal research and documents as well as a Glades area history collection. While the museum would operate somewhat separately from the library, pairing with the library made it very accessible since it was open during regular library hours. The museum sold many of Will's popular books about the Glades area, *Okeechobee Hurricane*, *A Cracker History of Okeechobee*, and *Swamp in Sugar Bowl*: and *Pioneer Days in Belle Glade*.

In 1979, following the sudden departure of the library's director, the city found it challenging to locate a replacement. Since Belle Glade is a somewhat remote, rural location and the economics of the area have changed drastically over time, it was difficult to find a professional librarian willing to work in the area with the salary offered. The library had recently hired a new children's librarian, Phyllis Lilley. She moved from New York after completing library school and heard that Florida was a great place to find employment and career growth opportunities. Even though Lilley had expressed interest in the job, the city was reluctant to hire her due to her inexperience; ultimately, they chose to offer her the position.

Almost daily film screenings, a new circulating video collection, fine amnesty days, local art exhibits, and children's story hours are just a few of the programs Lilley continued throughout the early 1980s. There were even programs to educate citizens about HIV (Human Immunodeficiency Virus) since Belle Glade was the location of Palm Beach County's first outbreak in 1981.

In an effort to counteract a tax hike for the 1987 year, the City of Belle Glade proposed merging its library with the Palm Beach County Library System. On average, it would cost city taxpayers roughly $0.34 per $1,000 if the county were to provide the service. In addition to saving money, the county offered to automate the entire collection into its computer system, provide bookmobile services to parts of the city, and increase staff. The city would retain ownership of the building (but lease it to the county) and the attached museum. The library officially became the Belle Glade Branch of the Palm Beach County Library System on October 1, 1986.

Some were concerned that a Belle Glade Branch meant the library would become more of a cookie cutter version of the other branches with less emphasis on the local community. However, with the addition of advanced computers and access to countywide shared resources due to courier service, it became clear that the library had made a wise decision.

Because of the library system merger, services improved significantly during the 1990s. More staff allowed for better hours. As the Internet began to gain traction, the library was among the first places in town where people could access a wealth of information using databases subscribed to by the county.

As time went on, however, the 1960s-era facility was beginning to show its age. Funded by a bond voted by taxpayers to improve Palm Beach County Libraries, the county began removing asbestos from the building, as well as adding new lighting and air-conditioning in the 1990s. A story continues to circulate among staff members about how Lilley (now the branch manager) had complained about the carpeting being in bad shape. The county offered to replace it with used carpeting from another branch undergoing remodeling.

Another bond was issued through the taxing district in the early 2000s to further update many existing branches and replace some. Belle Glade was slated for a 17,000-square-foot replacement. The current facility, at roughly 7,000 square feet, was far under the state's recommended size for a library serving a city the population of Belle Glade.

In 2005, Hurricane Wilma ransacked the area, including Belle Glade's Civic Center and its municipal pool on NW 4th Street. The damage was severe enough that the city demolished the complex and left the land vacant. In the planning stages for the new library, officials decided to use the land to create a new civic center for the city. The civic center would be in the library facility but operated by the City of Belle Glade. The library would continue to operate under the Palm Beach County.

The new LEED (Leadership in Energy and Environmental Design) certified building with energy efficient features opened in March of 2013. The library featured a large room lit naturally by skylights centered above the computers, bookcases, and a large circulation and reference desk. Spacious study rooms surround the perimeter of the library and a large children's section adorns the south side of the building.

The library features several works of art, thanks to Palm Beach County's Art in Public Places program. Miami mosaic artist Carlos Alves and ceramics

BELLE GLADE LIBRARY BRANCH. Belle Glade Library mosaic at the newly opened library in 2012. *Courtesy of the PBCLS.*

artist JC Carroll created a circular floor tile at the entrance commemorating the city's long-time motto, "Her Soil is Her Fortune." They also added a modern spin on the mural, stating, "Knowledge is our future." Andrew Reid designed several twelve by twenty-four foot murals inside the library skylights that highlight important historical aspects of Belle Glade. The old library building still lives on as an expanded Lawrence E. Will Museum of the Glades.

Pahokee

The Pahokee Public Library dates back to January 27, 1938 when the Everglades Business and Professional Woman's Club met to discuss what they were going to do with a small collection of books they had collected over the course of the previous year. A newly formed Pahokee library board and Reverend Fred Martin agreed to set aside a small room at the Methodist Church for a circulating library for town residents. Woman's Club secretary, Miss Marian Meredith took on the task of overseeing the new library called the Everglades Public Library.

In October of the same year, the clubwomen met to discuss a better permanent downtown location in the Gold Building for the library as well as the possibility of using Works Progress Administration funding to hire a full-time librarian to manage the collection. They decided to change the name of the library to the Pahokee Public Library and hired Miss Juanita Erler as the WPA librarian for the town.

In the midst of World War II, the library was an active site for town residents wanting to keep up to date on the international situation. The library yet again needed a larger space. The city responded in assisting the Woman's club in securing and remodeling a new downtown location—the J.B. Thomas Store building on Bacom Point Road. With the growth in space, a new committee was set up to aid in raising money for the purchase of new materials.

LOULA V. YORK PAHOKEE PUBLIC LIBRARY. U.S. Sugar representatives at the 1966 groundbreaking. *Courtesy of the PBCLS.*

In a repositioning that makes the Pahokee Library the most frequently moved library in the history of libraries in Palm Beach County, the library relocated from its downtown store front to a larger space inside the Pahokee City Hall. In the mid-1960s, Harry T. Vaughn—President of U.S. Sugar, which had a large mill in the nearby unincorporated and now nonexistent area of Bryant—presented a check in the amount of $80,000 to donate a civil building to be selected by town residents. Vaughn felt the money was a symbol of their commitment to wanting to be part of the Pahokee community. Since most of Pahokee's municipal buildings at the time were in good shape and the library had never had permanent quarters, residents felt the money was best used to build a permanent library facility. Vacant land at Bacom Point Road, already owned by the city, was selected as the site. Vaughn performed a similar donation for a library in Clewiston at the same time with the same premise.

Vaughn turned down the honor of the library named in his honor, although the library in Clewiston named their library after him. The library was instead named after the late Loula V. York, who had been a teacher in the Glades area for over forty years. Architect Chester A. Cone designed the $68,000 building. The remaining money would be used to purchase new furnishings for the facility. The new library facility was dedicated with a celebration on March 8, 1968. Mrs. C.M. Todd, Pahokee librarian, spearheaded the effort to relocate the library in the weeks before. With volunteer assistance from the community, furniture was set up and the building lavishly decorated.

For over twenty years after the library's completion, residents enjoyed the growth in collection (much still through donations), as well as knowledgeable, friendly staff. In response to the HIV outbreak in the Glades in the 1980s, GIFT (Glades Informed Families Together) donated a collection of videotapes discussing drug abuse highlighting topics such as cocaine, heroin, and alcohol. Videos to educate people about sexually transmitted diseases such as AIDS were also part of the donated circulating collection.

In early 1987, the Pahokee City Council began discussing the cost of operating the library. Changes in technology and the need for the library to continue to grow were becoming a financial burden on the local government. Continuing to operate the library at the same growth levels would have cost taxpayers too much money. Belle Glade had just joined the library system the year before; citizens were happy with the results, and the idea of transforming the Pahokee Public Library into a county branch seemed attractive.

Library director Jerry Brownlee, of the county library system, gave a presentation to the council one evening highlighting what the library would gain, noting that current benefits enjoyed by residents would not be impacted, but enhanced. Computers and better staffing with more accessible hours was attractive to council members. The council concluded they would save an estimated $43,000 a year for the city.

Dorothy Harvey, Pahokee librarian, knew the building had begun showing its age and there were also many benefits library patrons would be able to enjoy. However, she did not want the library to lose its close connection with residents and she was an advocate of making the decision quickly. In an interview with *The Palm Beach Post*, she said there were many improvements needed, and neither the county nor the city did anything about it while they were in negotiation.

Initially, the city was uncomfortable with what they called "blank spaces" in the agreement with the county. Therefore, the referendum did not even make the ballot in 1987. The city continued to encounter problem after problem when its own budget was short about $3,500 to make necessary repairs to the building to keep it operational. U.S. Sugar again stepped in to assist with the shortfall, but was not willing to do it again.

Talks of merging the library with the county were much more successful in 1989; residents passed the referendum that year. The library's annual budget would now increase from the $72,000 a year the city spent to $150,000 a year that the county would spend on the facility and its collection. The Pahokee Loula V. York Memorial Library became the Loula V. York Branch of the Palm Beach County Library System on Oct 1, 1989.

Like the experience Belle Glade had a few years prior when they merged with the system, computers were brought in, the library fully automated, new staff hired, and many more programs for children and adults were planned. The library would now be open almost fifty hours per week.

The initial agreement was similar to Belle Glade's; the county would pay a small sum each year for use of the city-owned building and land, but when the city needed money in 1992, they sold the facility and land to the county.

When taxpayers voted in favor of a bond to improve library service in the early 2000s, the library was not a priority for renovation because it was not the busiest location. However, Mother Nature had other plans. When Hurricane Wilma in 2005 severely damaged the building. Much of the collection inside the building was moistened and unable to be preserved. The facility was extensively remodeled and new furniture, bookshelves, carpeting, and an entirely new collection was purchased. The entrances were reversed to the back instead of using the original entrance against the main road. Modern facades were also installed at the new entrance.

Pahokee remains a very small but diverse community, according to the Palm Beach County Library System website. Today, the branch has an emphasis on Spanish materials as well as a sizable children's collection and countless events each month. The town had its own struggles in recent times. There is even talk of unincorporating Pahokee altogether. Residents, however, can rest assured their library will continue to prosper and be a focal point to the small community for years to come.

South Bay

The rural Glades community of South Bay was incorporated in 1941. It is the smallest and westernmost municipality in Palm Beach County. It never had a proper library, but when the Palm Beach County Library Taxing District was established in the late 1960s, it was one of the municipalities to pay into it. Residents also frequented the Belle Glade Public Library a short distance away, which had been in existence when South Bay was incorporated. For many years, the Belle Glade Library allowed South Bay residents to use its services free of charge.

When the library system set up bookmobile services in the late 1960s, South Bay was one of the first municipalities to actively use it. The bookmobile provided service once a week in the area. The bookmobile service remained in place throughout the 1970s and the library system shakeup around that time.

PALM BEACH COUNTY LIBRARY SYSTEM MOBILE LIBRARY.
Servicing the Glades area in the 1970s. *Courtesy of the PBCLS.*

By the late 1980s, the town had grown to nearly 3,500 residents, most having little income and limited transportation. In 1986, Mayor Clarence E. Anthony he asked the Palm Beach County government to consider establishing a permanent facility in the town. He also claimed that having no physical presence other than the occasional bookmobile was a disservice to children in the community whose parents often couldn't get them to the library in Belle Glade. He also urged his fellow town commissioners to write letters to the county explaining the need for a library.

Library director Jerry Brownlee agreed there was potential need for a library in South Bay. Brownlee was able to get the county to agree to match $200,000 toward the building of a library if a state grant the town wanted to obtain could match the other $200,000. The effort failed. For a time, Anthony and his commissioners in South Bay contemplated trying to raise the money themselves and pulling out of the taxing district to establish their own municipal library. This effort was also unsuccessful.

In 1989, the city attempted to get money to match the county's offer again. This time, commissioners were armed with letters from the town's children explaining how much they would benefit from a library in the community. Because of the small size of South Bay, if the town had its own library branch, most kids would be able to get there on their bikes or by walking.

In early 1989, with the help of State Representative Marian Lewis, the state granted South Bay the $200,000 it needed. The town commissioners began working alongside Jerry Brownlee and county planners to create a 4,000-square-foot building on vacant land next to city hall. It was important to the commissioners that the building look natural among the other municipal buildings in the complex.

In July of 1990, during the library's planning stages, and to the surprise of city commissioners and the library director, it became clear the plan contractors had been working on did not resemble other municipal buildings at all. Its cost also increased with the new design by another $200,000. Commissioners and the library system worked to modify the plan so that both county officials and South Bay officials would be happy with the outcome. Grand details such as skylights and archways were removed from the design. A simpler Bohemian/Georgian style with warm color tones, resembling the neighboring city hall, was chosen instead. The footprint of the design would remain the same.

Palm Beach County Commissioner Carol Roberts was very fond of Mayor Anthony's seven-year-long effort to bring a library to his community, even when it seemed impossible. Roberts convinced other commissioners to dedicate the library in his honor. Since he was only thirty-one at the time, he is the youngest person a county building has been named for to date.

Groundbreaking took place in early 1991 and the library opened to the public in May of 1992 as the Clarence E. Anthony South Bay Branch library. Despite being a small library, it remains an essential community resource and focal point. With numerous literacy programs and an active children's department, the library has been able to accomplish much of what Mayor Anthony worked to achieve for his community.

CLARENCE C. ANTHONY BRANCH LIBRARY. The Clarence C. Anthony branch of the Palm Beach County Library System at its 1992 grand opening. *Courtesy of the PBCLS.*

Part II
Academic Libraries

PALM BEACH JUNIOR COLLEGE LIBRARY. *Courtesy of Palm Beach State College.*

Palm Beach
State College Libraries

Janet DeVries and Penelope Brown

In order to fully understand the tremendous growth of Palm Beach State College from its 1933 genesis with forty-one students and a single building, to today's five campus locations with a collective enrollment of almost 50,000 students, it is important to revisit local history. Until the 1920s, Palm Beach County was primarily pine scrub and farmland. Lucrative pineapple plantations, orange groves, dairies, and truck farms dotted the landscape. The tiny settlements along Florida's east coast developed into beachside hamlets and small city centers. Up until the big land boom of the 1920s, the county's entire population numbered less than 20,000, with some joking that there were more cows than people living in the county. During the boom, developers, promoters, and investors rushed to purchase cheap land, parcel it out, and promote Palm Beach County as the last American frontier.

West Palm Beach witnessed the birth of neighborhoods such as Grandview Heights, El Cid, and Flamingo Park. Hotels, office buildings, restaurants, and theaters quickly grew to keep up with the population increase. As land values doubled, the county built roads, schools, and a hospital. Developer George Graham Currie dubbed WPB as standing for "Where Prosperity Beckons." Spirits were high as northerners headed down to claim their place in the land of sunshine.

In the late 1920s, the bubble burst on the land boom. Developers couldn't get materials shipped as quickly as promised, and projects fell behind schedule. Nervous speculators then began to demand their money. Hurricanes in 1926 and 1928, destroyed property, killed people, and dashed hopes. Prosperity gave way to the Great Depression.

Families living in the county couldn't afford to send their children away to college. The Palm Beach County Board of Public Instruction started Palm

PALM BEACH JUNIOR COLLEGE. Located on the Palm Beach High School campus, 1930s.
Courtesy of Palm Beach State College.

Beach Junior College as a solution for students to enroll in higher education while living at home. The college opened its doors in 1933 in a building on the campus of Palm Beach High School in West Palm Beach. The college classrooms, assembly hall, office and library were located in the two-story Mediterranean Revival-style building designed by William Manly King. High school teachers volunteered to teach some of the college courses, and Eleanor McNeil served as the librarian for both the high school and the college.

In July 1940, the school board appointed Pahokee resident Frances Howell, a recent graduate of Florida State College for Women, as the new librarian. Howell served as the librarian and freshmen advisor, stayed in a West Palm Beach boarding house, and visited her parents in Pahokee on weekends. The fall 1940 semester saw a record enrollment of over eighty-five students, more than double the original number.

The college outgrew its Palm Beach High School quarters after World War II, and moved to Morrison Field, a decommissioned United States Army Air

PALM BEACH JUNIOR COLLEGE LIBRARY. The library occupied a Quonset hut on Morrison Field, 1940s. *Courtesy of Palm Beach State College.*

ELIZABETH REYNOLDS, LIBRARIAN.
Courtesy of Palm Beach State College.

Force Base, which is now Palm Beach International Airport. The Army barracks provided a large space for classrooms and student activities. Students enjoyed the additional space for coeducational activities; sports, dances, fraternities and parties. There was even a swimming pool, as well as a spacious library with a growing collection. The library occupied a Quonset hut retrofitted with study tables and chairs, bookshelves, books, encyclopedias, newspapers, and magazines.

The Southern Association of Colleges and Schools granted accreditation to Palm Beach Junior College, and the college hired Kelsey City Elementary School principal Elizabeth Reynolds, a professionally trained librarian, as the head librarian. Student assistants helped to checkout and reshelf books. While teaching at Kelsey City, Reynolds strongly supported literacy and composition, and initiated the school newspaper, *Panther Tracks*. At the college, Reynolds served as the faculty advisor to many student organizations such as the Philo Club, Coed Club, and *The Beachcomber* (student newspaper).

Reynolds, ever-so-popular with students, had several caricatures of her printed in the college yearbook, *The Galleon*. In 1947 *The Palm Beach Post*

PALM BEACH JUNIOR COLLEGE. Lake Park Town Hall, 1950s. *Courtesy of Palm Beach State College.*

mentioned (perhaps in jest) how Reynolds greeted study-worn students at the library entrance with an aspirin and a glass of water. In addition to books and literature, the friendly librarian was well-versed in flower arranging; her floral displays adorned

PALM BEACH JUNIOR COLLEGE. Professor Watson B. Duncan, III (left) and the Galleon yearbook staff pose for a photo in the library at its Lake Park location, 1950s. *Courtesy of Palm Beach State College.*

the library and she presented workshops on flower arrangement throughout Palm Beach County.

When Morrison Field reactivated during the Korean War, the library and the college moved to the Lake Park Town Hall. Because of its frequent moves, the school earned the nickname of "the little orphan college." The restricted quarters resulted in lower enrollment; subsequently some faculty retired when their contracts were not renewed. Reynolds, the consummate educator and librarian, stayed with the college during the transition, taking on many roles and using her organizational skills and creativity to adapt and function in the smaller space. Reynolds directed the library through its many transitions. Upon her 1963 retirement, technology librarian William Chambers, a 1950 Palm Beach Junior College graduate, replaced her as the head librarian.

Another fledgling local college; Roosevelt Junior College, opened in the Roosevelt High School building in West Palm Beach in 1958. Created to provide educational opportunities beyond high school for the district's African-American students, the college opened with Britton Sayles as president and Paul G. Butler as dean and registrar. Its fourteen faculty members included two librarians, Margaret Marie Brown Richardson and Idella B. Wade.

The community school prospered for several years and was a source of pride for its students, faculty and administrators. The librarians worked closely with students, greeting every student by name. By its second year of operation,

166

ROOSEVELT JUNIOR COLLEGE LIBRARY. Students studying in the Roosevelt Junior College Library, 1960. *Courtesy of Palm Beach State College.*

the library had developed a well-rounded book collection and the students produced a yearbook and a school newspaper, called *The Hornet.* After graduating with two-year degrees, some students, many who were the first in their family to graduate high school, continued their academic studies at upper division schools such as Florida Agricultural and Mechanical University (FAMU).

In 1961, the Palm Beach County School Board activated integration. Mary Warren registered at Palm Beach Junior College, becoming the first African-American student. The following year, nineteen more African-American students applied; however, six of the students were denied admission because they lived nearer to Roosevelt Junior College.

The Civil Rights Act of 1964, Title VI, prohibited discrimination in any program or activity, including schools that received federal financial assistance, prompting the county school board to formally desegregate the county school system and close Roosevelt Junior College. Six professors, including librarians Richardson and Wade, and the library's collections, were transferred to Palm Beach Junior College, where they worked until their retirement.

Portraits of Richardson and Wade grace the current Palm Beach State College Lake Worth campus library. A few dozen books from the Roosevelt library collection are displayed in a case along with Roosevelt photographs, newspapers and yearbooks. Video interviews of Richardson, Wade and other Roosevelt faculty and students are preserved in the Palm Beach State College archives. Whereas the school lasted only a few years, its memory lives on.

In 1955, Palm Beach Junior College and the library relocated to its present site in Lake Worth. The Board of County Commissioners gave Palm Beach Junior College 114-acres of county land west of Lake Osborne, and the State of Florida funded the buildings. The library's temporary quarters during construction were in the administration building. The three-story library, part of the college's $2 million building boom, totaled $955,000 once outfitted with new books, periodicals, and audio-visual facilities.

Arnold Construction Company completed the library ahead of schedule. A college-issued press release praised the innovative, modern building and mentioned that it "climbed higher into the sky than any other building on campus." The library had central air-conditioning, which in the 1960s was still uncommon in many average homes. The reading areas were outfitted with superior lighting, and an interior elevator ferried freight, and students, staff and faculty with special needs.

Library director Wiley C. Douglass, hired to replace Chambers in 1966, secured $423,000 of the library's nearly $1 million total price tag through a grant from the Health, Education and Welfare Department. A Higher Education Act provision allowed publicly supported colleges to apply for reimbursement of up to forty percent of new library construction. The Library Learning Resources Center, as it was called, officially opened on August 22, 1966.

LIBRARY LEARNING RESOURCE CENTER. The Harold C. Manor Library on the Lake Worth Campus, 2012. *Courtesy of Palm Beach State College.*

Students marveled at the technologically advanced facility, and especially enjoyed the brand-new Xerox copier.

Palm Beach Junior College played a role in training Library Technicians. Library technology instruction originated when the State Department of Education approved a course in children's literature for teacher certification credit in 1967. Over fifty teachers enrolled in the class the first semester. The college then launched courses in General Library Procedures, Library Workroom Procedures, Non-Book Materials, and a practicum in Library Service and Technologies designed principally for library technologists, assistants, and others working in libraries.

Former biology professor Howard Baker and his wife established a library endowment in the late 1960s. The endowment was to provide funds to the library in the form of interest, for every year that the college stayed in existence. "I believe that I learned more from the city library than I ever did in high school," Mr. Baker said. "I decided that if I were ever in a position to help a library, I would do so." The Bakers' gift prompted others to contribute to the library endowment fund.

Douglass emphasized the importance of current research materials in a 1970 *Palm Beach Post* interview. He declared that in the time it took to publish a book, complete the purchase, and process it for library use, books in many subjects were already outdated when placed on the shelf. To afford students the most up-to-date resources, Palm Beach Junior College subscribed to sixteen newspapers, seventy-eight periodicals and had over 2,500 microfilm reels. The library had machines to view microfilm and microfiche, as well as micro-printers to copy film, and a much-celebrated video tape recorder.

Palm Beach Junior College opened its Boca Raton campus, located adjacent to Florida Atlantic University in 1971. Students, faculty and staff from all Palm Beach State College locations have library privileges at both Florida Atlantic University (Boca Raton) and Palm Beach State College's libraries.

The seventies also brought great advances in library technologies and resource sharing. In 1972, the library purchased a color closed circuit television system. The five-channel broadcast station, centrally located on campus, enriched student learning and limited the number of occasions media services technicians had to physically deliver and set-up a film and projector in the various campus classrooms.

Within a few years, media technology grew rapidly, as did the college enrollment. The Belle Glade Center opened in late 1972, housed in temporary quarters at first, until a permanent campus could be built. Library media services could now televise to sixty classes simultaneously via 23" color television receivers.

The college joined SOLINET, the Southeastern Organization Library Institutional Network, a network of ninety-nine colleges and universities in 1974. SOLINET membership opened the door to resource sharing and increased students' access from 85,000 titles to over one million. The computerized system shortened the process for interlibrary loans and generated catalog cards at the rate of about sixty titles per hour, a huge improvement over typing the cards by hand.

On March 17, 1982, the Lake Worth campus library was renamed the Harold C. Manor Library in honor of the college's second president. During Dr. Manor's tenure, which began in 1958, the college experienced high growth in enrollment, staff, coursing offerings and services to the community. In 1988 Brian C. Kelley replaced the retiring Wiley C. Douglass as the Library Learning Resources Center director and manager of all Palm Beach Junior College libraries.

Dr. Manor, who believed in "education for all kinds of people" predicted Palm Beach County's development patterns and guided the District Board of

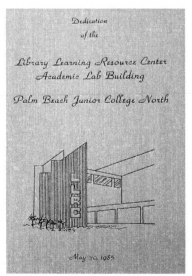

Trustees to purchase 109 acres of land on PGA Boulevard for future campus growth. The new north campus occupied a portable building at Palm Beach Gardens High School, and adjunct faculty taught evening courses. At the time, Tequesta, Juno Beach and Jupiter were small towns or unincorporated areas. By 1976, the college owned a mobile home on the Florida Atlantic University site at 45th Street and added full-time faculty to teach and to initiate a library. Librarian Ruth Dooley transferred from the Lake Worth campus to help with the project.

LIBRARY DEDICATION PROGRAM. May 30, 1985. *Courtesy of Palm Beach State College.*

Palm Beach Junior College North held the groundbreaking ceremony for the library and academic lab building on August 2, 1983. The college dedicated the facility two years later with Ms. Alice Zacherl serving as library director.

Novelist James Michener spoke at the library on June 4, 1982. In commemoration of this momentous occasion, Dr. Paul Sheldon, a longtime friend of the college and friend of Michener's, donated a collection of all of Michener's works to the library.

The college libraries employed an eReader program in 2008 by purchasing fourteen new first-generation Amazon Kindle tablets. For several years, the library had more eReaders than any college or university in the country and soon integrated a host of eReaders for loan including Kindle2, Kindle DX, Kindle3, Kindle Fire, Sony BW, Nook BW and Nook Color. In 2009, the library anticipated evolving technology and added the first-generation iPads, followed by iPad2s in 2014.

PALM BEACH STATE COLLEGE LIBRARY. Palm Beach Gardens Campus, 2010. *Courtesy of Palm Beach State College.*

The Palm Beach Gardens library received a major space redesign in 2009. Architect Leo A. Daly's firm designed a space with natural lighting, a monumental staircase, and updated technologies. Under the direction of library director David Pena, the Hedrick Brothers firm oversaw the transformation of the 49,000-square-foot project modernization project. The expanded library has enhanced media technology services, computer classroom study areas, student support services, offices and the latest in Wi-Fi and wireless technology.

By 2012, the Lake Worth campus library boasted over one hundred computers designated for student use as well as twenty laptop computers. Popular book titles were piloted in 2013; the collection was warmly received and swiftly propagated to include over 250 titles in English and Spanish. Library faculty and staff planned and created a formal college archives. Through a grant from Lyrasis, the library digitized important college history holdings including

COLLEGE ARCHIVES. The Palm Beach State College archives on the Lake Worth Campus, 2013. *Courtesy of Palm Beach State College.*

The *Beachcomber* student newspapers, *The Galleon* and *The Hornet* yearbooks, and college catalogs. These materials are hosted by the Internet Archive and are available to students and researchers both in the library and remotely via the library website.

Upon Brian Kelley's retirement in 2016, Palm Beach State College selected Robert Krull, a veteran professor/reference librarian over several external applicants to serve as director of the Lake Worth campus library and all college libraries.

The Belle Glade campus library's motto is "We've got you covered" In addition to loaning books, computers, calculators and eReaders, Angelica Cortez, director of the Belle Glade library, added circulating items such as umbrellas and mobile hotspots to meet her students' needs.

Palm Beach State College named its fifth campus after the college's outgoing president Dr. Dennis P. Gallon in recognition of his service to the college and the community. The Loxahatchee Groves campus opened as one building in February 2017. One room in the building is a shared space for the Student Learning Center and Library. The library is a work in progress with librarians available to help students with research. Students at Loxahatchee Groves have access to all books at Palm Beach State College as well as electronic resources including online databases, eBooks, etc. There is a limited and growing collection of equipment for checkout as well.

As Palm Beach County continues to grow, so does Palm Beach State College and its libraries. In order to expand access to material, and to improve user experience for students, staff and faculty, a new ILS (Integrated Library System) will be implemented at the Libraries of Palm Beach State College in 2018.

St. Vincent de Paul Regional Seminary Library

Arthur G. Quinn

St. Vincent de Paul Regional Seminary in western Boynton Beach opened in 1963 with philosophy and theology programs. The curriculum was designed for students who were accepted as candidates for the Roman Catholic priesthood. Most students were Florida residents. The library occupies a space at the north end of the main campus building. The first library director was philosophy professor Reverend Carey Leonard (1963-1965). He was succeeded by Reverend Leslie W. Sheridan (1965-1972), who also taught social studies and catechetics.

Sister Patricia Mary O'Brien (1972-1974) served as the third library director, followed by Reverend. John A. Crowley (1974-1983). During Reverend Crowley's tenure, the Seminary program became bilingual and multicultural, requiring collection development of monographs and serials in Spanish as well as in English. During Reverend Crowley's tenure, the library began outgrowing its current space. In 1980, a formal request to expand into adjacent areas for additional book stacks and storage was granted, increasing the library's space to 7,500 square feet. The fifth director, Brother Frank Mazsick (1983-1987) made an additional request to expand into more adjacent spaces in 1985 for the same reason. This time, his request could not be granted since the spaces were needed for instruction.

The sixth director, José L. Romo (1988-1996) played an important role in the planning and construction of the current library building, located north of the main campus building. A task force was created in order to consult with faculty, students, alumni, library staff, and architects following a 1989 accreditation visit by the Southern Association of Colleges and Schools. The accreditation team recommended construction a new library building. In 1992

ST. VINCENT DE PAUL REGIONAL SEMINARY LIBRARY. Aerial
view of the library shortly after its 1996 dedication. *Courtesy of the St. Vincent
de Paul Regional Seminary Library.*

the task force made its recommendation to the Seminary's faculty council
which approved and forwarded the final report to the Board of Trustees of the
Seminary. The Board accepted the proposal and hired Spillis, Candela and
Partners of Coral Gables as the library architect and Rick Mouw of Delray
Beach as the contractor.

That same year, the Seminary received a donation from the estate of Oscar
Schorp which covered most of the costs for the new library's construction.
Ground was broken in November 1994 and the new building was dedicated in
February 1996. The building includes administrative offices, and the library
space of 17,500 square feet is more than double the space of the original library.
As the library collection was moved into the new building during the summer
of 1996, the card catalog was phased out and replaced by an automated catalog.

More than once, it had been said that the original library was so small,
patrons would have to go outside to change their minds! The new library is
spacious and comfortable. Included in the new complex is a Rare Book Room,
housing nearly six hundred titles. Most of the books are from the nineteenth
century, although some titles date back to 1550. Also housed in the new library
is the Seminary Archives, a collection consisting primarily of documents and
photographs. The archives were established in 1986 by alumnus and former
history professor Reverend. Michael McNally. The archives department
operates from a separate budget but has been maintained by library staff for
the past twenty years.

Mr. Romo retired in 1996 and the seventh and current library director,
Arthur G. Quinn, succeeded him. Since then, information technology has

evolved, affecting operations and collection development. The first digital catalog used was Athena, it was replaced in 2010 with EOS, which is still in use. An eBook collection has been growing slowly since 2012 with the purchase of digital titles supporting the Seminary's curriculum of graduate level theology and philosophy.

The new library has also been used as a venue to host professional meetings for the Florida Theological Library Association, Association of Jewish Libraries and Catholic librarians of the Diocese of Palm Beach. Use of the library by patrons has also changed over the years. While use of physical resources has steadily declined, the library has become the preferred location for quiet study, away from the distractions of dormitories or homes.

A unique characteristic of the Main Library's collection has been the resources in Spanish, which number over fourteen thousand volumes in various formats. Serials in the Spanish language have also been a characteristic of the Seminary library with thirty-three current subscriptions from Spain and Latin America. Collection development of Spanish resources continues just as the Seminary's program continues to offer academic courses in the Spanish language.

Bibliographic instruction offered by the library has undergone changes over the years. Research has transitioned from print indexes and the card catalog to web-based systems accessible anywhere and at any hour. While digital sources are convenient and provide access to vast amounts of research, library patrons benefit from library instruction to efficiently utilize these resources.

The larger library allows the Seminary to display more statues and wall paintings. One unique are collection consists of laminated panels and a three-dimensional portrait of Our Lady of Fatima by Vietnamese artists.

At the library looks to the future of its services and its collection, it is anticipated that the availability of digital resources in theology and philosophy will increase, but never fully replace print resources. Library patrons of all ages prefer to hold a book in their hands to read for the sake of reading, and rely on digital resources to consume data for their practical needs.

Florida Atlantic University Libraries

Victoria Thur, Theresa Van Dyke, and Leslie Siegel

Overview

Established in 1964 as the first public university in southeast Florida, Florida Atlantic University (FAU) currently serves more than 30,000 undergraduate and graduate students on multiple campuses located along Florida's beautiful southeast coast in Broward, Palm Beach, and St. Lucie counties. FAU has ten distinguished colleges that offer more than 180 degree programs, including the Schmidt College of Medicine, and is home to one of the world's preeminent marine science education and research centers, the Harbor Branch Oceanographic Institute. The Jupiter campus houses the preeminent centers, Scripps Florida and the Max Planck Florida Institute for Neuroscience. FAU is taking its place among the world's great research centers and given the designation of a "High Research Activity" university by the Carnegie Foundation for the Advancement of Teaching. FAU was ranked 27th by U.S. News & World Report among all American universities for campus diversity, with 49 percent of its student body classified as minority or international students. In 2015, it earned the distinction of being a federally designated Hispanic Serving Institution.

With an annual materials budget of $3 million, FAU Libraries house approximately 3.7 million items and provide access to over 80,000 electronic journals, nearly five hundred databases, and a growing collection of e-books and streaming videos. The Libraries' Special Collections house many distinctive collections, including artists' books, sound recordings, print music, rare books and manuscripts, and University Archives. The S.E. Wimberly Library serves as a selective depository library in the Federal Depository Library Program and as a depository library in the Florida State Depository System. The Digital

Library creates online collections from unique materials from Special Collections and University Archives and serves as the University's repository for the intellectual output created on campus.

The Libraries offer multifaceted instructional services including workshops, research consultations, tutorials and webcasts as well as broad-based creative outreach programming that encourages student and public engagement. The Libraries maintain formal relationships with the Center for Research Libraries, the State University Libraries (through the Florida Virtual Campus) and area libraries in the Southeast Florida Library Information Network. The Libraries have an annual budget of approximately $8.6 million with over ninety faculty and staff to support its mission.

Early Years

During World War II and for ten years after, the fields surrounding Florida Atlantic University were once the home to the U.S. Army Air Corps, which operated a radar training school at the Boca Raton Army Air Field. By the early 1950s, the school closed and the fields abandoned. The idea to create a university was born partly out of necessity and partly from the dream of local businessman and politician Thomas J. Fleming, Jr. In the northern part of the state, there were well-established universities while the southern section lacked institutions of higher education. Mr. Fleming was able to use his considerable influence and powerful friends to lobby the Florida Legislature to use the abandoned airbase. On July 15, 1961, the Florida Legislature passed the measure and on paper created the university. The bond drive and popular slogan to support a fledging university became known as "Boca U in '62; open the door in '64."

Late in 1964, FAU inaugurated its first president Dr. Kenneth Williams and in October of the same year, the 36th president of the United States Lyndon Baines Johnson, dedicated Florida Atlantic University at Boca Raton. Local newspaper headlines heralded the opening as a new and experimental approach to higher education and the university's motto was "Where Tomorrow Begins." In the nascent era of space travel and technological advances, FAU was planned as a testing ground for innovative ideas using technology as a tool for pedagogy. FAU opened its doors to a class of 867 upper division undergraduate students on September 14, 1964.

Central to the experimental education program at FAU was the Learning Resource Center. The initial plans for the Center included space for testing and guidance clinics, a reading clinic, video viewing rooms, music listening rooms, museum and exhibit space, UHF television studios and transmission facilities, and counseling offices. The focus of the Learning Resource Center was the library. One of the first buildings constructed on the new campus, the library was to be radically different from the traditional university library incorporating the latest breakthroughs in technology. This new conceptual library was to serve as a model for libraries of the future.

In the early planning stages for FAU, a library taskforce was appointed to oversee the creation of the first computerized library and to find the right person to make it a reality. The taskforce found that person in Edward Heileger. At the time, he served as the university librarian at the University of Illinois charged with setting up the library at the new satellite campus in downtown Chicago. In 1962, Heileger co-authored a book about library automation, *Advanced Data Processing in the University Library*, and considered an expert on the applications of computer technology in libraries. FAU hired Heileger in June 1963 to implement his ideas and research. He had fifteen months to employ staff, amass a collection, and oversee the development of the computerized system that would catalog, inventory, order books and journals. His plans included an automated checkout system, inter-library loan, inventory controls, ordering and receiving, and a computerized collection catalog. Instead of the conventional card catalog, he proposed a computer-generated catalog bound and mounted on swivel stands at various locations across the university.

Heileger faced an uphill battle in the implementation of his ideas. Among

other things, the library building was designed to serve the needs of the university, not a library. The first floor housed the offices for the College of Social Science, Student Affairs, Office of the Registrar, Admissions, and the computer complex. A corner was reserved for the library office that processed incoming books.

THE S. E. WIMBERLY LIBRARY AT FLORIDA ATLANTIC UNIVERSITY. 1970s.
Courtesy of Florida Atlantic University Libraries.

FLORIDA ATLANTIC UNIVERSITY LIBRARIES. Two students search the author section of the card catalog. The FAU Library attempted to eliminate the card catalog system when it first opened, but it quickly returned to the more conventional method of access to library holdings. Photo by Monroe Causley, 1971. *Courtesy of Florida Atlantic University Libraries.*

The library occupied the middle three floors of the five-story building and was designated a Federal Depository in 1963, as well as a State of Florida documents depository. The offices of the President, Dean of Academic Affairs, the College of Business, the College of Education, and all the offices of Administrative Affairs were housed on the fifth floor. Library staff worked tirelessly filling the new faculty requests for journals and books and getting them on the shelf before the doors opened on September 14, 1964. Ultimately, Heileger and his staff faced hard decisions about what could be purchased within the fiscal restraints, a situation that continues to this day.

Heileger's dream of a fully automated library was truly visionary, but seriously ahead of its time. The costs of bringing a computerized library to fruition were staggering and unfortunately, the State of Florida did not provide the allocation or appropriation of funds needed to make it happen. Staff began to fall behind in processing the new books because they were too busy contending with the computerized aspects of the catalog. In 1967, Edward Heileger left FAU and was replaced by H. William Axford as the new library director. The computer catalog was scrapped and a card catalog installed. From 1967 to 1970, Axford reorganized the library into a more conventional mode of operation. By 1969, as the population of students increased the need to serve those students required the construction of new buildings across the campus.

SMOKING AND STUDYING. Two students study together at a table in the stacks in 1970. Smoking was permitted in the library until the early 1980s.
Courtesy of Florida Atlantic University Libraries.

Eventually, all of the non-library departments moved into new offices in other buildings on campus.

After three years of Axford's leadership, there was a new library director, Peter Spyer-Duran. Spyer-Duran oversaw the expansion of the library into the vacated spaces but quickly realized that the building was too small for the growing university and student population—by 1973, the student body increased and the library served 5,632 students. He library space and submitted a new design for a large addition. Funding for the addition was not available; the decision to name the library in memory of Dr. S.E. Wimberly, former Vice President for Academic Affairs at FAU, went ahead and on November 1, 1974, the building was formally dedicated in his memory.

Era of Growth

By the time Harry R. Skallerup joined the staff as library director in 1977, the library had fifty-two employees, a budget of nearly $900,000, and half a million books, periodicals and manuscripts. Very quickly, the new director began to lobby for a library addition to house the growing collections and student population of 9,388 students. In 1979, Skallerup and Dr. Kenneth Michaels, Vice President for Academic Affairs, initiated planning for a new library addition. At the same time, the efforts by President Glenwood Creech to obtain priority consideration for FAU's request for funds were successful and assured construction. By 1983, President Creech retired and FAU welcomed Dr. Helen Popovich as president; she was the first woman to lead a public university in the State of Florida. In 1984, FAU admitted lower division undergraduate students a move that increased the enrollment significantly. Construction for the library addition began in 1984 and was completed in

November 1985. The contents of the old building were moved into the new addition so that the old structure could be completely remodeled. The renovation was complete and ready for students in July 1986. The addition, designed by Spillis, Candela and Partners, and Stinson-Head, Inc., was featured on the cover of the December 1986 *Library Journal*.

In 1987, Dr. William Miller became Dean of Libraries. The university and library went through major growth spurts in his twenty-seven-year tenure. During that time, technological advances transformed libraries across the nation. Heileger's dream of a fully automated library finally became a reality. On the first floor, stacks filled with books and journals were replaced with computers where students could access electronic journals and databases. In addition, during Miller's tenure FAU built new campuses in Davie, Dania Beach, Jupiter, and Port St. Lucie. The Downtown Fort Lauderdale, Reuben O'D. Askew University Tower, campus was expanded with the addition of the Florida Atlantic University/Broward Community College Higher Education Complex, a twelve-story high-tech facility. Joint-use libraries were established at Port St. Lucie, BCC/Davie, and with Broward Main Library at the downtown Ft. Lauderdale campus along with the library at the Honors College in Jupiter and a library at Harbor Branch Oceanographic Institute.

Miller held a core belief that specialized and distinctive collections increased a library's visibility and he pursued projects and programs to enhance FAU Libraries. The only collections of prominence and the first donated collection were the personal papers and manuscript archives of Theodore Pratt. He is best known for novels set in lush and lavish Florida landscape and revolve around Florida's peculiar quirks such as *The Barefoot Mailman, Flame Tree, Big Blow*, and *Mercy Island*. Five of his thirty-five novels were made into movies. During Miller's tenure, Special Collections expanded its holdings and collections focusing on the Floridiana, American Civil War, WWII, and Judaica materials. In 1998, Mata and Arthur Jaffe donated their collection of 2,800 artists' books which became the foundation for the Arthur and Mata Jaffe Collection: Books as Aesthetic Objects. The center revolves around the Book Arts Gallery, which houses the collection and is a hybrid of a library and an art gallery. JCBA's inspires patrons to take a cue from artists' books, that is, to see things differently, explore content, and encounter the unexpected. In 2002, the Judaica Sound Archives began as a volunteer project dedicated to the preservation of recorded Jewish music. The Recorded Sound Archives (RSA) includes more than 150,000 donated sound recordings including vintage phonograph records and more than 21,000 Jazz albums. RSA has a robust digitization operation for all types of sound recordings. Alongside the creation of RSA, Miller actively collected Jewish print sheet music and created the department, which became known as Music, Performance and Education to promote the sheet music from shelf to stage.

Another distinctive collection is the Marvin & Sybil Weiner Spirit of America Collection. Mr. Weiner spent sixty-five years combing through bookstores, estate sales and catalogs in a tireless effort to add to his collection. Publications in the collections span six centuries and Weiner amassed over 13,000 items, including rare books, manuscripts, pamphlets, and historical newspapers. Weiner was particularly inspired by Benjamin Franklin, and he considered this Founding Father to be his mentor. During the year that marked the 300th anniversary of Franklin's birth, Weiner donated his collection to FAU. The gift established FAU as the major resource center in the southeastern United States for the study of the American Colonial period.

In 2011, Mrs. Marny Glasser donated the Harold L. Glasser Collection to Special Collections. Mr. Glasser, a World War II bombardier who became internationally known during his twenty-seven-year career as president of Miss Universe, Inc., was accomplished in both business and law. He was a native New Yorker and received his B.A., J.D. and L.L.M. degrees from New York University, Columbia Law School, and Harvard Law School. Most notably Mr. Glasser had a distinguished military career serving overseas in World War II as a bombardier, achieving the rank of 1st Lieutenant. His collection spans his military service, law career, and the Miss Universe pageant.

As database use and electronic accessibility greatly improved, there was a growing need to use technology to display special collections materials. By the mid-2000s, the FAU Digital Library was created and its early mission was to digitize Special Collections and make them accessible via the web. Now, the FAU Digital Library has robust digital collections that highlight not only special collections and university archives materials but also showcase faculty and student scholarship in a variety of formats.

The Paul C. Wimbish Wing

In 2005, construction began on a new addition to house these collections. The Paul C. Wimbish Wing, a five-story, 20,000-square-foot addition was constructed on the east side of the original 1963 library. The project was funded with generous donations from Virginia and Peter MacEachron and their son, John MacEachron; the family of the late Paul C. Wimbish, for whom the wing

COLLECTIVE MEMORY. The "Collective Memory" sculpture
by Dirk Cruser (1940-1996) outside the library entrance after
its 1985 expansion. Photo by Dan Forer, 1986.
Courtesy of Florida Atlantic University Libraries.

is named; Mata Jaffe, the late wife of benefactor Arthur Jaffe; numerous benefactors of the Levine-Weinberger Jewish Life Center and Hillel of Broward-Palm Beach; and the FAU Student Government Association. This new space provided the library with much needed space to hold exhibitions highlighting special collections, teachings students, and community engagement.

A New Beginning

In 2015, Dean Carol Hixson was hired to lead the FAU Libraries into a new era that centers on student services, dedicated student spaces, and renewed vigor for faculty and student scholarship. The libraries serve over 30,000 students on the Boca, Jupiter, and HBOI campuses and through partnerships with Broward College in Davie and the Broward County Library System in Ft. Lauderdale. Within the past two years, Dean Hixson spearheaded comprehensive cultural and organizational improvements to the S.E. Wimberly Library. Under her leadership, the library's many departments, with various purposes and outreach programs, became unified in their purpose and mission. The library has always been a space on campus for students. Under Dean Hixson's direction, students are truly in the forefront of library planning, management, and direction.

In November 2016, the dean held a two-day strategic planning meeting for all the library personnel which set a new precedent for a more inclusive and

FLORIDA ATLANTIC UNIVERSITY LIBRARIES. Students work on their assignment on the 2nd floor in the west addition to the library in 1990. The atrium and lobby of the 1985 expansion were the prime points of architectural impact of the new addition, adding a sense of openness to the library space.
Courtesy of Florida Atlantic University Libraries.

transparent management of the library. Everyone was encouraged to create a vision and mission that focused on library patrons and community—locally and virtually. The new vision for the FAU Libraries is student-focused and service-centric, with proactive engagement across the university and the broader community. The library opened up more individual and group study spaces, created a Graduate Student Study Lounge, redesigned the main lobby with FAU branding and new furnishings, upgraded one of the computer labs, created a permanent video conferencing center and Special Collections teaching lab, and for the first time opened up the fifth floor as a multi-purpose study and presentation space.

A hallmark of Dean Hixson's leadership is open communication and accountability. This new direction has encouraged a workplace culture that emphasizes broad collaboration across library departments as well as the university. There is an air of excitement among library faculty and staff, with a shared vision clearly articulated during the Strategic Planning Retreat. The new Libraries Mission, as drafted at the retreat, reads: "As leaders at Florida Atlantic University, we connect people to knowledge and global communities of learning across time and space. Reimagining services and spaces, we enable users to explore, collaborate, educate, and create in their journey toward academic excellence and lifelong learning." After fifty years, FAU Libraries is "Where Tomorrow Begins."

Part III
Special Libraries

THE PALM BEACH POST LIBRARY. *Palm Beach Post*
librarians Virginia Lyon and Mary Dixon clip stories from
the day's newspaper for preservation in the archives in
the 1980s. *Courtesy of The Palm Beach Post.*

Richard S. Beinecke Medical Library, Good Samaritan Medical Center

Janet DeVries and Ginger L. Pedersen

Good Samaritan Hospital opened in May 1920 as the area's first full-service hospital, replacing the tiny six-bed Emergency Hospital opened in 1914. The thirty-five-bed waterfront facility was established as a voluntary, non-profit, non-sectarian hospital to serve Palm Beach County's growing community. At the time, the Palm Beach County boasted a population of 18,654. Over the next eight years, the hospital rapidly expanded and added one hundred additional beds. Twenty-five years later, in 1953, the hospital established its first medical library.

The library occupied a small space in the cafeteria and served as a combined doctor and nurses' library. The initial holdings included twelve medical journals and about five hundred medical books. A Medical Library Committee, representing the various medical specialties, was appointed to oversee the library and to approve new materials' purchases.

As the community grew, and the hospital acquired additional land, the hospital needed a designated library facility. The Richard S. Beinecke Medical Library, dedicated in 1968, was a gift from the Beinecke family in memory of Richard Sperry Beinecke (1917-1966), a Good Samaritan Hospital Association Board of Governors member. Beinecke had served as a director of the Sperry and Hutchinson Company (S & H Green Stamp customer loyalty program); his brother William was CEO and chairman of the board.

Noted Palm Beach architect John L. Volk designed the elegant Georgian Revival Style medical library building. The brick exterior displays marble columns two stories high and faces Flagler Drive and the waterfront. Volk gained fame for designing stately residential estates for many well-known Palm

BEINECKE MEDICAL LIBRARY. The library at
Good Samaritan Medical Center faces Flagler
Drive and the Intracoastal Waterway, 2017.
Private collection.

Beachers including the Vanderbilts, Duponts, Phipps, and Pulitzers; his local
commercial architectural designs grace much of Worth Avenue. Volk's other
significant local structures include the Palm Beach Town Hall, Poinciana Plaza
and Playhouse, and the Bath and Tennis Club.

A 1970 brochure described the library's many modern services including
paging service and music, reading lounge, interlibrary loans, audio-digest tapes,
photocopy service, and nurse's library.

The reading lounge held approximately two hundred medical journals, as
well as ten years of bound journals. In addition to its own research collection,
the library held a reciprocal borrowing agreement with other Florida medical
research libraries as well as with the National Library of Medicine in Bethesda,
Maryland.

The library had central air-conditioning and a special humidity control to
help preserve the books. It is not surprising that the sunken doctors' reading
room became a popular place for doctors and nurses to spend their breaks
relaxing and reading in the beautifully appointed library. Before the Florida
Clean Indoor Air Act was enacted in 1985, doctors and medical personnel were
drawn to the library's solitude and spent their smoking breaks amongst the
fruitwood shelving and walls. An Ampex Micro 85 cassette recorder and a
Webcor tape recorder allowed the doctors, nurses and medical students to
record and listen to tapes on various medical subjects.

DICTIONARY STAND. The Beinecke Medical Library retains its classic 1960s furniture and aura. *Private collection.*

Fifty years after its inception, the Richard S. Beinecke Medical Library appears much the same as it did when it opened nearly a half century ago. The original card catalog cabinets still contain cards with detailed bibliographic information. A desktop carousel holds library rubber stamps. A rare book collection and medical equipment, including a vintage copy of *Grey's Anatomy*, is displayed in a locked bookcase at the library's front entrance. Medical librarian Anjana Roy, who joined the Good Samaritan Medical Center staff in 2004, uses both the card catalog system and electronic databases. She asserts that although previous librarians and staff members have favored updating the library to new furniture and new technologies, she appreciates the classiness of the classic (and quiet) medical library.

CATALOGING SUPPLIES. Beinecke Medical Library's rubber library stamp collection. *Private collection.*

Society of the
Four Arts Libraries

Graham Brunk

It was May 1934 and Garden Club of Palm Beach members Mrs. Lorenzo E. Woodhouse (Mary Kennedy), Mrs. John Elliott (Maud Howe Elliott), and Mrs. Frederick Johnson (Mary Mackinnon) decided that more should be done in the Town of Palm Beach proper to generate interest in the arts. Initially, they set up a small organization known as the Civic Association of Palm Beach. By 1936, that organization would become an official nonprofit and renamed itself The Society of the Four Arts meaning drama, art, music, and literature.

In its early years the Four Arts primarily featured lecturers, art exhibits and a small library of donated materials. Until Addison Mizner associate architect Maurice Fatio donated his services to design a permanent building for the organization, the Four Arts held its events in the Embassy Apartment building ground floor on the corner of Ceiba Avenue (now Four Arts Plaza) and Royal Palm Way. Fatio claimed inspiration from the J.P. Morgan Library in New York when designing the building. On the building's first birthday in 1939, muralist Albert Herter revealed a series of murals on the stoop patio area of the building representing the Four Arts.

Initially intended as an unofficial reference library to complement the programs, by 1940, the book collection filled the Four Arts director's office in the new building. As the collection grew, and the Four Arts reached its fourth season, so did the interest in the library. Dr. George A. Waterman was appointed by the director of the Four Arts to become the first Library Committee chairperson. It was through Waterman's efforts that the library received its first permanent accessible space.

With the assistance of founders Woodhouse and Elliott, Dr. Waterman installed shelving in the second-floor lecture space. At the time, the space

THE SOCIETY OF FOUR ARTS LIBRARY. The Four Arts library building in 1938, shortly after its completion. Note the murals are not yet on the patio. *Courtesy of the Society of the Four Arts Library.*

featured a massive Mizner inspired cathedral style ceiling with matching chairs and tables for people to remain comfortable while using the library. It became very clear at this point that the significance of the library was recognized and that the society needed to hire a professional librarian to cultivate the collection. Four Arts member, Mrs. William Procter (whose husband's father founded Procter & Gamble), donated her own money to the organization to finance the salary for such a person.

The Society hired University of Illinois library school graduate Mrs. Herbert Gibson to run the library and employed Mrs. Samuel Heilner to help Gibson with clerical work concerning the library. Gibson worked at the library through World War II. Anyone was welcome to use the library, but the library charged a two-dollar fee for each book borrowed with one dollar returned once services rendered. World War II officers and soldiers who were on leave were able to circulate books free of charge. Gibson was able to work a schedule out to keep the library open all year round, a rarity in Palm Beach at the time.

As the Four Arts began to gain popularity and World War II ended, Four Arts President Dr. Joseph Gunster presented a Post War plan for expansion to committee chairs and the board of directors. The plan detailed giving the library the entire second floor of the original building and expanding the original building on both sides. This plan did not come to fruition; in 1947, the Four Arts abandoned the plan in favor of buying the vacant Embassy Club facilities across the street for $275,000. The new building was remodeled to house an art gallery, administrative offices, and a lecture auditorium. This now left the library to occupy the original building entirely on its own. During this time, Mrs. Thomas Duffy, an Ohio State University graduate, took over as director of the library.

Mrs. Duffy's tenure came with the incorporation of several special library collections. With the goal of attempting to be a very art centric library, the library gained the attention of Mrs. Frederick Guest. She had custody of famed South Florida architect Addison Mizner's personal library and scrapbook collection for which she felt was an appropriate use in the Four Arts Library. She donated the books to the town with the agreement that they remain in the custody of the library. The library continued to grow when Bethesda-By-The-Sea Bishop Nathaniel Seymour Thomas donated books to start a Floridiana collection.

Various Four Arts members contributed important literary works and books for simple entertainment from their collections to help the library continue to grow. Perhaps the biggest bump for the library came from the death of Edward Bradley. In 1946, the former Palm Beach mayor willed $25,000 to the Town of Palm Beach for the establishment of a library.

The Town of Palm Beach had never established an official library and until this time had an agreement with the City of West Palm Beach to allow town residents to use their well-established Memorial Library on Flagler Drive. It was no secret to the town at the time that many residents had grown fond of using the now rapidly growing Four Arts Library, which was more convenient than

THE SOCIETY OF FOUR ARTS READING ROOM. 1947.
Courtesy of the Society of the Four Arts Library.

the library in West Palm. Moreover, the library already had a steady collection consisting of nearly 10,000 volumes. The town agreed in 1947 to recognize officially in its budget a line item for dedicated funding recognizing the Society of the Four Arts Library as its official town library.

Around this same time, Dr. Edmund LeRoy Dow, treasurer for the Four Arts and president of the Historical Society of Palm Beach County, successfully negotiated with the organization to allow the historical society to be headquartered out of the library building. From this agreement, the historical society would store nearly all of their collection in the available space on the library's second floor.

In 1955, the town began seeing the Four Arts' impact on the community and in recognition, renamed Ceiba Avenue where the organization was located, the Four Arts Plaza. They also agreed to contribute an increased amount of $6,000 annually (today about $54,000) to the library operation.

The 1950s was a great decade for the library and the organization as a whole. The society hired Mr. Vincent Rapetti to direct the library after Mrs. Duffy's resignation. He led the library through a period of steady growth. With eight hundred registered borrowers, annual circulation was over 23,000 items. A new library assistant, Mrs. Irene Stevenson, joined the staff in 1954. She would become the Four Arts library's longest serving staff member remaining with the library until her 2005 retirement.

Rapetti also oversaw the creation of the children's library. Benefactors had donated a small selection of children's materials during the previous decade, but there was never a formal children's area or staff to manage it. In April 1956, Rapetti invited Florida State University Library School Dean, Louis Shores along with several faculty members to survey the library's services and offer recommendations for improvement. Among their recommendations was an improved children's collection, a better, more "child friendly" space to put the collection, and a staff member to oversee it. In that same year, the society hired Miss Rosemary Glenn as the first children's librarian.

The former Four Arts lecture auditorium on the second floor of the library had mostly remained as an extended adult reading room since taking over the entire building. Staff decided that this second-floor space would make a great children's room. A dropped ceiling replaced the cathedral style ceiling and central air-conditioning was added. This addition likely made Four Arts the first library (and among the first commercial buildings) with central air-conditioning in Palm Beach County. The former lecture stage was transformed into a story time area, 2,000 new books were purchased, and, new "child friendly" furniture was acquired. In 1956, architects Wyeth, King & Johnson designed a new wing downstairs with an elevator. Staff dealt with this loss of space by relocating the entire adult collection to the first floor.

In mid-1957, Rapetti left the Four Arts to direct the Technical Services Department at an Orlando area library. The society hired Mrs. Helen McKinney from Pensacola's library, who would remain with the library as its director for next three decades. McKinney also hired a new children's librarian, Mrs. Mable Gick.

THE SOCIETY OF FOUR ARTS LIBRARY. Children listen to story time at the Four Arts library in 1967. *Courtesy of the Society of the Four Arts Library.*

McKinney wasted no time assimilating into the alluring culture that is Palm Beach society. She learned to know her patron base very well and on a first name basis. In part, due to her friendship with well-known Palm Beach Junior College Professor Watson B. Duncan III, she worked with the college and enticed its students to join the Four Arts Library by offering a complimentary membership. Duncan also instituted a regular weekly book discussion series that continued into the summer even though the rest of the society mostly remained closed after season ended around mid-April. McKinney also coordinated an effort to participate in the state's interlibrary loan program, which allowed the library to summon a copy of a unique title for the patron from another area library.

Gick had similar success with her children's room upstairs. She even made a bold attempt that one might think of as difficult to track in the pre-computer days by allowing children to take out as many books as they wanted as long as

THE SOCIETY OF FOUR ARTS READING ROOM. 1947.
Courtesy of the Society of the Four Arts Library.

they promised to bring them back. The library was also responsible for screening films during the season. The adult library downstairs primarily focused on art films, while Disney films tended to be the most well attended upstairs on the second floor.

The Four Arts Library faces west towards downtown West Palm Beach overlooking the Lake Worth Lagoon. Over the course of its existence, the Society of the Four Arts had acquired the land behind the library, rescuing it from becoming a Winn-Dixie grocery store. There had long been established small demonstration gardens to the south of the library building, but throughout the 1970s, the sculpture gardens began to take shape and the patio surrounding the library grew to be a peaceful and serene environment for locals and tourists to frequent. Because the library is one of the main entrances to the gardens, it is often a great focal point for those just visiting, in addition to local library users.

Among the most notable features people fondly recall about the Four Arts Library and still recognize as significant to this day, are the two bronze panther statues that grace the library's entrance. While not unique pieces to the Four Arts, they were sculpted by Wheeler Williams, and after having spent some time in a personal residence, were donated to the Four Arts by Mr. Byron Miller and Mr. Andrew Jergens in 1933. It is unknown when Williams actually sculpted these and they have matching cousins at the Brookgreen Gardens in South Carolina.

The two panther sculpture's histories at the society are a rather comical one. When they were initially installed they were not anchored down very well and easily removable (even though they each weigh about 350 pounds). On one quiet summer morning in June 1962, someone discovered that the female panther sculpture had gone missing. Police found her in the median on Royal Palm Way just a short distance away and put her back in place. In 1980, someone must have been privy to the incident in 1962, but decided to take the other one. Instead of dumping it nearby, they threw the male panther statue into the Intracoastal Waterway. Once again recovered a short time later, both famous statues were anchored down and they have remained in place (except for a brief removal in 2017 during a renovation).

Throughout the 1970s and 1980s, the library continued to experience growth and be a major focal point of the organization. Most Palm Beach County schoolchildren (as well as many area private school students) could say they visited the Four Arts Library at least once, due to great outreach efforts with the schools. In the adult library, a steady, but growing art collection complimented the circulating collection of best sellers, records, and VHS tapes. A new area with a small upstairs loft was added in 1980. This offered more shelving space, additional office space, and a small staff break room.

At the close of the 1983-1984 season, McKinney announced her retirement. A small reception was held on the back patio honoring her twenty-seven years of service. Library committee chair Mrs. Hope Kent hinted that a new librarian had been chosen with an official announcement coming out that summer. Winnifred Romoser, a graduate of the now defunct University of Tampa School of Library Science, worked as a librarian at the North Palm

CHILDREN'S ROOM. Library staff and children show off their statistics for their first year of operation. *Courtesy of the Society of the Four Arts Library.*

Beach Public Library, Palm Beach Day Academy as well as *The Palm Beach Daily News* making her well-known among the Four Arts patron base. Having spent much time in Palm Beach in the past, she unsuccessfully applied for employment at the Four Arts Library twenty-four years earlier. McKinney had admired Romoser's continued drive for success and all that she had accomplished in that time and recommended her to the board of directors and the library committee as her suggested successor.

Romoser instituted the library's unique collection development policy for new acquisitions. She put in place a "patron driven model," a topic often discussed in library schools, but rarely implemented. Rather than using a lengthy committee to review each suggestion or have a sole librarian in charge of deciding what people should read, she relied heavily on patron suggestions. She would follow trends driven by the patron base locally, rather than traditional methods of using various library journals.

At the end of the 1986-1987 season, Romoser left the Four Arts. After a short search throughout the summer of 1987, Joanne Rendon was selected as the new director. A graduate of the University of Michigan's Library Science program, Rendon came to Palm Beach after having spent some time at Gwynold College near Philadelphia. Her approach was very different from past directors. While she maintained a special interest in English literature, it was very important to her that the library have a well-rounded collection covering all disciplines.

Rendon had some revolutionary ideas that were new to library science at the time. Rendon and children's librarian Evelyn Rand both curated their collections to include more books on science and technology and other current affairs. With the rise of computers and surrounding libraries quickly automating their collections, Rendon recognized the world of libraries and the way we consume information was beginning to change rapidly. She knew the library's importance relied on it being a notable focal point the community. She corralled her staff into learning more about their patron's reading habits, knowing everyone on a first name basis, and giving them an experience that was unmatched by the West Palm Beach Public Library across the water.

In the early 1990s, it became clear that the Children's Library was outgrowing its second-floor quarters. The society had also just completed the purchase of the Addison Mizner designed Embassy Apartment building across the street from the library. The Four Arts originally began in the lobby of this building in 1936. The plans called for a complete renovation of the structure, which included new administrative offices, a new president's apartment, as well

FOUR ARTS CHILDREN'S LIBRARY.
The new Four Arts children's library after its
move across the street in 1993.
Courtesy of the Society of the Four Arts Library.

as a new Children's Library. The Children's Library would be constructed in the center of the building, which was initially an open space. The center would feature skylights allowing natural light to grace the open programming space below.

Under the direction of recently hired head children's librarian Christine Coffman, the Children's Library moved its nearly 9,000 items across the street in November 1993. The new library was two thirds larger than the previous children's space and included separate sections for nonfiction and fiction books as well as a reference study room, and a craft room. An art gallery was also included where annual exhibits aimed at youngsters would be displayed. With these improvements, the Four Arts hired an additional staff member to assist with its operations.

The second floor of the "adult library" as it was now called, was reconfigured to become home to the growing fine arts collection along with a special room set up just for rare books. This would house the Mizner collection and other donated special collections.

With the rest of the collection needing to fit downstairs, Rendon had compact shelving installed in the lower two additions. Now VHS tapes, fiction, large print, and some nonfiction books could completely fit in the two new additions, as well as the reading room with plenty of space to grow.

Renewed interest naturally came with the new look of the Four Arts Libraries. Evening hours piloted throughout the 1990s during the season to complement evening events at the galleries and auditorium, but deemed unsuccessful. However, the Four Arts Library thrived during the day. A consistent flow of architects, decorators, landscape designers, and library aficionados found the library to be a great treasure. An architectural graduate student at the University of Nebraska even wrote her thesis on the special collections of Addison Mizner. Several novelists also spent time in the library researching and writing including Mark Hollingsworth's *Saudi Babylon: Torture, Corruption and Cover-Up Inside the House of Saud*, and Robert Mycal's *Palm Beach Confidential*.

In 1997, the library received a very sizable donation from Gioconda King in the name of her late husband Joseph King. The library in return was dedicated to them as The Society of the Four Arts Joseph and Gioconda King Library, or King Library for short.

At the close of the 2016-2017 season, the King Library closed for a much needed eighteen-month complete restoration. The two additions were demolished to make way for a new more sensible addition providing better office space for staff, more room for cataloging/processing and preserving materials, a more functional staff breakroom, as well as the addition of handicap accessible entrance, upgraded restroom facilities and a new elevator. The main reading room received a restoration treatment for future generations' enjoyment. Perhaps the most anticipated feature will be the restoration of the Fatio's original cathedral style auditorium ceiling on the second floor, which will become the Mary Hulitar Discussion Center, named for a generous trustee of the Four Arts.

Now under the leadership of Dr. Rachel Schipper, experienced librarian and former associate dean of technology and support services at the University of Florida, the library continues to remain a vital community focal point. Both libraries are now fully automated with a state-of-the-art integrated library system. Their participation in local library consortiums allow them to provide eBook services, host well attended book discussions including its preschool themed story hours, Florida Voices, Talk of Kings, and Page Turners book groups, making the Four Arts libraries a special gem in the heart of Palm Beach year-round for people all over the world.

Preservation Foundation of Palm Beach Library

Shellie A. Labell

The Town of Palm Beach has a unique history; the island's first pioneer families settled in the area surrounding Lake Worth in the early 1870s. The name Palm Beach is derived from the Providencia, a Spanish vessel which washed ashore in 1878, leaving behind a load of coconuts which were enthusiastically planted by early settlers.

Palm Beach earned its place on the map in 1896, when Henry Flagler's Florida East Coast Railway brought well-to-do tourists from the northeastern United States to Florida, where they were impressed by Florida's mild winters. The Town of Palm Beach was officially incorporated in 1911, one of the earliest towns incorporated in South Florida.

Palm Beach has always taken great pride in its architecture. By the early twentieth century, the town had acquired a world-class reputation for its elegant lifestyle dominated by the extravagant homes that surrounded its shores. Addison Mizner, Marion Sims Wyeth, John Volk, Joseph Urban, Maurice Fatio, and Howard Major–these were the six names celebrated as the foundational architects of the Palm Beach style.

For almost a century, the most influential architectural style in Palm Beach has been Mediterranean Revival, an amalgamation of Spanish Colonial, Italian Renaissance, and Venetian Gothic. Mediterranean Revival quickly became a beloved building style during the real estate boom of the 1920s. Pioneered by the vivacious Addison Mizner, this style expressed the romance and opulence of the times. In addition to Mediterranean Revival, Palm Beach architects favored styles including Shingle, Bermuda, Georgian Regency, Bungalow, and Art Moderne. These styles are beloved even today, and demonstrate the legacy of the talented and dedicated architects that continue to influence modern South Floridian architecture.

The Preservation Foundation of Palm Beach was founded as a private advocacy organization with the mission of engaging the Town of Palm Beach's population in the awakening historic preservation movement in the town. The Landmarks Commission was established in 1979 and a formal historic preservation ordinance was adopted by the Town of Palm Beach to save threatened structures. Within a year, a number of prominent citizens joined to create the Preservation Foundation of Palm Beach, a non-profit organization with the common goal of preserving the architectural history of Palm Beach.

The Foundation was officially incorporated under the laws of the State of Florida on January 15, 1980. By the 1970s, many of the magnificent mansions built in the early twentieth century were deemed outdated by developers, realtors, and even homeowners.

The first board members and officers of the Foundation were involved from the inception of the national preservation movement. LaBaron S. Willard, Jr. was one of the first Landmarks Commissioners and served as its chairman. He then became the first President of the Foundation. He served as a liaison between public and private preservation movements in Palm Beach.

Ambassador Earl E.T. Smith served as the highly respected mayor of the Town of Palm Beach from 1971 to 1977 and served as the first Chairman of the Foundation. The Town of Palm Beach and the Foundation would not have achieved their high standards and accomplishments without his persistence and innumerable appearances before the Town Council to win support for historic preservation. Through the generosity of hundreds of Palm Beach residents, the Preservation Foundation has been able to save the town's oldest extant structure, Sea Gull Cottage.

During the summer of 2004, the Preservation Foundation moved into a beautiful new headquarters on Peruvian Avenue that was built adjacent to Pan's Garden. The building was designed by Jeffery Smith, well-known Palm Beach architect and foundation board member. Hugh Davis was the contractor and Scott Snyder designed the interiors. The grand opening of the building was held in January of 2005, which also coincided with the 25th anniversary of the foundation.

The Preservation Foundation's Robert M. Grace Library houses a circulating reference collection of over 2,000 books and periodicals pertaining to historic preservation, structural and landscape architecture, urban planning, and local history. The Grace Library was named in honor of Preservation Foundation founder Robert M. Grace by his wife, Mrs. Jane Grace. Mr. Grace

PRESERVATION FOUNDATION OF PALM BEACH LIBRARY.
The Robert M. Grace Library at the Preservation Foundation of
Palm Beach. *Courtesy of the Preservation Foundation of Palm Beach.*

still serves as a Preservation Foundation trustee. Mrs. Grace currently serves on the Preservation Foundation's Executive Committee.

Also available to members are the Foundation's house files, which provide access to information and images on each structure in the Town of Palm Beach, appealing to current and potential homeowners, architects, real estate agents, and historians. The Grace Library is a beautiful reading room with a comfortable seating area that overlooks the scenic Pan's Garden. Members of the Preservation Foundation, students, and institutional researchers are invited to peruse the shelves for topics of interest.

The most significant collection of books in the Grace Library was donated by the Elson family in 2005. The library's collection complements the archival collections and advance the mission of the Foundation. The library's periodical collection includes archived Preservation Foundation newsletters and season event profiles from 1982 to the present.

In addition to the Grace Library's book collection, the Preservation Foundation houses myriad architectural drawings from prominent Palm Beach architects such as Marion Sims Wyeth, Belford Shoumate, and Henry K. Harding. Within these architectural collections are thousands of priceless architectural drawings, renderings, and photographs of Palm Beach residences and commercial buildings primarily spanning eight decades, from 1917 to 1986.

Palm Beach Post Library

Mary Kate Leming

In the late 1970s, the archives of *The Palm Beach Post* were kept down a long hallway past the Opinion department, a columnist's office and the workspace of the editorial cartoonist. It became a game for the newspaper's library staff to identify footsteps as they made their way down the hall.

Often, there were a set of distinctive steps that would reach the library door, then stop. No one stepped in.

The staff believed these belonged to Lois Wilson, the recently deceased head librarian. She had suffered from pulmonary problems for some time and had a severe asthma attack at the end of a long work day and died at Good Samaritan hospital. It was believed she had fully intended to return and left unfinished work.

The staff took some comfort in believing Lois, who died in her forties, was still around and would come back to check on her beloved library.

Lois cherished her job as a newspaper librarian and researcher and set a high benchmark of professionalism for everyone who followed. She had worked previously at the *Miami News* and made the daily commute to West Palm Beach from Tamarac, where she lived with her elderly parents. If the footsteps heard down the long hallway were those of Lois, she was visiting a place and a job she loved.

For years, newspaper archives and libraries were known as "the morgue." It was the place where journalists joked that newspaper stories went to die. That was a misnomer, of course, as the archivists worked hard to not only preserve the news stories—and photographs —for future reference, but to help reporters and editors to retrieve these files along with other facts and information.

This was not always easy, as the library was often located in leftover space in far corners of the newsroom. When Lois was in charge, the library was small and crowded with any new file cabinets placed wherever she could find the space. This meant the collection did not stay in alphabetical order, so requests for information from reporters and editors tended to be, "Ask Lois. She remembers everything."

File cabinets where fundamental to early news libraries. Each day's newspapers (the library supported both *The Palm Beach Post* and the *Evening Times* until 1987 when the *Evening Times* was merged with the morning *Post*) were sliced and diced into "clippings" that would be stamped with the date and publication and then filed into multiple locations depending on key elements in the news story. They were also kept organized by the byline of the writer.

These were then carefully folded into envelopes and filed into row after row of cabinets. At some point, when microfiche technology was new, many of these were filmed and stored in this space-saving format. There were clippings in this format dating back to 1916 when the *Post* became a daily newspaper.

The newspaper was also archived in its complete form. First in binders that could be flipped through to see news and advertising placement, and later on microfilm. Converting newsprint to microfilm was done in-house for many years with a large camera set up in the art department. The film from the camera was then sent to a local company that would convert it to microfilm. Eventually the process was all done off-site. This collection reflected the entire newspaper, but was retrievable only by date.

THE PALM BEACH POST LIBRARY. *The Palm Beach Post* archives in the late 1970s, when it was known as the morgue. *Courtesy of The Palm Beach Post.*

After Lois' death, a copy editor at the *Post*'s sister paper *The Palm Beach Daily News* (known locally as The Shiny Sheet) asked for the open library director's position. When Rich Ploch took over the library's management, the library was moved to a larger space near the newsroom where the file cabinets could be put back into alphabetical order. Rich was declared a genius by the newsroom for this effort. The clipping files were then accessible by everyone.

In the early 1980s, Florida's population growth spurred the start of a newspaper war among the three South Florida daily newspapers. This increased the quantity and quality of news coverage from Miami to the Treasure Coast. As a result, the Palm Beach newspapers grew in size and circulation and new positions were added to the library staff. Long-timers like Bev Jones (formerly Ramsey) and Gail Reece (formerly Ewing) were the anchors who kept the daily work up-to-date and maintained friendly relations with a sometimes stressed out newsroom.

Rich then hired Manny Gonzalez from the paper's purchasing department. His contributions to the library were immediate and would be important in the coming years.

During Rich's tenure, he stewarded the library's transition from a place to "keep" information to a place that "shared" knowledge. In the new, larger space — with a renewed focus on assisting the newsroom — the library became a place where reporters enjoyed hanging and hiding out. It was also frequented by historians, true-crime and gossip writers and professional researchers employed by popular authors. At least a small part of Elmore Leonard's novel *Maximum Bob* came from clippings in the *Post* library.

Rich's journalism background and his focus on providing quick and accurate information to the newsroom was noted during a presentation he made at a Special Libraries Association meeting and Rich was hired away by *The Washington Post* to become the director of their large staff of researchers.

Before leaving *The Palm Beach Post*, Rich added an early Lexis/Nexis terminal to the library for online research. It required dial-up access and usage was billed by the minute. That red box marked a revolutionary change in newspaper libraries: To become searchable, newspapers had to become digitized.

The final versions of stories created on the reporter workstations were stored electronically, indexed by software and had searchable keywords assigned by the library staff. Gradually, the library staff shifted from clipping and filing stories to indexing electronic stories. Their involvement with this digital transition gave them insights into data management that helped them to become expert online researchers.

It was at the very beginning of this digital transition when I arrived to manage the *Post* library. Although the transition to digital was not easy for everyone, the benefits to the newsroom were obvious and well respected. Besides the Lexis/Nexis red box, the library began to compile subscriptions to numerous online databases and worked with the newsroom to compile and build internal databases. Since the online databases were still subscription and dial-up, the library became the clearinghouse for gathering outside information for the newsroom.

The library became the home for the first "smart" computer in the newsroom. During the William Kennedy Smith rape trial, this was used to compile a database of information on the jury members—helping reporters to locate them quickly once the verdict was read.

Finding people became a research specialty for the library staff. As data collections could be built or acquired, they were pursued as valuable sources of information in those pre-Internet days. These included databases of School District employees, voter registrations and even a low-tech collection of driver's license registrations on microfiche that was organized phonetically. One of the most popular was of Palm Beach County pet registrations. This included addresses and phone numbers of everyone who registered a pet and was helpful to reporters trying to track down an especially elusive source.

Still, not everything the library did was focused on research or data indexing. When the *Post*'s parent company decided to close the *Miami News* in 1988, I became concerned that the archives of a newspaper that had covered Miami for most of the twentieth century would end up in a landfill. The *Miami Herald* had an agreement to keep the *News'* digital story collection online, but there had been no agreement on the clipping files or the photo collection. The photography collection held some of the earliest images from South Florida, including major hurricanes, the Mariel boatlift, Muhammad Ali training in Miami and of John F. Kennedy before he flew to Dallas in November 1963.

A deal was arranged between the management of the *Post* and Cox Newspapers for us to move the majority of the photo collection to West Palm Beach. With the support of *The Palm Beach Post* Editor Edward "Eddie" Sears and *Miami News* Editor Howard Kleinberg, a panel truck was hired to drive to the *Miami Herald* building on Biscayne Bay.

Manny Gonzalez and Mary Kate Leming used the back entrance off the loading dock to avoid notice by the Knight-Ridder-owned *Miami Herald* staff.

Although *The Herald* and the *Miami News* had a joint operating agreement (and shared the building), the legal ownership of the archives had not been finalized. Therefore, they quietly met with *Miami News* Publisher David Kraslow and Editor Kleinberg to determine which photos should be given to the archives of HistoryMiami and which should move to the *Post*. Over the next several days other library staff joined them to pack the collection. Once finished, there were over six hundred boxes of photographs and about a dozen boxes of newspaper clippings.

Hardworking Manny Gonzalez then spent much of the next several years working to glean this collection for the most historic and important images. During those years, Manny did manage to take one long lunch break—to run to the courthouse to marry the pretty switchboard operator who worked downstairs. He came back to the office after the ceremony and continued to glean photos.

Packing these boxes in the recently vacated *Miami News* newsroom was a haunting experience. Journalists had left sweaters hanging on their chairs and half-filled cups of coffee and family photos on their desks. There were journalism awards hanging on the wall. It was as if the entire newsroom had just vanished. While we were packing boxes, the elevator dinged that it had arrived, but no one stepped off. There were no footsteps. We had to wonder who was making one final visit.

Soon after this collection was acquired, and competition between the newspapers grew more intense. *The Palm Beach Post* moved into a new building with seemingly endless space. When the building was christened in 1995, the library space had an office for the director, a reference desk, shelves for a reference collection, and roomy work areas for the digital archivists, who now also indexed photographs for retrieval. The library staff included about a dozen employees around the turn of the twenty-first century. The old hand-cranked moveable shelving, which had been essential space savers in the old location, were replaced with contemporary moveable shelving that eliminated the beat-up old filing cabinets.

The new moveable shelving created long, narrow storage aisles and often the library staff would hear muffled yelps as someone began to crank as another person was still between the shelves. These were believed to be accidental incidents—most of the time.

As the Internet revolutionized the information world, I stayed with the newspaper's parent company, but moved away from the print newspaper and into their interactive division. Prior to making this career change, I had the luck to hire Sammy Alzofon, who had been working at the *St. Petersburg Times*, to manage the digital archiving department along with researcher-extraordinaire Michelle Quigley. These hires (and others) left the library/research department in good hands.

After Alzofon became the library director there were several changes in how the library serviced information delivery to the newsroom. This included moving the reference desk out into the newsroom to be better positioned during breaking news.

At the Internet continued to change modern life, print newspapers began to suffer a loss of readership and revenue. Craigslist strangled classified advertising and little-by-little advertisers began to shift their dollars toward online.

By the time the economic downturn hit in 2008—and more than three hundred people retired or took buyouts at Palm Beach Newspapers, Inc.—few of the library staff remained. By 2009, the newspaper discontinued human-assisted indexing of photos and stories. Photo indexing moved to the Photography department and text indexing became almost completely automated.

MARY DIXON. *The Palm Beach Post* librarian Mary Dixon indexes newspaper stories in the *Post's* electronic archive in 2008. *Private Collection.*

Just prior to the buyouts, the archives of *The Palm Beach Daily News* had been brought up to contemporary standards with the help of long-time Post librarian Mary Dixon. But after the historic Shiny Sheet building was sold to The Breakers in 2010, the photo and clipping collection was boxed and moved across the bridge. It was kept near the Shiny Sheet's temporarily relocated offices in the *Post* building.

By that time, there was no one remaining in a library management position. The last two librarians still performed research, but reported to various other newsroom departments.

As reporters began to do more and more of their own research online, these librarians shifted into social media and data-driven research and analysis roles. Their data expertise made them valuable to the investigative team—which at one point moved into the vacated Post library space for the privacy of a separate area to do long-term projects out of earshot of the general newsroom.

Eventually, the investigative team moved back into the newsroom, but the researchers stayed on as an important part of a team that has won many state, regional and national journalism awards. Today, one librarian—Melanie Mena—remains on staff doing research, contributing to investigative work and picking up some of the library housekeeping work that is still required of a working newspaper. Her position is a rarity in all but the very largest U.S. newspapers.

For now, the photo collection remains at the *Post*, but the text archives (dating back to 1916) are available to the public only through www.newspapers.com. This collection includes *The Palm Beach Daily News* and the *Miami News* archives.

The archives of *The Palm Beach Daily News* are now locked in the former office of Pulitzer Prize-winning editorial cartoonist Don Wright in the Opinion department of *The Palm Beach Post*. With national interest in President Trump's "winter White House" just across the bridge, the door is frequently being unlocked for access to this valuable collection.

Just down the hall, the more spacious *Palm Beach Post* library space is now used primarily as a getaway spot for informal meetings and private telephone conversations. Reporters describe the room as empty and "morgue-like"—an ironic throwback to its traditional name.

Hopefully, when the time comes for the *Post's* parent company to part with the old hard-copy collections in the building at 2751 South Dixie Highway, someone will find a home for these valuable historic resources. Too much history is there to be delegated to the landfill.

And any ghostly footsteps heard in that nearly vacated end of the newsroom? They could be from any of the librarians and staff who had the good fortune to work at *The Palm Beach Post* library: a place and business we all loved and enjoyed during many years of exceptional journalism and innovation.

Genealogical Society of Palm Beach County Library

Genealogical Society of Palm Beach County

A group of individuals interested in tracing their ancestors organized the Genealogical Society of Palm Beach County on May 6, 1964. Monthly meetings were held in various locations, genealogical procedures were taught, and books and other materials were shared by members. The society incorporated in 1966 as Palm Beach County Genealogical Society. Their quarterly journal, *Ancestry*, began production for the information of members and to exchange with other genealogical societies around the country. It continued in paper format until the end of 2014, when it switched to electronic format for a year before ceasing publication. Ancestry changed to a monthly membership newsletter format.

When book donations increased to the point of requiring library space, the West Palm Beach City Library offered a place for the genealogy society to meet and to house their collection. This was their home for the next forty years, at first in one small upstairs room, and then downstairs into two rooms. When Bruce M. Lewis of Lewis Publishing Company, West Palm Beach, retired he donated his collection of genealogical and historical volumes to the society, along with shelving and file cabinets from his office. Florida Atlantic University in Boca Raton contributed a sizable collection of books on Boston and New York. Many individuals made book donations in honor of friends or as memorials. By this time, the library had over 8,000 volumes, magazines, maps and other materials. It had become the largest and most complete genealogical research library in South Florida. The non-circulating collection continued to grow and keep up with the times, moving from microfiche readers to computers.

When the City of West Palm Beach announced the building of their new library, the plans did not include space for the genealogy society and its holdings. They had to find a new home and reached an agreement with the

215

GENEALOGICAL SOCIETY OF PALM BEACH COUNTY
LIBRARY. 2017. *Private Collection.*

Palm Beach County Public Library System to rent space for the collection and
for the society activities. The society moved in a large modern library space in
the Main Library on Summit Boulevard in West Palm Beach on February 1,
2008. The collection now includes over 13,000 books, digital resources, and a
large periodical collection.

The Genealogical Society of Palm Beach County is an all-volunteer
nonprofit non-profit educational organization, supported by membership dues,
donations, and a trust fund. They receive no government funding. In addition
to their print and digital collections, the library offers its members computers
and Wi-Fi, and subscriptions to several online databases including Ancestry
Library Edition. Their monthly programs and seminars provide educational
information and an opportunity to network with others.

Lake Worth
Little Free Libraries

Paige Turner

Andrew Carnegie is regarded as the Patron Saint of Libraries. As a young teenager, Andrew emigrated from Scotland to America with his family. They sought to escape the crushing poverty and despair that the industrial age had wrought among self-supporting home-based craftsmen in his hometown of Dunfermline. Andrew's father, Will, a handloom weaver, struggled to find a place for his family in the busy world of machinery that had come to dominate their ancient homeland. He saw and lamented the conditions under which his fellow laborers worked, prompting Will and Margaret Carnegie to sell everything they owned and bring their sons to Pennsylvania in 1848.

Young Andrew joined the throngs of immigrants working in the New World factories. He educated himself with books borrowed from a neighbor who opened his extensive private library to them as an act of kindness. Andrew read voraciously, worked tirelessly, and developed the skills needed to advance in one industry after another, eventually making a great fortune. By the age of thirty-five, Andrew Carnegie was one of the wealthiest men in the world. Carnegie never forgot how instrumental having access to a library was to him. He believed there could never be a more productive investment than the founding of a public library and spent over $50 million to establish 2,509 public libraries all over the world, 1,679 in the United States.

Nearly 140 years later, Todd Bol of Hudson, Wisconsin wanted to honor the memory of his mother, who served as a teacher for thirty years. Bol built a miniature replica of a one room school house and set it on a post in his front yard with a sign on it announcing "Free Books." Friends and neighbors loved the idea and asked Todd to build small book exchange boxes for them. Two years and some forty book boxes later, Todd and his friend, Rick Brooks saw possibilities to improve the community, increase literacy, and bring books to those who had limited access to public libraries. They formed a non-profit organization named "Little Free Library" and aimed to establish 2,510 Little Free Libraries, one more library than Carnegie had established.

By 2011, there were more than four hundred Little Free Libraries; in 2012 that number had increased tenfold, far surpassing their original goal. By 2015, more than 25,000 Little Free Libraries had been established in over forty countries around the world. A photo of one of these small libraries went viral on Facebook, and the idea of the Little Free Library spread like wildfire throughout the community of Lake Worth, and the Lake Worth Little Free Library project was born. There are currently over one hundred Little Free Libraries within walking distance of every resident in the City.

The project began at Lake Worth's City Hall, where the idea was presented to city manager Mike Bornstein. He enthusiastically endorsed the idea and cleared the way for the planting of these Little Free Libraries in public parks, greenways, at the beach, the Snook Island nature preserve, the public boat ramp, as well as at private homes and elementary schools throughout the city. Initial funding came through grants awarded by the Palm Beach County Office of Community Revitalization and by the time the funds became available, nearly fifty Lake Worth residents had signed up act as stewards of these Little Free Libraries. By the time the first shipment of Little Free Libraries arrived at the city's utility warehouse, sixty-five neighbors participated in unpacking and painting them in one day.

Additional Little Free Libraries were funded by private individuals, local businesses, and non-profits, and the number of Little Free Libraries in the City of Lake Worth grew to more than fifty in the first year. A generous group of artists in Lake Worth stepped to donate their time and talent, building the appreciation of art, literacy and community upon which Lake Worth thrives.

Hundreds of neighbors have donated tens of thousands of books for grown-ups and for children alike. A $5,000 grant awarded by the Lake Worth Community Development Corporation funded $15,000 worth of Spanish and Creole language children's literature. Publishers and book distributors fell under the spell of Little Free Libraries and offered tremendous discounts. The Palm Beach County School District currently provides Lake Worth Little Free Libraries with books no longer needed by the district. Palm Beach County's school district was the first to embrace the Little Free Libraries, and in the summer of 2017, the district supplied more than ten thousand children's books to the Little Free Libraries' collection.

LAKE WORTH LITTLE FREE LIBRARIES. The City of Lake Worth has nearly 100 Little Free Libraries making grassroots community project a model for other cities and towns throughout the continent. *Courtesy of the Lake Work Little Free Library Project.*

When the initial grant money was exhausted, the people of Lake Worth pitched in. Each Lake Worth Little Free Library is funded by the generosity of the Friends of the Lake Worth Library community group. Local businesses and neighborhood associations have funded over half of the Little Free Libraries in the city and continue to offer their support for promotion and maintenance. The Lake Worth Community Redevelopment Agency even 'wrapped' one of the electrical switch boxes with a photo collage of Little Free Libraries, and a local bench advertising company has donated space on bus stop benches reminding their Lake Worth neighbors to "Take A Book, Leave A Book." *The Lake Worth Herald,* Lake Worth's oldest extant business, has published dozens of stories about the Little Free Libraries. *The Herald* has donated thousands of printed bookmarks and other materials used to promote the Little Free Libraries.

Through close partnership and cross promotion with the Lake Worth Public Library, Little Free Libraries in Lake Worth have made "Take A Book, Leave A Book" a familiar and beloved motto for sharing Lake Worth's most valuable asset: literacy, art, and above all, community. Little Free Libraries are happy ambassadors for the city's public library, practicing reciprocity at every turn.

The Lake Worth Little Free Libraries project is registered as a non-profit organization in the State of Florida. Each Lake Worth Little Free Library is

LAKE WORTH LITTLE FREE LIBRARIES. Little Free Library at the Bryant Park boat ramp. The library is decorated with nautical flags. *Private Collection.*

chartered and registered with the original organization. Book exchanges are not a new concept, but directors of the Lake Worth Little Free Libraries project believe in the importance of the work that has made these small book boxes a world-wide phenomenon with over sixty thousand Little Free Libraries currently operating in more than seventy countries around the world.

The Little Free Libraries project is an entirely volunteer-driven effort committed to enhancing literacy and building on the strong community that Lake Worth has always enjoyed. There are more than one hundred stewards who tend the Little Free Libraries in the City of Lake Worth. The stewards' primary purpose is to encourage their neighbors to spread the message that everyone who sees a Little Free Library is aware that it belongs to the entire community. Lake Worth residents have embraced this project wholeheartedly, responding with generosity when a call is issued for more book donations.

The Lake Worth Little Free Libraries project was able to grow quickly and enjoy such success because of a committed and deeply engaged community. Lake Worth has shown itself to be fertile ground for a project that depends on the kindness and generosity of so many. People and businesses have contributed funds to the project, asking only that a Little Free Library be planted in any neighborhood where it is needed. Many Little Free Libraries have been funded in memory of the donor's loved ones. The success of the Lake Worth Little Free Libraries project has inspired several nearby communities to initiate their own similar projects. Palm Beach County has a rich heritage of providing its communities with outstanding public libraries, and is well on its way to becoming "Little Free Libraryland."

A Message from Todd H. Bol

TODD H. BOL, Creator and Executive Director of Little Free Library. *Courtesy of Todd H. Bol.*

I am honored to be able to celebrate one hundred new Little Free Libraries in your community. I am touched and proud, and pray many other communities follow your literacy leap forward. When it comes to literacy, there is work to be done. According to the Children's Literacy Foundation, in low-income neighborhoods in America, there is only one book for every three hundred children; the Reading is Fundamental organization states that sixty-five percent of United States fourth-graders are reading below grade, but if a child has just twenty-five books in their home, they will complete two more years of school than a child from a home without any books at all.

I would like to share a few stories that reflect the spirit of Little Free Library and provide context to why the City of Lake Worth's accomplishment of building one hundred Little Free Libraries is so significant.

A few years ago, I felt a tap on my shoulder and turned around to see the former Governor of Wisconsin, Jim Doyle. We were attending a Wisconsin Reading Association conference, where Little Free Library was receiving an award, and Governor Doyle's wife was receiving a lifetime achievement award. Governor Doyle said to me, "My wife and I love Little Free Library. You know what, Todd—what's going on in America is not us. We are not this divisive or this polarized. Little Free Library is more about who we are. We reach across the aisle, we reach across the street, and we pick each other up. We do not care who someone is or where they are from, we pick them up and make their life better. This is who we are as Americans."

In 2010, I was exploring the idea of Little Free Library and trying to find support for the concept. We had only moved three or four Little Free Libraries in six months—pretty dismal results. I was thinking of quitting and throwing in the towel.

I had about thirty Little Free Libraries sitting in my backyard soon to be covered in the snow as winter was approaching. As I was thinking about unwinding this Little Free Library initiative, I heard a piece on National Public Radio (NPR) about Dr. Martin Luther King, Jr. He was asked, "What would you do if you were going to die tomorrow?" He said, "I would plant a seed, because a seed can grow, change, and produce a better tomorrow."

I realized this was the solution I needed; to strategically give away the thirty Little Free Libraries in the backyard. In other words, to plant seeds of literacy and community. This strategy worked. We gave away the Little Free Libraries to organizations and individuals that represented key markets, players, and advocates. The media and the public started to support us and we grew to more than 60,000 Little Free Libraries in 2017.

Lake Worth, Florida, stands as a great example of this growth as a seed of change, which exemplifies a better example of who we are as Americans. A town of about 30,000 people stepped up and built one hundred Little Free Libraries and brought together the community. The mayor's office, the library, local artists, teachers, students and neighbors, neighbors, and more neighbors. The Lake Worth community became what George Bush the first called one of the great shining lights of America. Lake Worth is a prime example of what a community can do together. It is also an example of how a community can become a better place, as neighbors connect with books and new conversations as they gather around the Little Free Libraries.

But just what is the magic of a Little Free Library?

Once, after a presentation I made, a man approached me and said he understands Little Free Libraries—it's all about air conditioning. He proceeded to say he was sixty-something and, when he was a kid, his parents and grandparents all read on the front porch. He played with his friends in the fields, streets, and sidewalks, and everybody knew everybody. Then we got air conditioning. We went in the house, shut the doors, locked the windows, turned on the TV, and it went downhill from there. Thus, the digital divide began. It took over fifty years, but with Little Free Libraries, we are talking again.

In my past life, I created a nursing scholarship company, and at one point I was in Mumbai, India at a hospital. I was in a gymnasium-sized room that had about fifty beds with several people by each bedside and one nurse. I asked the nurse how she could take care of all of these people. She said she was from India, and they are a poor country; they will never have all the resources that they need to properly take care of the patients. The Indian nurse continued to say, "See all of these people by the patients? These are friends, neighbors, relatives, and loved ones. I teach them to take vital signs, feed them, and care for them. We call them 'watchers,' and you would be surprised how well we do with watchers."

The moral of the story is, we likely will never have all the resources we need, but when all else fails we have each other to depend on and build a better place—a better community. Our traditional education systems, schools, libraries, and parents likely will never have all the financial resources necessary to reach our shared literacy goals, but when we all work together, we can take steps forward. You may not be able to solve literacy issues in your country, state, or even your city, but you can take care of your neighborhood's Juan, Suzie, Mohammad, and Billy.

This is very similar to civil rights, feminism, or other social consciousness movements. You must believe you can create change and you are personally responsible to make the change. Our traditional educational structures need to be augmented and supported by each and every one of us in order to reach desired literacy goals that we all read well together. We all do better when we all read better.

The Lake Worth community has stepped up and said: We are talking again and working together to fix our own community around a book, a conversation. We are also moving forward to really make a difference as a shining example for other communities. As I understand, almost forty other Florida communities are inspired to follow in Lake Worth's footsteps.

While the seed has been planted, the greatest deeds are ahead. How will these beautiful Lake Worth Little Free Libraries become ongoing contributors to literacy and art, and serve as a significant part of the community's fabric for years to come? I am a big believer that each community and each individual must ask, how am I part of the village?

Now that the door is opening to improved literacy and community life, how will this Little Free Library neighborhood be expanded and accelerated and become an even better story of a great city?

This is a chapter that you need to write. We can only share what others have done, such as:

Start an Action Book Club, read stories to neighbors, start a neighborhood pen pal club, participate in Bookoween, make sure every child has six new books every summer. You can have book swaps and book-based potlucks, share and cook family heirloom meals, share tools, start a community garden, or read books to neighborhood pets. Make sure all buses, meals on wheels, churches, and police cars have mobile Little Free Libraries. Start sister Little Free Libraries, urban and rural, across the state, country, and globe. Remember that wherever people shall gather, there shall be books.

Peace on earth will only ever happen if we know and care for each other, and it is my hope that the great community of Lake Worth has taken a beautiful step forward. We all do better when we all do better, and you're well on your way.

Joel M. Starkey Library, Compass LGBT Community Center

David Scott

Compass LGBT Community Center in Lake Worth, as it is known today, had its beginnings in 1988 with the creation of the Stop AIDS Project of South Florida, Inc., as part of the national effort to educate the public about the spread of HIV. The Stop AIDS program grew over the following four years and in 1992, with private contributions and local funding from the Children's Services Council of Palm Beach County, the original group of volunteers established Compass Inc. as the gay and lesbian community center of Palm Beach County.

In its early days, Compass established the Joel M. Starkey Library in recognition of South Florida's prominent pioneer gay activist. Starkey (1946-1992) was the founder of The Southern Gay Archives, which later merged with the Stonewall Library in Fort Lauderdale. He also published *The Southern Gay Liberator* newsletter during the 1970s. He was a strong advocate for civil rights and equality for the LGBT community. Starkey's generous donation of his personal book collection allowed Compass to significantly expand its library holdings in the early 1990s and make the collection available to the LGBT community at large.

The library has relied heavily on book donations to grow its collection throughout the years, yet remained a simple, uncatalogued browsing collection up until 2015. After an extensive weeding process, the collection was cataloged and made available online through the Compass website. Today, the Joel M. Starkey Library is largely a popular LGBTQ print collection focusing on LGBTQ authors, themes, subjects, self-published and biographical works. The collection of 1,500 volumes includes LGBTQ-themed fiction and non-fiction, self-published works, children's literature, and biographical monographs.

JOEL STARKEY LIBRARY AT COMPASS GLCC.
Courtesy of Compass GLCC.

This collection continues to grow through donations of new LGBTQ-related material, much of which are not available in other local municipal, county or academic libraries.

Strier Library of
Temple Beth Tikvah

Sandra Gottesman

Begun in the summer of 1989 with bare shelves at the rear of the synagogue's daily chapel, today the Strier Library of Temple Beth Tikvah in Greenacres has more than double the original cases, yet they are overflowing in their ability to house this ever-growing collection of Judaica materials.

Shortly after the synagogue, the first building owned by the congregation, opened in 1989, an inquiry was posed to its then president. "How can we, the people of the Book, not have provided a place for our Jewish books in our new home?" With that one question, a spark was kindled in first the president; it spread next to the board of directors and then, like wildfire, it ignited a commitment in the membership. An endowment to begin a Judaica library was secured from the family of a recently deceased member whose passionate dedication to Judaica knowledge would now be most fittingly remembered by the library to be named in his memory.

A selection policy, based on established professional criteria and geared to the determined library needs of their rabbi, cantor, membership, faculty, and students in the adult education programs and the local community, was filed with the board. At the same time, an outline was drawn up of the projected phases of growth which would have to occur in order to create not just a collection of books looking for readers but a viable Jewish heritage educational center.

The Strier Library, like all newborns, came into the world needing guidance, support, and a large dose of love. Sandra Gottesman, a former school librarian who, though she had no prior Judaica librarianship background, learned on the job, providing guidance. Under her direction, the equipment necessary for a well-organized library was purchased. The "layette" included

STRIER LIBRARY AT TEMPLE BETH TIKVAH.
Card catalog. *Private collection.*

everything from pencils and paper clips to bookends, a card catalog, and even a book cart. An initial but temporary volunteer staff that finally totaled eighteen men and women gathered daily to sort, mend, stamp, cover, apply call labels and the innumerable tasks large and small needed to process the many books which were immediately donated to begin the collection. On a good day, four to six typists would be pounding away as they typed the catalog cards. Others waited to file them in those pristine drawers. Right from the start, all books were classified according to the Weine Classification Scheme for Judaica Libraries. This was a perfect choice for the Strier Library; the Jewish version of the Dewey Decimal System would be easy for both patrons and volunteer staff to use because of the familiarity most had with the Dewey system and because the Weine system was designed for smaller libraries. When the very first book was ready to be placed on the shelf, the librarian—while holding this treasure aloft—carefully led a conga line around the room crowded with volunteers working at not only the library table but as many card tables as could be fitted into the remaining space. Curious visitors often added to the many workers, visitors who frequently were put to work and who soon became enthusiastic supporters of the project.

It quickly became apparent that hand-me-downs could not be the exclusive components of the collection; certain basic works as well as current materials were missing. Thus, new books were ordered, using reviews in both secular and Judaica publications of note and recommendations of colleagues but always focusing on the ascertained needs of patrons. This would build the core collection of Judaica reference works, nonfiction titles encompassing the beliefs and practices of Judaism, our people's history, biographies, sociology, arts and crafts, and literary heritage. In addition, popular fiction with a strong Jewish thread was added as the "honey" with which to attract patrons.

Among the very first expenditures were that which proved to be the most fortuitous: The Strier Library became a member of the Association of Jewish Libraries. The international organization encompasses universities, research organizations, day schools, community centers, and synagogue libraries both large and small. This resulted in a plethora of information about methods, programs, materials, books, videos, and more, as well as an introduction to colleagues from around the globe who shared tips through the resulting networking as well as gifts of duplicate items from their own collections.

Once the core collection of books had been processed and cataloged, the next planned library phase was addressed. A magazine and newspaper section was set aside for both purchased and donated issues, for no book can offer insights and information about current affairs as promptly as periodical publications.

Though Temple Beth Tikvah's membership is comprised primarily of senior citizens, it was deemed important to allocate what was quickly becoming limited shelf space to a representative juvenile collection. Grandparents who needed ideas as to which books to purchase as gifts or to read to their visiting grandchildren would use these. The juvenile collection would also be available to students, parents, and teachers from the regional religious school. Most of these volumes were "freebies" secured by the volunteer librarian Sandra Gottesman who had become a judge for the American Jewish Libraries' Sydney

STRIER LIBRARY AT TEMPLE BETH TIKVAH.
Check-out card with logo. *Private collection.*

BOOKS WITH PROCESSING NOTES. *Private collection.*

Taylor Book Awards Committee and a reviewer of both adult and juvenile books.

The next logical progression in developing a well-rounded collection which would meet the needs and wants of patrons was to offer videos for curriculum enhancement, special programs, and home viewing. The seventy-five videos included documentaries, dramas, and comedies, primarily in English but also including noteworthy ones in Hebrew, French, Italian, and more, with subtitles for foreign languages.

With new sections and a growing book collection, new shelving had to be built to accommodate the growing collection, and grow it must. No library can remain static; new and important materials must be added to keep abreast of current learning. Effort as well as monies had created what soon became known as one of the best Judaica libraries in this area of South Florida. The library's financial needs were not included in the synagogue's annual budget but were met by drawing up a set amount from contributions made to the library fund, continued and diversified ways Strier library. A logo has been employed which portrays a Magen David composed of adjacent open books, featuring the motto, "Read and Remember."

Within the library itself, a bulletin board and themed book displays present an ongoing invitation to all who visit. To facilitate ease of use by the patrons and to simplify its operation by volunteers, the entire collection bears color-coded spine labels. Red signifies reference works which do not circulate; blue, nonfiction; clear, biographies; green, juvenile literature, both fiction and nonfiction; yellow, fiction; and orange, videos. The card catalog offers guidance to its use and contains numerous cross-references to help in locating materials. Transferring all cataloging information to a computer system, and bringing the library database online, is still in the planning stages. Today, this relatively small, well-rounded collection is truly achieving its goals. It has definitely become a source of pride, sharing our rich Judaica heritage.

Finnish Library and Reading Room

Sirpa Aho and Janet DeVries

In the 1930s, a large influx of immigrants from Finland flocked to Florida, lured by the mild winter climate. In 1935, a group of new Finnish Americans organized a Finnish Club in Lantana to host dances, picnics and other social gatherings. In 1944, club members updated the name to the Finnish Tourist Club. In addition to social events, the group's primary purpose was raising money for widows and orphans.

The Finnish library at the then Palm Beach Community College, Lake Worth, opened on April 5, 1990. Jaako Laajava, cultural attaché from the Finnish Embassy in Washington, D.C. performed the ribbon cutting. Arne Aaltonen representing the Finnish Chamber of Commerce presented the library's director, Brian C. Kelley, with the first donated book. The college's library provided the space for the Finnish library and the Chamber of Commerce sought donations, monetary and in-kind, to supplement the collection. The Chamber opened the library with five hundred books and donations totaling $10,000.

The Finnish library's collection was truly unique, not only in size but in quality. The Finnish Embassy in Washington sent books, as did Finland and Finnish Communities in Canada. From its inception, the Finnish Chamber of Commerce managed the Finnish library along with Finlandia Foundation Florida Chapter representative, Katariina Westman. The most valuable aspect of the Finnish library was that because the University of Indiana had cataloged the entire collection, students and researchers throughout the United States could access the collection through an interlibrary loan service.

The Finnish Chamber of Commerce formed a committee in the mid-2000s to facilitate the transfer of the library and donated monies from the Chamber to the Florida Finlandia Foundation. In 2012, Palm Beach Community College was growing and transitioning into a four-year college. The college no longer

THE FINNISH LIBRARY AND READING ROOM. The Finnish Library and Reading Room is located on the second floor of the Finland House (Suomi Talo) in Lantana. *Private Collection.*

had space for the Finnish library's collection, which had grown to approximately 4,000 books and transferred the books to the Suomi Talo (Finland House). Volunteer librarians curate the collection, housed in the library reading room on the Finland House's second floor.

Jewish Genealogical Society of Palm Beach County Library

Barbara S. Nowak

In 1991, The Jewish Genealogical Society of Palm Beach County, Inc.'s (JGSPBCI) library had modest beginnings in the home of Mona Morris, the association's co-president and first librarian. As a mobile library, Mona transported the books from her house to the monthly membership meetings. Library hours were an hour before and one-half hour after the monthly meetings. The library was initially a collection donated by the membership, supplemented with used book purchases. The library began acquiring new genealogy library resources such as reference books and CD-ROM databases that required computer access. An example was an early CD of eastern and western U.S. telephone numbers. Members would telephone President Al Silberfeld who would do the research; five numbers for one dollar and any subsequent research cost one dollar for each additional ten names.

By 1997, the collection had grown. It was evident that the Society needed a permanent library location distinct from a member's residence. Carol Raspler found a home for the collection on a permanent loan basis, at the Molly S. Fraiburg Judaica Collection at Florida Atlantic University (FAU). The association's newsletter, *Scattered Seeds*, noted, "With that opportunity also comes an obligation on the part of each ... member." The new library needed volunteers to aid with cataloging, computer research, and bookbinding. Members Sylvia Nusinov, Jackie Fineblit, and Ben Karliner volunteered in the Special Collections Department at FAU. At FAU, the Society had a bank of bookcases along a wall in a small room inside of another room with Judaica books. The collection was only accessible by appointment.

Members had difficulty accessing the library due to the university campus parking restrictions. Members could obtain visitor parking passes three times per semester; however, it required a visit to the campus police each time. In an attempt to overcome the parking challenges at FAU, Irv Skorka and Ben Karliner searched for a new home that they found at the Rose Merry L. Plough Media Resource and Reference Center in Boca Raton. The Plough Center, located in the Phyllis and Harvey Sandler Center for Jewish Life Enhancement on the Levis Jewish Community Center campus in Boca Raton was a better fit for the Society. Parking was easy; the library was large and welcoming.

Ben Karliner, Dennis Rice, and Al Silberfeld packed and moved the books while Sylvia Nusinov and Jackie Fineblit shelved the collection in the new home, a bank of shelves along one wall. In 2005, librarian Irv Skorka inventoried all the books, assigning them a catalog code on the local computer, and then labeled and shelved them. The association had built up a substantial research collection of mostly member donated materials including generic genealogical research guides, along with more area specific research manuals, atlases, encyclopedias, as well as Jewish Community and Genealogical Societies Newsletters.

One of the codicils in the Memorandum of Understanding with the Jewish Community Center was that the JCC had priority access to the library for their programs, even if the JGSPBCI was already on the schedule. As the JCC grew, their many activities began to impact access to the library. Consequently, in 2015, Membership Chairperson Eric Sharenow and association Secretary Ina Getzoff began searching for a new home to house the collection. They found Temple Shaarei Shalom (TSS) in Boynton Beach. President Cindy Potter-Taylor and President emeritus Dennis Rice collaborated with Rabbi Fertello to make this new partnership a reality. After lengthy discussions with the Rabbi and the temple administrator, both sides agreed to the arrangement.

The association now had a receptive home with sufficient flexibility for the group to access the library space in addition to relatively easy parking. Boynton Beach is centrally located to the membership, resulting in more foot traffic. In addition, the interest in moving into the synagogue space seem to stimulate the synagogue's library committee into organizing their collection. Part of the agreement with the synagogue was that the Society would purchase bookcases which matched the synagogue's, for the collection. In addition, the Society joined forces with the synagogue, splitting the purchase costs of library cataloging software.

As of June 2016, the collection is now housed at Temple Shaarei Shalom, Boynton Beach. Dr. Barbara S. Nowak, the present library coordinator, reclassified and cataloged the collection to match TSS' choice to use the Weine Classification Scheme. The Weine system is an alternative library organizational schema designed specifically for Jewish collections. The Weine system is, however, not designed for genealogical research. As a result, Barbara Nowak made appropriate modifications for a genealogical collection. She and president Cindy Potter-Taylor spent the summer of 2016 re-cataloging and shelving the associations' collection of approximately four hundred volumes. After a year of working with the collection, some minor cataloging changes and a final inventory of the collection made sure all books were correctly entered into the computer system.

JEWISH GENEALOGICAL SOCIETY LIBRARY. The library in its home at Temple Shaarei Shalom in western Boynton Beach. *Courtesy of Barbara Nowak.*

Another major project for the library is working in partnership with the Genealogical Society of Palm Beach digitizing the collection of community and Jewish Genealogical Association's newsletters. Digitized versions will be uploaded to the library computer. While these newsletters are a great source of information, they become unwieldy when the collection includes hundreds of pages of un-indexed information. Digitization of this collection will make research more efficient with the use of a search command. To reciprocate for the time and effort in the digitizing project, the group has agreed to facilitate a series of beginning lectures for the Genealogical Society of Palm Beach around the county in local library branches.

The new home at TSS has revitalized the mentoring program. One day a week at the library, the librarian and other knowledgeable community volunteers provide help and guidance. Assistance can be as simple as teaching members about available computer databases to working through the shelved materials. This new home has once again become a lively and very active research library.

Part IV
Library Consortiums and Literary Festivals

Bookfest! of the Palm Beaches: A Literary Festival

Virginia K. Farace

In 1991, a new literary event came to Palm Beach County: BookFest! of the Palm Beaches–A Literary Festival. It was founded and produced by the Palm Beach County Library Association (PBCLA), which is a professional organization of librarians, paraprofessionals, institutions, Friends groups, trustees, and volunteers—all interested in providing quality library service.

In what became an annual event for ten years, the library and literary communities of the Palm Beaches came together to celebrate the joys of literature and reading and the recognition of the essential role of libraries in fostering and supporting a lifelong interest in the marvelous world of books.

Inspired by the Miami Book Fair, held in November, BookFest was held in the spring. It was a labor of love by local librarians, booksellers, Friends, and volunteers. *The Palm Beach Post* was a major sponsor. The Cultural Council of Palm Beach County started offering advice mid-way through the decade and took over the management of BookFest in 1998.

Timeline and Highlights

April 19-21, 1991:

The first event was held at the Exposition Centre of South Florida Fairgrounds. The dates were selected to coincide with National Library Week; the theme that year was "Children Who Read Succeed" and briefly "Read Succeed." The festival had a strong component of children's literature and an emphasis on Florida authors. Among the over two dozen authors who appeared were the following big names: Stephen Birmingham, author of twenty-five best-selling books including *Those Harper Women*, *The Auerbach Will*, and non-fiction social histories such as *Our Crowd* and *Real Lace*; Ben Bova,

BOOKFEST COMMITTEE. Taken outside the Palm Springs Library
when tee shirts were delivered during a 1991 BookFest meeting. Front row:
Virginia Farace (with arms outspread), Cathy Benson-Brown, Vicki Webber.
Back row: Sally Bailey, Angelica Carpenter, Steve Eisenstein, unknown,
Anne Mojo, and Karen Batchelder. *Courtesy of Virginia K. Farace.*

prolific author of seventy-five science fiction and non-fiction books about
space and technology, whose non-fiction book, *The Beauty of Light*, was voted
one of the best science books by the American Library Association three years
prior; Rob MacGregor, who wrote the book version of *Indiana Jones and the Last
Crusade*; and finally, Patrick D. Smith, author of *A Land Remembered* and other
historical fiction. In the 1970s, his work had been nominated three times for
the Pulitzer Prize and in 1988, his lifetime work was nominated for the Nobel
Prize for Literature. Smith was inducted into the Florida Artists Hall of Fame
in 1999.

More than twenty book exhibitors as well as Friends groups and local
organizations had booths. The first year's budget was close to $70,000. Over
12,000 people attended the free event. The fairgrounds charged one dollar per
vehicle for parking.

April 24-26, 1992: The event was held at the Exposition Centre of South
Florida Fairgrounds. BookFest received two grants: The William Bingham
Foundation for $12,000, and The Community Foundation for $2,000
(earmarked for children's activities).

Major authors included Peter Matthiessen (National Book Award winner);
Carl Hiaasen; Robert Lacey; Lucia St. Clair Robson; and Cherokee Paul
MacDonald. In addition to author speeches, there were panel discussions, book

signings, folk singing, and performances of As you Like It by the Palm Beach Shakespeare Festival. Angelica Carpenter and her mother, Jean Shirley, appeared as authors of two biographies for young readers: *Frances Hodgson Burnett: Beyond the Secret Garden* and *L. Frank Baum: Royal Historian of Oz*.

Attendance was about 15,000 and admission was still free, although the fairgrounds charged two dollars per car for on-site parking.

April 22-25, 1993: The event was held at the Exposition Centre of South Florida Fairgrounds.

Major author was Dominick Dunne (who writes about the rich and famous murder trials).

Kermit Christman, producing artistic director of the Palm Beach Shakespeare Festival, presented Zoo Story by Edward Albee, starring William Katt (television star on Perry Mason).

April 22-24, 1994: The event was held at the Exposition Centre of South Florida Fairgrounds.

Best-selling Florida authors were Edna Buchanan, Carl Hiaasen, Robert Lacey, and Paul Levine. National multicultural authors included Virginia Hamilton, a children's author who won the National Book Award, the Newberry Medal and the Coretta Scott King Award; and Cuban poets Angel Cuadra and Uva Clavijo.

Palm Beach Shakespeare Festival presented a new play called Edgar, depicting the life of Edgar Allen Poe by award-winning playwright Jack Yuken. Several panel discussions were presented on writing and getting published. Over one hundred exhibitors offered thousands of new, used, and rare books for sale. Attendance rose to about 17,000 and admission was two dollars per person with free parking.

February 17-19, 1995: BookFest moved outside to Old School Square, Delray Beach.

The cost was almost double doing the event outside. Most booths were under tents that leaked when it rained. The highlight was the arrival on horseback of two male models who posed for the covers of romance paperbacks, and were sponsored by the Florida Romance Writers organization. As in years past, there was a children's section with entertainment, music, and storytellers. Attendance was free but due to location and rain, the attendance was reduced to 12,000.

March 22-24, 1996: The event returned to the South Florida Fairgrounds. BookFest almost went broke the previous year. It had no reserves left because of the rain and poor attendance in Delray. Nevertheless, the committee pulled it together back at the Fairgrounds. Authors' groups such as the Florida Romance Writers, the Mystery Writers of America, and the Society of Children's Book Writers and Illustrators helped. They also found authors willing to waive fees to participate. The writers' associations wanted the festival to survive. The theme this year was mystery and romance. Mystery writers included Carol Higgins Clark, daughter of Mary Higgins Clark; also, South Florida authors Paul Levine and James Neal Harvey. Top romance writers included Heather Graham, whose books have appeared on the *New York Times* bestsellers, list and Marilyn Campbell, noted for her "bizarre outfits" at the festival. The most recognizable author was Olivia Goldsmith, author of *First Wives Club* and *Flavor of the Month*.

Cartoonist Mort Walker, creator of *Beetle Bailey*, demonstrated how to draw cartoons. True crime authors included Aphrodite Jones, Stuart McIver, and Cliff Linedecker. The attendance was about 18,000 and children's activities and authors continued to be popular.

April 18-20, 1997: South Florida Fairgrounds

The theme was diversity. There were more female than male authors this year. Included were actresses Janet Leigh and Jean Marsh; poet Laurel Blossom; mystery writer Caroline Garcia-Aguilera, and novelist Jane Heller. At the urging of Dr. William E. Ray, president of the Cultural Council of Palm Beach County, the Palm Beach County Library Association paid for a fundraising consultant, Peg San Felippo, who was housed at the Cultural Council offices. Her mission was to develop a fund-raising arm for BookFest called Ex Libris. From 1991 through 1997, Randy Pytel, staff member at the Palm Beach County Library System, designed the posters and tee shirt each year and they became collector's items. BookFest was awarded a John Cotton Dana Library Public Relations Award for the graphic designs.

March 13-15, 1998:

The Cultural Council of Palm Beach County and Dr. William E. Ray, President and Chief Executive Officer of the council, took over the management of BookFest. It moved to a 37,000-square-foot air-conditioned tent on Flagler Drive in West Palm Beach. Librarians continued to volunteer. Valet parking was available. Dominick Dunne was named Palm Beach Author

Laureate. The council hired Robin Spillias as project director to work full-time on BookFest from January to March.

Admission was raised to five dollars, attendance was low at 5,000, and the Cultural Council reported a loss of $34,000.

March 19-21, 1999: Cultural Council moved BookFest back to the Fairgrounds.

More than fifty authors appeared, including novelists Robert B. Parker, James Patterson, and Stuart Woods. The event focused on children and families, featuring storytellers and activities. Admission was three dollars for adults and two dollars for seniors; children under twelve were admitted free as usual. Attendance was very low at 3,600.

April 8-9, 2000: A more focused, two-day event was held by the Cultural Council at Levenger Company headquarters in Delray Beach. Levenger was a mail-order firm with the motto "Tools for Serious Readers." The company donated its three meeting rooms. The event offered only the books from about thirty authors who were speaking, rather than all of the booksellers and antiquarians of year's past. The author laureate was Peter Matthiessen, writer of several historical novels set in the Everglades. Other authors included Tim Dorsey and Randy Wayne White. New workshops included Turning Fiction into Film and Photography for Publication.

Admission was free but seating was limited. Attendance was 2,000; however, the event broke even because of a grant from the Lattner Foundation. This was the final year of a decade-long literary event as the Cultural Council voted to end its management.

Library Memories

Angelica Shirley Carpenter

In 1989, people who lived in West Palm Beach did not usually go to Miami. It was too far, too dangerous, and there was nowhere to park. I wanted to go to the Miami Book Fair, held annually each November. Somehow, I convinced the Florida Public Library Association to charter a bus and sold enough seats for an excursion.

Wearing hats and sunscreen, we day-trippers shopped through a couple of streets that were closed off to cars. The sidewalks were lined with booths selling new and used books, some run by library Friends' groups. Signs advertised talks by famous authors. Why, this is like a big library program, I thought.

"We could do this," I told my friends, Virginia Farace and Vicki Webber. Why didn't they slap me? Instead, we went home and formed a steering committee.

"People in Palm Beach County don't read," helpful souls assured us, but we were librarians and we did not believe them. We called on Gail Howden, community relations director for *The Palm Beach Post*, and she agreed that the *Post* should be our major sponsor.

That first BookFest, held April 19-21, 1991, at the South Florida Fairgrounds, had a budget of about $65,000, scrounged by various means from governmental sponsors and private donors. We offered almost a hundred booths. In the second year, Randy Pytel, staff artist at the Palm Beach County Library System, designed an Andy Warhol-ish poster of glamorous women reading; his posters later won a prize from the American Library Association.

Literary people loved our fair. BookFest kept growing, and one year the managers of the South Florida Fairgrounds invited some of the organizers, including Virginia, Mary Baykan, and me up to a second story window overlooking the main floor. Why we did not take a photo, I will never know (this was before cell phones). Maybe we were too dazzled at the sight of the huge hall below, packed with people. Even the aisles were full; we had to study the booth layout to understand where they were. I think our biggest annual attendance was about 20,000 over a three-day weekend.

Author Gregory Maguire spoke at BookFest soon after *Wicked* came out.

244

He had put himself through college playing the piano, and somehow, he spotted a piano at BookFest. I asked him to play "This is All I Ask," written by my great-uncle Gordon Jenkins. He happily obliged and then he teamed up with the Florida Romance Writer's president who was a former cabaret singer. Wherever we went that weekend, they found a piano and then played and sang that song for me.

In 1999, I took a job in California and moved away from South Florida. When I came back in 2000 to visit friends, a woman stopped me in the grocery store. "Do you know what was wrong with BookFest this year?" she demanded.

"No," I said, "I don't. I don't live here anymore. I'm not involved in BookFest." Secretly, I was proud that she loved the original BookFest and wanted to make it better.

COALA–Cooperative Authority for Library Automation

Charlotte Olson

In the early 1980s, libraries began to automate, using computers to handle jobs formerly performed by staff. Services were expanding. Boynton Beach City Library's annual circulation count was about to exceed 300,000 items and by the end of 1984 the figure would top 400,000.

Boynton Beach and the West Palm Beach Public Library were both members of the Library

Cooperative of the Palm Beaches. Boynton Beach library director Virginia Farace and West Palm Beach director Pete Daniels hoped that the Palm Beach County Library System would be able to include the two city libraries in the Dataphase automated system implemented at the county.

The Boynton Beach and West Palm Beach city councils started setting aside monies in fiscal year 1981-82 and 1982-83 with additional monies added each fiscal year to fund the automation project. Meanwhile, the county's problems with implementation delayed the cities' entry into the system and finally, in early 1983, the county notified the cities that the Dataphase System did not have space to include the city collections.

After much research and a detailed needs assessment, Farace received city approval to investigate the new SIRSI automated system. In Athens, Georgia, she met with the founder, designer, and owner of this state-of-the-art system, Jim Young. She also met with the director of the Georgia Tech University Library, the only library at that time to be actually using the SIRSI system. The director guaranteed that the Georgia Tech Library would continue to use, develop, and support the SIRSI system if by chance the company failed, which he believed would not happen.

In 1984, Boynton Beach City Library and West Palm Beach Public Library collaborated with the Delray Beach Public Library Association to form a partnership that would jointly undertake library automation. Delray Beach director Leslie Strickland also recognized the advantages of sharing costs and resources. By fall 1984, the three governing entities formed COALA, the Cooperative Authority for Library Automation, and COALA signed a contract with SIRSI.

The SIRSI System operated a library software package called Unicorn on a single Zilog 8000 server that ran the UNIX operating system. All three libraries used the software; each was able to operate independently using parameters which applied only to that library. The purchase cost of the central site hardware and software was divided equally among the three libraries. Because communications at that time used telephone lines and multiplexers, the most economical location for the central equipment was in the Boynton Beach Library, about mid-way between West Palm Beach and Delray Beach.

Boynton Beach support services librarian Charlotte Olson took charge of the main system and she coordinated conversion from the old card catalogs to new, automated records. She remembered thinking how amazed she was that three library directors, three city managers, three attorneys, and three governing bodies agreed on this partnership.

The SIRSI hardware and software was updated many times over the years. The West Palm Beach Public Library withdrew from COALA and the Palm Springs Public Library, Lake Park Public Library, and North Palm Beach Public Library joined COALA. All five libraries still control their own policies and patrons can access just one collection or all five of the COALA member libraries in one search. The Palm Beach County Library System switched to SIRSI at a later date and COALA hosted demonstrations for their staff.

Retrospective Conversion of the Boynton Beach Library Collection

Virginia Farace

All three SIRSI owners came to Boynton Beach to install software. Jim Young, SIRSI President, was the trainer. Vice President Mike Murdock managed the hardware. Jackie Young, Jim's wife, also a vice president, assisted.

Because the library could not afford OCLC (an expensive library database), the director had to find a way to convert paper files to computer files before using Unicorn. Staff looked up Library of Congress or International Standard Book numbers on microfiche for all titles in the collection. A staff member would take a shelf list drawer (which listed books by call number), look up title after title in the microfiche, and note a number on each shelf list card. Then a librarian (Janet Ivey and Jane Northup) would search the number in other library software and import the record. Charlotte recalls, "We only had one IBM PC at the time." After about a year of entering this information, staff had completed most of the Adult collection. The data was then sent to SIRSI who uploaded the data into Unicorn.

When the library went live on Unicorn, circulation staff had to register every adult patron. The system used receipts for due date slips printed with the book title and due date. Most patrons liked the receipts. Staff spent the next year creating brief records for the adult books that were not yet loaded into Unicorn. At the same time staff created brief records for the children's collection. The library went live with the checkout of children's materials about a year later.

Later the library was able to overlay the brief records with full MARC (machine-readable cataloging) records from Autographics.

SEFLIN's First 30 Years: A History of Innovation and Leadership

Dr. William Miller

The Southeast Florida Library Information Network (SEFLIN), during its first thirty years, has advanced the missions of its member libraries and allowed them to do, together, things that would have been impossible to achieve individually. From its earliest days, the member libraries—academic institutions and public libraries—have viewed SEFLIN as a mechanism for research, development, experimentation, and innovation. Quite often, SEFLIN pioneered initiatives that were later adopted by the other multi-type networks or statewide. On occasion, SEFLIN has begun programs of national and international significance, emulated widely by other networks and state agencies throughout the United States.

Library Services and Technology Act (LSTA) funding was the foundation of SEFLIN, and the other Florida multitype library networks with the support of State Librarian Barratt Wilkins. After the three-year LSTA planning grant, SEFLIN was incorporated. The directors of member libraries developed a membership dues structure that was high enough to support the projects they wanted to achieve. Member dues, federal LSTA grants and after 1993, the State Library Cooperative funding allowed SEFLIN to grow and innovate.

With the support of the members and board of directors, SEFLIN has always been characterized by a willingness to innovate and take chances. For instance, in 1986, in its earliest days, when fax machines were a new technology, SEFLIN purchased one for every member library. Prior to 1986, it took at least three days for requested articles to get from one library in the region to another. With the fax networks, 24-hour information sharing became the standard. When SEFLIN libraries received fax machines, the university and college administrators who wanted to send or receive a fax had to go to the library director's office to do so, raising the library's profile as a high-tech hub at that time. In time, fax machines ceased to be rare, and the centrality of the library as a place to go for faxing wore off, but it had left an impression on those in charge. This became the pattern for one SEFLIN-supported innovation after another.

One of SEFLIN's most iconic achievements was the FreeNet. In 1994, when email and public computing were largely unknown, the Board began discussion leading to the implementation of a FreeNet, based on the National Public Telecommuting Network. It is hard to realize, now, that it was considered highly unorthodox for libraries to become involved, and many looked suspiciously on this enterprise. However, SEFLIN jumped into this new program with both feet, using librarians at member institutions to train the public, and maintaining hardware and software to support public access. For a time, SEFLIN was the second-largest purveyor of email in South Florida, and every public official became aware of this innovation.

Before the FreeNet, there were no other public email services available. SEFLIN's profile has never been higher, and institutions basked in the knowledge that their library was a member of an innovative organization providing such valuable public service. Other multitype networks in Florida soon began offering similar services. SEFLIN won an NTIA Grant for FreeNet training in 1995, and an outstanding project award from the Southeastern Library Association (SELA) in 1996.

SEFLIN FreeNet email predated Hotmail, Yahoo, and Gmail. As these new, free email services began to appear, the public had other options. By 2001, the board decided that its work in this area was done. They decided to transition the effort to virtual library services, including "My Library Service" which amalgamated a variety of online resources for the public. Once again, SEFLIN's role was that of innovator and pioneer.

As early as 1986, SEFLIN was pioneering the linking of member library catalogs through "SEFLINK." The first phase involved a print and microfiche Union List of Serials, which moved to CD-ROM in 1988, and then finally to an online list, "SE@L," in 1989. It was eventually migrated to an Autographics product named "SHELLS" (Serial Holdings Electronic Library Lists) in 1999, in cooperation with the Central Florida and Panhandle regions, thus becoming a resource covering much of Florida. Such lists were common in regions throughout the country, but this was only a prelude to something much more cutting edge, an actual online link, which enabled people to see the catalogs of their own library and those of other member libraries.

This second phase of "SEFLINK" provided computer links to the catalogs of the two state university libraries (FAU and FIU), the Miami-Dade Public Library, the Broward County Library, and the Palm Beach County Library System. "SEFCAT" was born, and the public could have dial-up access to 11.4 million volumes in the linked catalogs. When the University of Miami Libraries were added in 1990, twelve million more items were added, more than doubling the size of the combined index. As more member libraries initiated online catalogs, a major benefit of SEFLIN membership was that each member's online catalog was added to the SEFLINK database. The SEFLINK database predated by many years other networked linked systems.

However, the very clunky SEFLINK software required original programming every time a new update to a library's catalog was implemented. Technology changed dramatically in the 1990s and the entire system was eventually superseded. As hard as it is to appreciate in retrospect, during its time in the early 1990s, SEFLINK provided users at member libraries and beyond with a level of bibliographic access rare at the time. Starting in 1991, SEFLIN also mounted a collection of non-proprietary databases such as ERIC and other non-proprietary databases for the public.

In the mid-1990s, the SEFLIN FreeNet replaced SEFLINK and continued to offer access to library catalogs, the Union List of Serials and the government databases. In addition to the library catalogs and free email, the FreeNet offered access to local information added by community information providers from our libraries and from schools, businesses, non-profit organizations, and other local organizations.

Technology continued to change and by 2001, such databases became more easily accessible to the public and through individual library web sites. FreeNet information services were absorbed into the next phase of access for resource sharing based on federate searching. Launched in 2001, "My Library Service" allows library users for the first time to search several catalogs at once instead of one at a time. A Spanish-language version, "Mi Servicio Biblioteca," was mounted in 2003. This collection continued to serve the public until 2009 as access to OCLC's WorldCat became easier and more accessible to the public.

From its earliest days, SEFLIN member libraries desired to share resources, and this was indeed one of the requirements of membership. This sharing was accomplished in several ways. Beginning in 1986, SEFLIN operated a courier van service among all members and contracted with the Broward County Library existing van delivery service. SEFLIN delivery used the visual pink bags to contain the materials. This was an extremely important benefit of membership, and at that time, no other region in the state had such a service. Eventually, this became a statewide service, contracting the management to the Tampa Bay Library Consortium. SEFLIN maintained the local delivery service for several years before the pink bags were replaced by the orange bags of the statewide ground delivery service.

An important avenue for resource sharing has always been the library card program, which from SEFLIN's earliest days has given the users at member academic libraries the right to borrow materials at other member academic libraries. SEFLIN also fostered the implementation of a multitype library card (the Sunshine Library Card) within Palm Beach County in 2008. Statewide cards are common in the United States but Florida has yet to take this step. However, the borrowing privileges made available through SEFLIN remain active and successful, and demonstrate, if any demonstration were still necessary, that providing such access helps users without harming the lending libraries.

A major benefit of SEFLIN membership has always been continuing education for staff at member libraries. From its earliest days, SEFLIN has offered classes on a wide variety of topics, many centering on technology as the field underwent rapid change. Through the 1990s, SEFLIN's continuing education relied on face-to-face workshops, often at a central location at the Broward County Main Library. Beginning in the early 2000s, SEFLIN pioneered the introduction of independent self-paced online education. SEFLIN paid for "Element K" technology training for staff of member libraries, and even became a reseller of this product to FLA and ALA. In 2006-07, WebJunction coupons and Neal-Schuman online classes supplemented the self-paced courses. In 2008, SEFLIN's online offerings expanded to include webinars through SEFLIN Connect. In the annual continuing education needs surveys, there has been a change from reluctance to learn online to a strong preference for the flexibility of learning online.

As SEFLIN continuing education became more individualized, SEFLIN transitioned to online registration. In 2004, SEFLIN introduced the Community of Learning Program website to manage registration, evaluation surveys and student transcripts. In 2010, SEFLIN closed the Community of Learning web pages and introduced a new web site for its membership records and online registration.

Another important avenue for education is conferences. From 1996 to 2007, the "Energize" conferences, organized by the Reference Committee, were an important avenue for staff learning, focusing on technology and drawing a wide audience from both within the membership and from staff at other area libraries. The SEFLIN annual regional conferences continue the tradition.

Reference Committee members presented a poster session at the 2008 American Library Association Conference in Anaheim entitled "No Travel Required: Planning a Regional Conference for Local and New Librarians." Starting in 2011, SEFLIN began a separate, online "virtual conference," also focusing on some aspect of technology such as resource sharing, mobile devices, e-books, and the user experience. The virtual conferences draw an international attendance.

Facilitating the virtual conference, a variety of webinars, virtual committee meetings, and other online interactions is SEFLIN Connect, actually Adobe Connect. SEFLIN has made virtual meeting rooms available to member libraries as an online conferencing service since 2009. This tool has enabled committees to carry out the business of the organization without incurring expensive and needless travel.

Important as educational and networking avenues for member library staff have been the many committees, interest groups, and discussion groups that the organization has supported. This allowed members with similar interests or job responsibilities to meet in person and more recently, online to exchange ideas. Traditionally the geographic location of South Florida made it expensive to send staff to participate when committee work was done at national and state conference levels. The local committees and discussion groups presented an equivalent professional outlet and served as a way for library staff to develop innovation and leadership.

SEFLIN committees reflect the truly collaborative nature of SEFLIN. Library directors have encouraged staff participation and involvement in committees, discussion groups, etc. Directors encouraged staff time to attend meetings, serve in leadership roles and design collaborative projects and services through SEFLIN. In the early days, committee meetings rotated among libraries, allowing committee members to observe and learn from other libraries. Committees were formed around interests such as Cataloging, Children and Youth Services, Circulation and Access, Collection Development, Government Documents, Interlibrary Loan, Library Administration and Management, Preservation and Conservation, Reference, Serials, and Technical interests. After 2001, many of these groups became informal discussion groups.

Another series of activities not characteristic of most other local networks has been SEFLIN's support of international librarianship. In 1998, SEFLIN hosted the 28th ACURIL Conference in Miami, and in 2002 cosponsored an IFLA Summit on Library Cooperation in the Americas.

In 2002, several Armenian librarians were hosted. In 2003, six SEFLIN library directors visited Jamaica and toured various libraries to explore possibilities for cooperation. Grants were also given from 2004-2007 for member librarians to attend ACURIL and IFLA. In 2006, SEFLIN hosted a Technology Summit for visiting librarians from the International Library, Information, and Analytical Center (ILIAC) representing Russia and former Soviet republics.

Because of SEFLIN initiatives, several book exchanges and interlibrary loan support are offered by member libraries to libraries in Armenia, Iraq, and Nigeria.

Leadership training has been a consistent focus of SEFLIN professional programming. In 1997-1998, SEFLIN pioneered a yearlong Sunseeker leadership program, designed by then-executive director Elizabeth Curry. Sunseekers trained junior staff with an eye toward enabling them to undertake more responsible positions over time. This program, like so many others, was superseded and in 2008 was enfolded into the State Library's similar Sunshine State Library Leadership Institute. In the ten years, over 140 SEFLIN library staff members became Sunseeker graduates. Many have gone on to job advancement, including library directorships.

A number of initiatives over the years are consistent with SEFLIN's DNA. The organization has always fostered the ability of member libraries to recruit staff, such as underwriting a booth at American Library Association Conference Placement Centers. In 2005, SEFLIN staff created a database to display available positions in Florida libraries, which it now maintains for the entire state, as the "Florida Library Jobs" website.

SEFLIN has experienced flush years and lean years, and has been able to progress in both environments thanks to a succession of executive directors who have continually innovated and performed with utmost professionalism, while also keeping careful control over the organization's finances.

Kathleen Imhoff helped the organization begin its life and gain independence and early success. Richard Luce led the technological innovations of the 1980s. Elizabeth Curry initiated the FreeNet and much of the continuing education and leadership efforts, and Tom Sloan oversaw the growth of the organization at its height, with a particular focus on international initiatives. As he was leaving, the economic downturn of 2008 hit the organization hard and some member libraries had to drop out. Current executive director Jeannette Smithee has successfully managed the downturn and kept the organization vital with a much smaller staff than her recent predecessors have had at their call. The organization's dues and expenses have been greatly reduced, but it still has the ability to innovate in response to members' needs and interests, and remains a vital part of the South Florida library world, with impact beyond our immediate service area.

SEFLIN BOARD PRESIDENTS

1988-1989 Cecil Beach, Broward County Library
1989-1990 Laurence Miller, Florida International University
1990-1991 Carol Roehrenbeck, Nova Southeastern University
1991-1992 Frank Rodgers, University of Miami
1992-1993 Samuel Morrison, Broward County Library
1993-1994 William Miller, Florida Atlantic University
1994-1995 Brian Kelley, Palm Beach State College
1995-1996 Doug Lehman, Miami Dade College
1996-1997 Jerry Brownlee, Palm Beach County Library System
1997-1998 Margaret Ellison, St. Thomas University
1998-1999 Donald Riggs, Nova Southeastern University
1999-2000 Julia Woods, Broward College
2000-2001 Raymond Santiago, Miami-Dade Public Library System
2001-2002 Zenaida Fernandez, Miami Dade College
2002-2003 Brian Kelley, Palm Beach State College
2003-2004 Laurence Miller, Florida International University
2004-2005 William Miller, Florida Atlantic University
2005-2006 Virginia Farace, Boynton Beach City Library
2006-2007 Robert Cannon, Broward County Library
2007-2008 Raymond Santiago, Miami-Dade Public Library System
2008-2009 Estrella Iglesias, Miami Dade College
2009-2010 John J. Callahan III, Palm Beach County Library System
2010-2011 Christopher Murray, Mandel Public Library of WPB
2011-2012 Laura Probst, Florida International University
2012-2013 Lydia M. Acosta, Nova Southeastern University
2013-2014 Steven Baker, Palm Beach Atlantic University
2014-2015 Craig B. Clark, Boynton Beach City Library
2015-2016 Anne Prestamo, Florida International University

OVERDUE IN PARADISE

2016-2017 Douglas Crane, Palm Beach County Library System
2017-2018 Amy Filiatreu, Lynn University

SEFLIN CURRENT AND PAST MEMBERS

American Intercontinental University
Ana G Mendez University
Art Institute of Fort Lauderdale
Barry University
Boca Raton Public Library
Boynton Beach City Library
Broward College
Broward County Library
Brown Mackie College – Miramar
Carlos Albizu University
Delray Beach Public Library
DeVry University
Doreen Gauthier Lighthouse Point Public Library
Encore Computer Corp
Everest Institute
Everest University
Everglades University
Florida Atlantic University
Florida International University
Florida Keys Community College
Florida Memorial University
ITT Tech. Institute – Deerfield Beach
ITT Tech. Institute – Miami
Johnson and Wales University
Jose Maria Vargas University
Keiser University
Lake Park Public Library
Lake Worth Public Library
Lynn University
Mandel Library of West Palm Beach
Martin County Public Library System
Miami County Day School
Miami Int'l University of Art & Design

Miami Dade College
Miami-Dade Public Library System
Monroe County Library System
North Miami Beach Public Library
North Palm Beach Public Library
Northwood University
Nova Southeastern University
Palm Beach Atlantic University
Palm Beach State College
Palm Beach County Library System
Parkland Public Library
Richard Sullivan Public Library of Wilton Manors
Riviera Beach Public Library
School District of Palm Beach County
Seminole Tribe of FL Library System
Society of Four Arts Library
St. John Vianney College Seminary
St. Thomas University
Trinity International University
University of Miami

April is for Authors Month

Helen Zientek

April is for Authors, an authors' festival for authors who write for children and young adults, provides a countywide literary experience bringing together authors, teachers, students, families and the community to share their love of books.

Created in 2011 by dedicated Palm Beach County educators, Helen Zientek, a retired library media specialist and Sue Slone, a retired elementary school principal, as a way for students to interact with their favorite authors. April is for Authors provides not only a valuable experience for children, but also an opportunity for authors to connect with their audience, as well as key decision makers in the local literacy programs. For the first four years, the April is for Authors event was a program under the Russ Corser Foundation associated with the Kiwanis Club of Singer Island Sunrise. To celebrate its fifth year, the organizers decided to create the April is for Authors Foundation Inc., and filed the paperwork to be a 501(c) (3) entity.

The original partners for the event were the School District of Palm Beach County, the Literacy Coalition of Palm Beach County, the Palm Beach County Library System, and the Kiwanis Club of Singer Island Sunrise. Additional partners included the Mandel Library of West Palm Beach, *The Palm Beach Post*, Barnes & Noble Booksellers (Legacy Place), and the American Association of University Women (Northern Palm Beach County branch). Loyal financial sponsors included the Children's Services Council of Palm Beach County, the Cultural Council of Palm Beach County, the Otis Willits Charitable Foundation, Publix, Florida Power & Light, and the Palm Beach Kennel Club.

Prior to the event, schools in Palm Beach County are encouraged to book the invited authors for school visits. Approximately 20,000 school age students each year see authors in their schools. Every year, the April is for Authors Foundation sought funding to pay for author school visits to Title 1 schools and to bring students from Title 1 schools to the event.

Nothing quite like this existed in Palm Beach County, indeed South Florida. It started as an idea, a dream, to bring kids' authors to Palm Beach County. To put a signed book in the hands of a child or a teenager to foster a love of reading, to encourage learning. Isn't that a wonderful dream? It is all about kids leading literate lives and loving books!

Author Biographies

Lois Albertson

Lois Albertson was named Director of the Town of Highland Beach Library in 2016. She previously served as the Director of Staff Development Services at the Southeast Florida Library Information Network (SEFLIN) for five years. She tries to appreciate all genres, but really only wants to read psychological thrillers. When she is not at the library, you can find her paddle boarding or at the beach.

Susie Rambeau Best

Susie Rambeau Best was born and raised in West Palm Beach. The history enthusiast researches West Palm Beach landmarks and buildings and promotes historic preservation. Susie volunteered at the Henry Morrison Flagler Museum in Palm Beach in high school, and in 2011 created the "Save the History of West Palm Beach" Facebook group.

Todd H. Bol

In 2009, Todd H. Bol built the first Little Free Library book exchange as a tribute to his mother, a teacher and lifelong reader. Today, he serves as executive director of Little Free Library, a 501(c) (3) nonprofit organization. There are now more than 60,000 Little Free Libraries around the world, in all fifty states and eighty countries. The organization has been honored by the Library of Congress, the National Book Foundation, and others, for its impact on creating access to books and bringing communities together.

Penelope Brown

Penelope Prosise Brown was born and raised in West Palm Beach and graduated from the Palm Beach Junior College Library Technician program. She began her career at PBJC, working at the Lake Worth Campus Library Learning Resources Center for forty-seven years thus far. She has volunteered at the Palm Glades Girl Scout Council and helped set up an Archives Section there. She likes to scrapbook and donates crochet baby blankets for sale in a local hospital gift shop for nursing scholarships.

Graham Brunk

Graham Brunk was born and raised in West Palm Beach and holds a strong interest in literature, local history and technology. He's worked as a Media Archives Assistant at the Lynn and Louis Wolfson II Florida Moving Image Archives, the Mandel Public Library of West Palm Beach, The Apple Store as a "Product Expert" and at the Riviera Beach Public Library. Brunk, who recently graduated from Florida State University with a Master's degree in Library and Information Science and holds a Bachelor's degree in Public Administration from Florida International University is the Technology Librarian at the Joseph and Gioconda King Library at the Society of the Four Arts in Palm Beach.

Donna Clarke

Donna Clarke is a Volunteer Librarian at the Briny Breezes Library. She was formerly an early childhood teacher who worked in special education, pre-kindergarten, kindergarten and first grade before retiring to Florida. She has a Bachelor's in Education and a Master's degree in Teaching. She is the fourth generation in her family to call Briny Breezes "home" and has owned property there since 2001. Donna has been the Lead Librarian at the Briny Breezes Library since 2014.

Janet DeVries

Janet DeVries Naughton is a Librarian and Associate Professor at Palm Beach State College. Previously she served as the Archivist for the Boynton Beach City Library and the Delray Beach Historical Society. She holds a Master's degree in Library and Information Science from Florida State University, and is completing a Master's degree in History. She is the immediate past-president of the Boynton Beach Historical Society and is the author, co-author, or editor of nine local history books. Janet moonlights as a tour guide in a historic Florida cemetery.

Michelle McCormick Donahue

Michelle McCormick Donahue was born in Miami and raised in Delray Beach. She is President of the Hypoluxo Island Property Owners Association and author of its *Brown Wrapper Historical Newsletter*. She serves as Vice President of the Delray Beach Historical Society and works as a realtor with Douglas Elliman. Michelle received a Bachelor's degree in Communications from Loyola University in New Orleans, and a Master's degree in Management from

St. Thomas University in Miami. She previously worked for the *Miami Herald* and *The Palm Beach Post* before joining the headquarters of Blockbuster Entertainment in Corporate Training and Development.

Virginia K. Farace

Virginia Kapes Farace is Library Director Emerita of the Boynton Beach City Library where she served for thirty-five years before retiring in 2006. She has a dual Bachelor's degree in Journalism and English Literature from Rider University and a Master's degree in Library Service from Rutgers University.

Vicky Fitzsimmons

Vicky Fitzsimmons has been with the Boca Raton Public Library for twelve years, serving as Reference, Instructional Services, and now Digital Librarian. She earned a Master's degree in Library and Information Science from Florida State University and is a life-long Boca Raton resident.

Dawn Frood

Dawn Frood, a native Floridian, started her library career as the Glades Adult Literacy Specialist for PBCLS and is currently an academic librarian. She was awarded the ELSUN scholarship (Education of Librarians to Serve the Underserved) which provided an educational experience with an emphasis on outreach to multicultural library patrons. She holds Master's degrees in Library Science and Information Systems and Technology. Dawn has served on the Palm Beach County Library Association Board as the Director for Academic Libraries, chaired the Nomination committee, co-chaired both the Technology and Bylaws committees and is the current president.

Shellie A. Labell

Shellie A. Labell is the Director of Archives at the Preservation Foundation of Palm Beach. She was formerly the Archivist at the Delray Beach Historical Society. She has earned a Juris Doctorate from Barry University School of Law, as well as a Master's degree in History. She is currently working towards a Master's degree in Library and Information Science through Florida State University.

Mary Kate Leming

Mary Kate Leming is the executive editor and owner of *The Coastal Star* newspaper in south Palm Beach County. She was formerly the New Media

Editor at *The Palm Beach Post* and worked in several editorial capacities for Cox Interactive Media. The majority of her career was spent as Library Director at *The Palm Beach Post*, where she worked for more than twenty years. Prior to joining *The Palm Beach Post*, she managed the news library at the *Boca Raton News* and worked in public and academic libraries in Florida and Illinois. She has a Master's degree in Library and Information Science from the University of South Florida.

Karen Mahnk

Karen Mahnk has lived in Florida for over forty years. She earned a Master's degree in Library Science from Florida State University. Her career includes serving as Law Librarian for several prominent Miami law firms; she also served as a researcher for the Dade County Public Defender's office before relocating to Palm Beach County. She served the Town of Lake Park's library beginning in 2003 and has been the Library Director since 2010.

Suvi Manner

Suvi Manner grew up in Finland and moved to Palm Beach County in her teens. After nearly a decade working as a teacher and English for Speakers of Other Languages (ESOL) coordinator in the Palm Beach County Public School system, she worked as the Branch Manager and Librarian in the Palm Beach County Library System. Manner has served as the Palm Springs Library Director since early 2016.

Dr. William Miller

Dr. William Miller is the emeritus Dean of Libraries of Florida Atlantic University where he served for 27 years before retiring in 2014. Excellence in reference librarianship with a strong commitment to instruction was the hallmark of his long and distinguished career. The American Library Association's Reference and User Services Division selected Miller as the 2014 recipient of its prestigious Isadore Gilbert Mudge Award.

Jennifer Noel

Jennifer Noel is a Reference Librarian at the Mandel Public Library of West Palm Beach. She has a Bachelor's degree in History from Penn State University and a Master's degree in Library and Information Science from UCLA. Jennifer joined the staff of the Mandel Public Library in 2015 after a year of volunteering in the library's archives and has experience in both law libraries and academic libraries. She lives in Palm Beach Gardens with her husband, daughter, and cat.

Barbara S. Nowak

Barbara S. Nowak is the volunteer library coordinator for the Jewish Genealogical Society of Palm Beach County. Barbara has a Doctorate degree in Anthropology and formerly taught at the university level in both Iowa and New Zealand before taking on the position of Senior Research Fellow at the National University of Singapore where she was employed to research and evaluate reconstruction and re-development of impacted communities following the Indian Ocean earthquake and tsunami in 2004.

Sid Patchett

Director of the Lantana Public Library since 1996, Sid started his career as a Peace Corps volunteer in St. Lucia. After three years in the Peace Corps, he remained on the island for three more years, serving as the Librarian for the island's higher education complex. He also spent several years serving as the Librarian at the University of Papua New Guinea, the University of Malawi, and the Papua New Guinea University of Technology. Sid has earned a Master's degree in Library Science from Florida State University and a Juris Doctorate from the University of Miami. He is still working out what he will do when he grows up.

Dr. Ginger L. Pedersen

Dr. Ginger L. Pedersen is a native Floridian and grew up among the pines and palms in Jupiter Florida. She is an administrator at Palm Beach State College in Lake Worth, Florida, serving as Vice President of Information Systems since 2016. She has also served as Dean and Associate Dean at Palm Beach State. Her prior books include *Pioneering Palm Beach: The Deweys and the South Florida Frontier* and *Legendary Locals of West Palm Beach*. She earned her Bachelors, Masters and Doctoral degrees from Florida Atlantic University in Boca Raton, Florida. She enjoys researching the forgotten history tales of Palm Beach County.

Michelle Quigley

Michelle Quigley is a Reference Librarian at the Delray Beach Public Library. She was formerly the Archivist at the Delray Beach Historical Society, and before that, worked in the library at *The Palm Beach Post* for nearly 20 years, as Government Research Service Librarian for the Palm Beach County Library

System, and Law Librarian at Gunster Law Firm. She has a Master's degree in Library and Information Studies from the University of Wisconsin.

Arthur G. Quinn

Arthur G. Quinn was born in Levittown, New York and relocated to Holiday, Florida after graduating from high school. He pursued different areas of study and work, eventually settling on library science. He graduated with a Master's degree in Library Science from Florida State University in 1996. He now works for St. Vincent de Paul Regional Seminary as Library Director and resides in Boynton Beach along with his wife, Noemi.

Ellen Randolph

Ellen Randolph is the Public Services Librarian at Boca Raton Public Library after previous editions as a Rare Books Librarian and bookstore owner. She has a Master's degree in Library and Information Science from the University of South Florida, a Master's degree in Religious Studies from Florida International University, and recently completed the Camino de Santiago pilgrimage route in Spain.

David Scott

David Scott is the Manager of the Greenacres Branch Library of the Palm Beach County Library System. He earned a Bachelor's degree in History from the University of Waterloo and a Master's degree in Library and Information Science from the University of Western Ontario, both in Canada. David worked for London Public Library in Ontario throughout the 1990s and moved to South Florida to start his professional career with Palm Beach County in 1998. He has served on the Palm Beach County Library Association's Board and served as its President from 2015-2016.

Leslie Siegel

Leslie Siegel, a lifelong Florida resident, earned a Bachelor's degree in History from Florida Atlantic University, graduating with honors. She has been an Archivist in the Special Collections Department at FAU since 2003.

Rosa Sophia

Rosa Sophia is a freelance writer, novelist, and an editorial consultant with an educational background in automotive technology and marketing communications. She served as the official historian for the Village of North

Palm Beach from 2010 to 2014, and worked as a Library Clerk at North Palm Beach Public Library. She is currently a Library Specialist with the Martin County Library System, and is working on several history-related nonfiction projects. She lives in a cottage by the sea in Jensen Beach and is currently pursuing a Master of Fine Arts in Creative Writing.

Victoria Thur

Victoria Thur is the Head of Special Collections at Florida Atlantic University. She started her library career as a student assistant in FAU's Government Documents department and became a staff member in the Circulation department. She earned a Master's degree in History from Florida Atlantic University as well as a Master's degree in Library Science from the University of South Florida.

Paige Turner

Paige Turner is the voice for hundreds of volunteer stewards, artists, builders, book donors, and contributors to the Lake Worth Little Free Libraries project. Paige is an avid reader and enjoys a good mystery most of all.

Teresa B. Van Dyke

Teresa B. Van Dyke is the Special Collections Librarian at Florida Atlantic University. She has worked at the university's S.E. Wimberly Library since 1999, serving in various capacities. She previously served as the Historian for Miami-Dade County in the Historic Preservation Division. She earned a Master's degree in History from Florida Atlantic University as well as a Master's degree in Library Science from the University of South Florida.

———

Suggested Reading

Brink, Lynn. 1976. *A History of Riviera Beach, Florida*. Riviera Beach: Bicentennial Commission of Riviera Beach, Florida.

Curl, Donald Walter, Fred L. Eckel, and Historical Society of Palm Beach County. 1986. *Palm Beach County, An Illustrated History*. Northridge, CA: Windsor Publications.

DeVries, Janet. 2006. *Around Boynton Beach*. Charleston, SC: Arcadia Pub.

Drake, Lynn Lasseter, Richard A. Marconi, and Historical Society of Palm Beach County. 2006. *West Palm Beach, 1890 to 1950*. Charleston, S.C: Arcadia Publishing.

DuBois, Bessie Wilson. 1981. *Jupiter Lighthouse*. Juno Beach, FL: Southeastern Publishing.

Farrar, Cecil W., Margoann Farrar. 1974. *Incomparable Delray Beach: Its Early Life and Lore*. Boynton Beach, FL: Star Publications.

Gill, M. Randall, and Boynton Beach City Library. 2005. *Boynton Beach*. Charleston, SC: Arcadia Publishing.

Laurenti, Lynn Klein, Louise Hinton, and Crystal A. Bacchus. 2011. *Florida Atlantic University: Fifty Years and Counting - A Look Back*. Boca Raton, FL: Florida Atlantic University.

Linehan, Mary Collar, Marjorie Watts Nelson. 1994. *Pioneer Days on the Shores of L*

Marconi, Richard A., and Historical Society of Palm Beach County. 2013. *Palm Beach*. Charleston, SC: Arcadia Publishing.

Suggested Reading

McGoun, William E. 1998. *Southeast Florida Pioneers: The Palm and Treasure Coasts.* Sarasota, FL: Pineapple Press.

McIver, Stuart B. 1975. *Yesterday's Palm Beach, Including Palm Beach County.* Miami, FL: E. A. Seemann Publishing.

Patterson, Dorothy W., and Janet DeVries. 2008. *Delray Beach.* Charleston, SC: Arcadia Publishing.

Pedersen, Ginger, and Janet DeVries. 2012. *Pioneering Palm Beach: The Deweys and the South Florida Frontier.* Charleston, SC: The History Press.

Simon, Sandy. 2003. *The Amazing Story of Highland Beach: 8,000 Years of Change.* Delray Beach, FL: Cedars Group.

Tuckwood, Jan, and Historical Society of Palm Beach County. 2009. *Palm Beach County at 100: Our History, Our Home.* West Palm Beach, FL: Palm Beach Post.

Tuckwood, Jan, and Eliot Kleinberg. 1994. *Pioneers in Paradise: West Palm Beach, the First 100 Years.* Marietta, GA: Longstreet Press.

Index

Index

Index

Index